TIME TO GET TOUGH

TIME TO GET TOUGH

How Cookies, Coffee,
and a Crash Led to Success
in Business and Life

Michael J. Coles
and Catherine M. Lewis

Foreword by Jim Kennedy,
Chairman of Cox Enterprises

The University of Georgia Press   *Athens*

Published by the University of Georgia Press

Athens, Georgia 30602

www.ugapress.org

© 2018 by Michael J. Coles

All rights reserved

Designed by Erin Kirk New

Set in Miller Text

Printed and bound by Sheridan Books

The paper in this book meets the guidelines for
permanence and durability of the Committee on
Production Guidelines for Book Longevity of the
Council on Library Resources.

Most University of Georgia Press titles are
available from popular e-book vendors.

Printed in the United States of America

22   21   20   19   C   5   4   3   2

Library of Congress Cataloging-in-Publication Data

Names: Coles, Michael Joseph, 1944– author. | Lewis, Catherine M.,
    author. | Kennedy, Jim, 1948– writer of foreword.

Title: Time to get tough : how cookies, coffee, and a crash led to
    success in business and life / Michael J. Coles and Catherine M.
    Lewis ; foreword by Jim Kennedy.

Description: Athens, Georgia : University of Georgia Press, [2018] |
    xiii, 216 pages : illustrations ; 24 cm

Identifiers: LCCN 2018947522 | ISBN 9780820354620 (hbk : alk.
    paper) | ISBN 9780820354613 (ebk)

Subjects: LCSH: Coles, Michael Joseph, 1944– | Leadership. | Food
    industry and trade—United States—Biography. | Business
    enterprises. | Businessmen—United States—Biography. | Success in
    business—Biography. | Entrepreneurship. | Management.

Classification: LCC HD9010.C65 A3 2018 | DDC
    338.7/6640092—dc23

LC record available at https://lccn.loc.gov/2018947522

This book is dedicated to Donna, my best friend and the love of my life. Our lives connected by coincidence, and our first meeting was like a total eclipse. It happens rarely, and if you don't look up you can miss it. Fortunately, I looked up.

I'd rather be a could-be if I cannot be an are,

For a could-be is a maybe who is reaching for a star.

I'd rather be a has-been than a might-have-been, by far,

For a might-have-been has never been, but a has was once an are.

—Milton Berle (1908–2002), after

Robert W. Chambers (1865–1933)

Contents

Foreword, by Jim Kennedy   xi

Prologue: Step into the Valley   1

1   In the Shadow of Goliath   7

2   Hey Kid, Do You Want a Job?   16

3   It's All Sold   26

4   What Strike?   37

5   Do You Know How Many Cookies?   53

6   From Cookie to Counter   64

7   The Crash   73

8   Inch by Inch   83

9   Exit 666   96

10   TTGT   105

11   The Reckoning   114

12   That Was Pretty Fast   129

13   Building a Brand Religion   139

14   Fifty Percent to Go   151

15   This Is the Battlefield   157

16   Service, Service, Service   170

17   Love Spoken Here   181

18   The Last Five Miles   187

Epilogue: The First Law of Nature Is Growth   202

Acknowledgments   209

About the Authors   215

Foreword

Jim Kennedy CHAIRMAN, COX ENTERPRISES

*"What the hell
was that?"
Those were the
first words out of
my mouth.*

It was in the early 1990s, and I was competing in a
huge cycling event to support Northside Hospital
that was not officially a race. This was news to the
group of about thirty of the amateur racers, myself
included, who were treating it very much like one.
We were out front setting a pretty good pace down
a long hill in North Georgia on our way to Lake
Lanier. We were cruising along at about forty-five
miles per hour when a bullet with two bicycle wheels
sticking out of the bottom shot past us.

"What the hell was that?"

It turned out that it was Michael Coles on a
recumbent bicycle with an aerodynamic skin that
comprised the outer shell. No telling how fast he was
going, but it was definitely a lot faster than we were.
I was an experienced racer and was pretty competitive, but we were no match for Michael's speed. He
was riding the same bike that he used to win the
Race Across America in 1989 with Pete Penseyres,
Bob Fourney, and Pete's brother James. They held
the world record, crossing the United States in five
days, one hour, and eight minutes. And that was
Michael's third record—he had completed two solo
races from Savannah to San Diego in 1982 and 1984.

Later that morning, after we finished the hundred-kilometer ride, I met Michael for the first time. Small in stature, but obviously with a big heart, big lungs, and powerful legs, he had a huge smile that made you feel like a longtime friend. He had a big personality and an even bigger story. Michael was introduced to the crowd and talked for about ten minutes about the accident that nearly killed him in 1977 and how he used cycling to recover, all while building a multimillion-dollar cookie business. I have heard inspirational business stories before, but this one was different. Michael talked about how much you suffer on cross-country ultramarathon races and how your ability to push through the pain can help you keep going regardless of the obstacles you face. I remember him saying that he wasn't faster or better than other cyclists, he was simply willing to suffer more. He closed his remarks by talking about the importance of keeping your head down to finish the race, but also using that time to plan for the next one. This event was the beginning of a more than twenty-five-year friendship built around bicycles, fly fishing, artificial knee joints, business, and politics. You are about to find out that Michael knows a lot about all those things.

I have always liked working with people who played competitive sports at one time in their lives. My reasoning is simple: All athletes who have pushed themselves on the field of competition—whether it be swimming, cycling, or running—have endured a period where they must dig down deep to overcome fear and pain to reach the finish line. In 1995 I interviewed a candidate to join our board of directors at Cox Communications named Janet Clarke who played ice hockey at Princeton University. She was an executive at R. R. Donnelley in Chicago, and we bonded over the fact that we spoke the same language of sport. The skills that made her successful on the ice translated into the boardroom, and she became one of our most effective directors.

Michael had that same kind of grit and determination, and his pursuit of three long-distance cycling world records illustrates his ability to overcome great physical trauma and focus on what appears to be an unattainable goal. He did the same thing for the chocolate chip cookie business, making a tasty treat into a national obsession. His dogged pursuit of perfection helped transform that industry. He commits the same energy and effort to running and building businesses, to serving his community, and to mentoring a new generation of leaders. If you are entering the business world, you will read this book and see yourself in his story. The difference between Michael and hundreds of other entrepreneurs is his determination. He simply puts his head down and fights until the battle has been won. He made it big, and his story will inspire you to do the same.

Who knew?

TIME TO GET TOUGH

Prologue

Step into the Valley

I was so close to setting a new ultramarathon cycling record that I could almost taste it. It was the eighth day of the 1983 race, and I was in Arizona, only 488 miles from San Diego. All of the elements for victory were in place. I had trained hard. I had assembled the right crew. I had done all the things that were necessary to break the record I set the year before. At thirty-nine years old, I was in the best shape of my life. I was going faster than I ever thought possible. If I stayed on this pace, I would cross the entire United States in nine days. You could hardly drive much faster.

But instead of breaking the record that year, I broke my collarbone. I was blown off my bike by a dust devil—one of those menacing whirlwinds called "ghost spirits" by the Navajo. Formed when hot air near the surface rises quickly through a small pocket of cooler low-pressure air, they create a funnel-like chimney. Most are weak and dissipate within a minute of forming, but others can grow to be large and intense, with concentrated winds that become quite dangerous. When the dust devil struck me and I started falling, I knew it was bad. I hit the asphalt and heard a loud, unmistakable crack—and there I was again, splayed out on the highway. I had been there before, broken and bleeding. In 1977 I was nearly killed in a motorcycle accident, riding home on a damp August evening six weeks after opening Great American Cookies. My partner, Arthur Karp, and I had started the cookie company with only $8,000, and it had become more successful than we ever could have imagined. Then, in a moment, everything changed.

Once again I was facing something unexpected, daunting, and larger than life. I found myself in the shadow of Goliath, the latest of the giants that have haunted me for so many years. But I was not going to be defeated by that dust devil when I was so close to reaching my goal. While waiting for my collarbone to be x-rayed, and even before I told my wife Donna, I started sketching out what I needed to do to prepare for the next race. The doctor told me I could start training immediately, as long as I kept pressure off my shoulder. When I got home, I set my bike on an indoor trainer and started a new regimen that felt eerily familiar. It was only a few years since I first climbed on a stationary bike while trying to recover the full range of motion in my legs after my nearly fatal motorcycle accident. Now I was broken again, but I was back on the bike.

It was a painful process. I needed a stool to get onto the seat. Even the lightest pressure on my right arm brought excruciating pain, so it took everything I had to just stay upright. I finally resorted to saying out loud, "You've got to do this. You can't waste any time. It's time to get tough." When I finished that first session, I grabbed a piece of paper and scrawled with my left hand TTGT and taped it on the bathroom mirror. Later that day I told Donna that I needed to make signs with that slogan to put around the house. This was before personal computers were common, so I hired a graphic designer who hand-painted fifty of them on four- and two-inch-square card stock. I posted them everywhere, even inside the refrigerator. I gave them to my crew and placed them on all of my bikes and all over my office. Every time I felt like giving up, the abbreviation for "Time to Get Tough" slapped me in the face. And it made all the difference.

The David and Goliath story has always intrigued me, but not for the reasons you might expect. Many who reference the Old Testament tale focus on David's victory over the Philistine giant. A brave but ordinary man overcomes extraordinary odds and wins. But for me, the most important lesson is not that David defeated Goliath but rather that he had the courage to step into the valley without knowing the outcome. He defied everyone's expectations. The result was not as important as the initial decision to act.

We each face our own Goliath-like challenges, whether it is trying to start a business, change careers, or go back to school. The first question to ask when facing such a challenge should not be "Will I succeed?" The real question is "Do I have the courage to start—to step into the valley?"

I have defied labels my entire life and had to muster the courage to face plenty of Goliath-like challenges. Because my father went bankrupt when I was ten years old, I started working while still in elementary school. We were poor, and people often set limits on what they thought I could achieve. That just gave me more incentive to prove them wrong. As a child, I was considered out of control. Now I am considered free-spirited. I was often told that I did not work well in groups, because I always told everyone else what to do. Now I am lauded for my leadership skills. Nobody believed I would be successful, because I often tried to do things a different way. Now that's called entrepreneurial spirit. Labels change, but I learned early on not to let them define me. The greatest disappointments in life come from failing to try something new or stand up to a challenge, and the greatest accomplishments come from going beyond what is expected.

By most conventional measures, I am successful. Peeling away that superficial veneer of accomplishment, though, reveals a pile of missed opportunities, false starts, and painful defeats. Ironically, some of those times have been the most satisfying, memorable, and victorious moments of my life, even though by most standards I failed. I have learned that glory does not reside in the final outcome; success presents itself in the journey. I am not the first person to realize this timeless truth. President Theodore Roosevelt made a similar point in a now-famous speech titled "Citizenship in a Republic," delivered at the Sorbonne in Paris on April 23, 1910:

The credit belongs to the man who is actually in the arena, whose face is marred by dust and sweat and blood; who strives valiantly; who errs, who comes short again and again, because there is no effort without error and shortcoming; but who does actually strive to do the deeds; who knows great enthusiasms, the great devotions; who spends himself in a worthy cause; who at the best knows in the end the triumph of high achievement, and who at the worst, if he fails, at least fails while daring greatly, so that his place shall never be with those cold and timid souls who neither know victory nor defeat.

Roosevelt's man in the arena is beaten and bloodied but not deterred. He is defiant in the face of daunting odds and finds value and worth in striving, not just in winning.

Several months ago I was at an event with Donna. I was wearing a suit and a crisp white dress shirt. I had spent quite a bit of time deciding which cuff links to wear, trying a few different options until I was satisfied. When I arrived at the dinner, one of my friends commented on the knot of my tie—not the tie itself, not the perfectly selected cuff links, nor the suit I had chosen. I had given a great deal of thought to those selections. His comment was about the knot. Why, I wondered, so much attention on the knot? People rarely wear ties these days, and even fewer comment on them.

A few days later I was meeting with an entrepreneur whom I was advising about starting a new business. As a mark of his gratitude, he sent me a note thanking me for my time and advice. The first line of his email read, "A man who takes the time to tie a proper necktie is impressive. I tell you it's a dying art." I was startled. I had just received two comments in the same week about my ability to tie a tie. This seemed like an odd coincidence. Over the years, I have heard people remark about my ties, but receiving these two so close together struck me in a different way. What was so notable about achieving the perfect knot? I remember standing in front of my mirror thinking about it. Suddenly I recalled being in front of a similar mirror watching my boss, Irving Settler, knotting his own tie.

I began working for Irving, a Miami Beach clothier, at the age of thirteen in 1957. One Thursday evening about a year after I started, I was in the store while he was getting dressed to go on a buying trip to New York

City. He took down a large hatbox and reached in to remove this gorgeous gray Resistol hat. Now, this was a time when hats were still a very important part of a man's wardrobe. Not in Florida—it was just too hot to wear them. But New York was a different story, and Irving handled that hat as if it were a piece of fine china. His delicate touch, suggesting that grabbing it too fast would destroy it, made his respect for the hat obvious. Finally he put it on the counter next to the mirror and turned his attention to his tie. I watched him for about half an hour tie it, untie it, and do it again. Each knot looked fine to me, but Irving was not satisfied until he had created a perfect double Windsor knot pulled tightly with a dimple at its tightest point. Each side of the dimple was perfectly symmetrical. It was simple and elegant—the sign of a well-dressed man.

Irving owned and managed Dorwins, a men's and young men's clothing shop on Washington Avenue. He built his business from scratch and spent a lot of time with me as an apprentice. I learned a lot about business from Irving, but even more about how to live a good life. So as I stood behind him watching this tie drama, I had to ask, "Several of those knots looked just fine. Why do you keep redoing it?"

He looked at me and said, "Yes, they were good. But they were not great. They were not perfect." He went on to explain, "Kid, never accept good. If you do, you will never know your full potential. And you never know how people are going to judge you. If your clothes are not right—if even the smallest detail is not attended to—you might lose their respect. Make sure everything is perfect, and people will know who you are."

These fairly simple lessons about perseverance, practice, and perfection helped me start Great American Cookies in 1977; helped me set three world records cycling across America; helped me grow companies such as Male Slacks and Jeans, Caribou Coffee, Charter Bank, and BrandBank; helped me run for Congress twice; and helped me chair the Georgia Film Commission, the Kennesaw State University Foundation, and the Walker School, and serve on the Board of Regents of the University System of Georgia.

My life and career have been about turning obstacles into opportunities, tragedies into triumphs, and poverty into philanthropy. I decided to tell my story not to boast about my accomplishments but rather to demonstrate that there is no single winning formula or straight line to success. I do not have an Ivy League pedigree or an MBA from a top-ten business school; I was not selected for a prestigious internship at a Fortune 500 company early in my career. Instead I started several entrepreneurial ventures as a teenager and worked my way up from sales clerk to store manager to national sales manager in the clothing business before founding my first company. I never imagined that I would one day write about my life. Why would anyone be interested in the story of a poor kid who never went to college? But then I started to see a pattern. At the end of every talk I give, I have a group of entrepreneurs, MBA students, and business leaders peppering me with questions: What did your early failures teach you? How did you start the cookie company? What motivated you to race your bike across country, and how did those races change your approach to business? What would you have done differently? They are essentially all asking different versions the same question: What can I glean from your successes and mistakes to help me reach my goals?

In the chapters that follow, I tell the story of what I have learned over the past half century from my own life and from the worlds of history, business, and sport to help answer those questions. In the epilogue I distill those stories into ten lessons that can help you as you face your own challenges. Life cannot be measured simply in terms of winning and losing. It is measured by the kind of courage you show along the journey. So step into the valley with me.

1

In the Shadow of Goliath

I started my business career young, and by the time I was twenty-five I thought I knew all the answers. The problem was that I didn't know all the questions.

I was ten years old when I found myself looking into the basement window of our former house in the Buffalo suburb of Kenmore. I used my hand to wipe away the grit that had built up during the four years we lived there. I peered through the smoky glass. With no other light than the morning sun, I was able to make out the vague shadows of my train set and other toys that had been left behind. Magazines and papers were strewn about the floor. I had ridden my bicycle from our new apartment in Buffalo back to Kenmore. It was only a little over a mile, and took about ten minutes, but it felt like a world away.

Just a few days before, I had come home from school and found all of our belongings packed, the car loaded, the house empty, and my parents waiting for me. We had lost the house and needed to move into an apartment across town near the University of Buffalo. My father and brother had loaded most of our belongings in a truck while I was at school. I had no time to gather many of my toys, notably my train set in the basement. And we probably would not have had room for it anyway. The most devastating news was that my parents

7

had arranged for a family down the street to take my dog Lucky because the apartment did not allow pets. I had had her for four years; my father had surprised me with her when I was six. My mother hated dogs, so the gift was a really big deal. Lucky was my dog, my best friend, and I fed her, walked her, played with her. She followed me around constantly and even slept on my bed. Giving her away was the most heart-wrenching thing I can remember doing as a child, but I knew I had no choice. I gently placed my beloved cocker spaniel next to her food and water bowl in my red wagon and pulled her down the street. It was the longest, saddest walk I had ever taken. The family we gave her to had a child two years younger than me. Even though they were really nice and would give her a good home, it was a terrible moment. I managed to control my emotions on the way to the house because I did not want the boy to see me cry, but on the walk back tears streamed down my face.

Looking through that basement window, I did not understand why this had happened so suddenly. Why had everything changed overnight? Scared, confused, and unable to comprehend these strange new events, I felt alone and isolated. My safe and secure childhood in Kenmore had been taken from me. Nothing was certain anymore. My life was taking another course, and it would be forever different. As I knelt on the ground staring through the window, I was not aware that I was standing in the shadow of the giant Goliath.

My father, David Coles, was born in the United States, but his family came from Russia. They had emigrated through France and eventually settled in New York. My father's older brother was killed in World War I, and his father died from tuberculosis when David was eleven. As the oldest male child, he went to work after completing the sixth grade. This was not a casual job for spending money—it was to support his mother and two siblings. He started collecting rags with a pushcart, and later a horse-drawn cart enabled him to expand his scrap business. My mother, Leja, was born in Poland, but as she came through Ellis Island she was given the name Lena. She hated it her whole life and went by Lee. Her father had come to America first and later sent for my grandmother and my mother in 1920, when my mother was six years old. The rest of my mother's family was killed in the Holocaust. My grandfather, who lived into his nineties, never recovered from that tragedy.

My parents married in 1932, when my mother was eighteen and my father was twenty. My brother, Gerald (Gerry), is nine years older than me, and my sister, Elaine, is halfway in between. We were all born in Brooklyn, but my family moved to an apartment in Buffalo, New York, in 1949 when I was five. I was excited to start first grade at my new school, but after a week I was put back into kindergarten because of the timing of my birthday. In the New York City school system, students started first grade at age five; in Buffalo it was six. My sister and brother were both held back as well. I had already made some new friends, but when I was pulled out of first grade, those friendships ended. The transition was traumatic, made worse by the fact that my former first-grade friends started calling me "kindergarten baby."

At this point my father was working as a driver for an import-export company that required frequent travel around the region and into Canada. The move to Buffalo allowed him to spend more time at home. He was still gone quite a bit, but in the summer he sometimes asked me to go with him. I would gather up my comic books and toys and my favorite pillow and jump in the truck. To this day I remember sleeping with my pillow on my father's lap while he drove to New York City. We were not wealthy, but we were comfortable in my earliest years. I did not know it at the time, but thinking back I remember that when Gerry turned sixteen, my father bought him a Studebaker. Getting a car as a teenager would be a big deal today; it was almost unheard of in the 1950s.

My father was doing well, and in 1950 we bought a house and moved out to Kenmore. We had always lived in apartments, so this was a big change for the whole family. The house seemed huge, and for the first time in my life we had a backyard. When I was six, my father came back from a trip to New York and surprised me with the six-week-old puppy that I named Lucky. She was all black and the sweetest, cutest cocker spaniel I had ever seen, and I was responsible for housebreaking her. My father planted a garden in our backyard, and I remember having homegrown vegetables on our dinner table for the first time ever. There were a lot of children my age in our neighborhood, and we spent most of our time outside playing in each other's yards—building forts and climbing trees. Caught up in the postwar housing boom, Kenmore was growing fast, so we saw the fields we played in transformed into subdivisions. This was a period of tremendous change in America, and I witnessed much of it through a child's eyes. Three years after moving to Kenmore, my father started his own company. Not long afterwards, there was a fire at his warehouse. He did not have insurance, and he was bankrupted overnight. I was only ten, and it took me a while to realize what was happening.

We left Kenmore and moved to a two-flat house, divided into an upstairs and downstairs apartment with a garage, in Buffalo at 218 Englewood Avenue. I did not want to move, but at first not much changed. We had lost the house, yard, my dog Lucky, and some toys, but we still had most of our household possessions. The apartment felt familiar because we had the same dining room set, the same television, and the same beds. My mother worked hard to make everything feel as normal as she could, though our meals became less elaborate, we no longer went shopping for new clothes, and there never seemed to be any extra money. My father always believed that he would rebound, and looking back now, we were probably living beyond our means.

The move to Englewood Avenue happened a month into my fourth-grade year. I remember this vividly because that was the year I was supposed to learn cursive writing. I discovered that my new school taught cursive in the third grade—so I had missed a whole year of instruction. When I got into my new classroom, the teachers thought I was slow. I was embarrassed to tell them that I had not yet learned cursive, so I had to use the border around the classroom that had both block and cursive letters as a guide. During exams, I had to look up to figure out how to write each individual letter. As a result, I could never finish a test. Up until this point, I had always done well in school. Because my parents were so preoccupied with my father's situation, they did not realize what was happening. Finally my mother and I went to meet with the teacher, and I had to confess that I could not write in cursive. With some extra help I brought up my grades, but to this day I still print everything that I write.

It was while living on Englewood Avenue that I launched my first entrepreneurial venture, hoping to raise a little bit of spending money. In October I offered to rake neighbors' leaves. Leaves do not have to be raked the moment they hit the ground, so I could manage five or six houses by myself, working on a house or two at a time. Yards could be raked every week or so, and even though the work was hard, it turned out to be a lucrative business throughout the fall.

As winter approached, I assumed I could shovel snow for the same customers to keep my income stream alive. But snow, unlike leaves, had to be removed instantly. I couldn't spread the work throughout the week but had to do all the houses in the same day. I was small for my age and quickly realized that I could not handle the work alone. However, I was really good at getting the work and negotiating a favorable price.

That gave me an idea. If I could get the jobs and hire friends to share the work, I could manage things so we all made more money. I started recruiting neighborhood boys to help. We were paid fifty cents to clear each driveway and a quarter for each sidewalk. If we did both, customers sometimes paid us a dollar. Five friends helped me shovel the snow, and I took a percentage of the money to manage the whole process. The system worked pretty well, because many of my friends were too shy to ask for the work, while I loved trying to persuade the neighbors to hire us. By the third snowstorm, we had increased our houses to ten. Had my family remained in Buffalo, we probably would have ended up with a full-blown snow-removal business that rivaled the city's crew—at least we thought so. This enterprise taught me that it was important to hire a good team. I also learned to play to my strengths. While I couldn't do all of the heavy lifting alone, I was good at marketing and building a customer base.

My first foray into retail followed a similar trajectory. When I was eleven, I wanted a Tru-Action Electric Football Game that had been invented in 1947 by Norman Sas. Tudor Metal Products and Tudor Games was one of the first companies to make a profit in the electronic games business. This football game was played on a vibrating metal field that was modeled on an electric car race game that the company sold. The vibration helped move miniature plastic players down the field. It was an instant hit, and every boy in America seemed to want one. It was the 1950s, long before video games were invented, and it seemed like the coolest game around. Electric Football cost about five dollars, which was a fortune for a toy.

I told my parents about the game, and they said that if I earned the money, I could buy it. Raking leaves and shoveling snow depended on the seasons, so now I needed a plan for the warm-weather months. After thinking about it for a few days, I realized that there were some old toys, books, and household items in our garage that nobody seemed to be using. My career in retail was about to begin.

I set up two small tables outside our detached garage and created a sidewalk sale with old toys that I had managed to save from our move from Kenmore, comic books, and assorted household items. I began to draw a crowd, as I was selling things for spare change. Even some of my best items went for a quarter. It was not long before I had sold almost all of my merchandise. When I counted up the change, I realized that I only had a little more than three dollars. I was so excited about my new venture that I had not given my approach much thought. I knew how much money I needed to buy the football game, but I had not considered how much merchandise I needed to sell or what prices I needed to set to reach that goal.

In the meantime, several of my friends in the neighborhood saw what I was doing and set up their own sidewalk stores. Pretty soon there were five of them on my block. I had run out of merchandise, and now I had plenty of competition. I needed a new plan. I took my red wagon and went to see what my neighbors were doing. One boy was selling the same kind of books and toys that I was, but his items were newer and in better shape. I looked over what he had for sale and quickly figured out that, with the three dollars I had earned, I could buy all of his merchandise. If I resold the items for higher prices, I could make more money. I offered the boy two dollars for everything, and he happily accepted, because two dollars seemed like a fortune to a ten-year-old boy. Together we loaded it all into my red wagon, and I headed back to my house. On the way I met another kid with the same variety of merchandise. I only had $1.50 left, so I had to school myself quickly in the art of negotiation. I offered him a dollar for all of his merchandise. The promise of a crisp one-dollar bill was appealing. After some back and forth, we agreed on $1.25. We filled up the wagon, and I walked home.

I did not realize then that I had learned two valuable lessons that day. The first was: Do not start a business without a clear goal in mind and a plan for how to reach it. That is as important for a kid's sidewalk store as it is for a Fortune 500 company. The second lesson was that I had over-paid for my first buyout. I had a lot to learn about the art of negotiation. Even so, my efforts paid off, and I did get the electric football game. More important, though, my career in business had begun.

In the two years after my father's bankruptcy, we fell deeper and deeper into debt, which required that we move into an even less expensive apart-ment and even further reduce our expenses. My father owed money to nearly everyone in town, and soon his wages were being garnished. When we lived in Kenmore, I remember my mother creating elaborate home-cooked dinners; now we often had only enough money to eat noodles. The situation became so bad that my father decided to move the family to Florida because the state had more favorable laws for debtors. One cold January night before my thirteenth birthday, we packed what we could fit in the family car, a Hudson Wasp. My brother was at the University of Buffalo and elected to stay behind to finish college. Our family had already mailed invitations for my bar mitzvah, but we moved to Miami Beach before the ceremony could take place. This time we did not take any of our belongings, because we were moving into a 350-square-foot one-bedroom apartment. The rent was about fifty dollars a month, and the dilapidated building was filled with palmetto bugs, those large flying cockroaches that are so common in South Florida. There was no air-conditioning. I had to share a room with my sister, and we did not get along. She was eighteen, and I am sure she did not relish sharing her space with her thirteen-year-old brother any more than I did. For most of my childhood I roomed with Gerry, and we were really close. Now he was grown and had moved out. So much had changed so fast, and the tension between my parents was exacerbated by close quarters. I started to do everything I could to stay out of the house. Moving to Miami Beach was jarring, but also eye-opening.

I could continue to believe that this was just a temporary situation, or I could face the reality of my father's bankruptcy, from which he never recovered, and start to find my own way. If I had to pinpoint a major turning point in my young life, this was it. I no longer had a stable home that I could depend on; we were on the brink of disaster.

My father had some business contacts in Miami Beach, and his sister lived there, so he hoped they could help him find work. His last job in Buffalo was working at Delgato's, an appliance store near downtown. He proved to be a great salesman and thought he might find a similar job in Florida. One night, while he was still searching for a job, he received a call from Nick Delgato asking him to come back to Buffalo to work for him. Two days later Nick showed up in Miami Beach, still hoping to persuade him. But we were there to stay.

The first Saturday that we were in Miami Beach, I rode my old Shelby bicycle around the neighborhood to explore my new surroundings. I came to Flamingo Park and saw a crowd gathered at the track. I had stumbled upon a bike race. There were only four competitors, and when I walked up to the fence to watch, one of the organizers asked if I wanted to join the mile-long race, which would be four laps around the track. I looked over at the other kids and at their shiny new English racing bikes; they had three-speed models that probably weighed thirty pounds. There I was on my old Schwinn knock-off that was at least twice as heavy. But I was the new kid and thought this might be a way to make some new friends. I joined the others at the starting line, and when the gun went off, my competitive juices started flowing. I never looked behind me or even looked up; I just pedaled as hard as I could. When I started the fourth lap, I could see the other riders ahead of me beyond the white ribbon. I thought I was so slow that they were holding the ribbon to stop me, so I began to slow down so I would not break it. Then I heard the crowd screaming: "Go, go, go!" I quickly realized that the other bikes were not ahead of me—they were behind me. I had lapped the field. I won the blue ribbon, but I did not make any friends that day.

I remember riding home and having nobody to tell what had happened. Our lives were in complete disarray. Gerry was still in Buffalo, so I no longer had his support. When my father went bankrupt three years earlier and my parents started fighting, anytime I found myself in the middle of their screaming matches, I could always turn to my big brother. Now he was gone, and my sister was out trying to make her own way. I was left alone, and I knew that in the face of this new reality, my little racing victory was pretty insignificant. But I really liked to ride. In Buffalo I used to go long distances, sometimes so far that my father had to come pick me up in the dark, miles from home. I was not very good at baseball or football and was usually the last one picked for those teams. But, by God, I could ride a bike.

2

Hey Kid, Do You Want a Job?

About a month after moving to Miami Beach, my father landed a sales position in the appliance department at Sears, and I found a job as a beach boy at the Georgian, an oceanfront hotel. This was not a casual job but real responsibility, to help our family survive. On one hand I was proud of what I could contribute, but I was also resentful. I never participated in after-school activities, had no time for sports or parties, and missed out on much of the social life my friends enjoyed. There was nothing romantic about the work. I woke up at five a.m. during the week and laid out mats and put up umbrellas before going to school. After the afternoon bell rang at school, I returned to the hotel and put the umbrellas and mats away and swept the grounds. I made a dollar a day during the week, and two dollars on the weekends because of the increased volume of work. It was hard work, and I had no choice but to do it.

Six months later I left that job because of a hurricane. The day after the storm, I came in early and found that the wind had blown literally thousands of pounds of sand into the swimming pool. In fact, the whole pool deck looked like a beach. My boss met me at five a.m. with a shovel and told me to start digging out the pool. I began working, and he kept yelling that I was not going fast enough. I kept wondering why he did not get in to help me. I was doing the best I could, but nothing seemed to please him, so I quit. That day I was hired by the hotel next door where my friend worked, the New Yorker, for the same wages. On weekends I worked for our landlord as an apprentice, learning plumbing, electrical work, and carpentry. I kept five dollars a week for lunches and school supplies and gave the rest to my parents.

In that first year of living in Miami Beach, I met a person who would have a tremendous influence on my life. I had discovered a clothing store at 1574 Washington Avenue named Dorwins King of Slacks (later renamed Dorwins Ivy Shop) that had really up-to-date merchandise, and I soon began shopping there when I could save up a little money. Sometimes I just visited the store because one of my friends worked for the owner, Irving Settler. Irving was a brilliant businessman, but also a difficult and exacting boss, so none of his employees kept their jobs for long. Signs in the window looking for a new stock boy were a pretty regular thing. Although he was the most quick-tempered person I ever met, Irving was also one of the smartest. He loved the clothing business, and he was a real visionary with an impeccable sense of timing, style, and marketing. I loved watching Irving. He and I shared an appreciation for clothes—and built a friendship on that common interest. As a teenager, even though I did not have any money, I liked to hang around Dorwins to window shop, enjoy the air-conditioning, and meet the other customers. Irving knew I could not afford most of what he sold, but he let me try on slacks, sport coats, and shirts anyway. I remember once when my mother's parents were visiting from New York, my grandfather gave me some money to buy clothes. This was a big deal because our family was really struggling, and I had not had new clothes for a while. So of course I went to Dorwins.

On the Saturday that I stopped to buy something, I was quickly drawn into a loud argument that Irving was having with my friend Steve. The way it sounded, Steve was going to be Irving's next victim. Irving was yelling and waving his hands around as his face turned redder and redder.

Steve was silent and terrified. I was embarrassed to be witnessing such a lashing, but just as I turned to leave, Irving spotted me.

"Hey kid," he yelled. "Do you want a job?" (He knew my name but still called me "kid" or Mikey.)

In that split second I realized that he was giving me an opportunity to work in an air-conditioned store that offered an employee discount on the clothes that I had been admiring for nearly a year. I would no longer have to bake in the hot Florida sun in the afternoons. Without even pausing, I said, "Sure."

Turning back to Steve, Irving said, "You're fired. Get outta here."

He grabbed me by the shoulder and said, "Kid, you're hired." Now, Irving knew me. I had been hanging around his store for some time, and he understood how much I liked and appreciated clothes. I started that very afternoon. I was thirteen years old, and it was 1957. Irving paid me fifty cents an hour, and it was a great job. I felt bad for Steve but was happy to have the opportunity. I was unsure it would last, so I kept my morning beach job for another year, because I knew Irving and had witnessed how easily he had turned on my friend. I also continued to work as an apprentice for the landlord in my building, but my main job after school was at Dorwins.

Irving had come up the hard way, and after I worked for him for a while, he told me his life story. A child of poor immigrants, he grew up in Scranton, Pennsylvania, during the Depression. He moved to New York City at the age of seventeen to work for a hat shop called the Mad Hatter in an era when men still wore hats. By the time he was twenty years old, he was running his own hat store. I once asked him how he found the courage to open his own business so young. He joked, "Well, I knew the business, and I found that people wanted to pay me what they thought I was worth. And I wouldn't work for that little money." When Irving first arrived in Miami Beach, he worked at Windsor King of Slacks. Several years later the owner sold him the business, and he had to work his way through the existing inventory over a period of time to transform it into a men's and young men's fashion store. The man who sold the business financed the sale to Irving, so if Irving missed a payment, he would lose everything. That helped explain why he was so protective of the store—every penny mattered.

The store's name was born of necessity. When Irving bought Windsor, he took the block letters that made up the original sign and rearranged them to spell Dorwins because he could not afford a new sign. Like many entrepreneurs, Irving started the store without much money. At first he catered to older men by selling dress slacks and suits, sport jackets, dress shirts, and ties. When he hired Steve, he was trying to attract younger people aged thirteen to twenty-five, so he changed his tagline to "The Smart Shop for Young Men" (and later "The Style Shop for Men and Boys"). There were Ivy Shops that catered to this demographic opening up all over Miami Beach, including several high-end stores on Lincoln Road, such as the Dinghy and the Stag Shop, and one across the street from Dorwins on Washington Avenue called Henry Steig's. Irving could see that younger men were becoming increasingly fashion conscious, and he saw the opportunity to tap into that new market.

Together, over the next year, we completely transformed his customer base, and the business exploded. I had a wide range of friends in school, and many of them started shopping at Dorwins. This was a big windfall for Irving, and he knew it. On Saturdays you could hardly move around the store, it was so crowded. I thought this was terrible, and I told him that we needed a bigger store. His reply was "It's a lot better to have a busy little store than a big empty one."

Years later I came to appreciate why he worked me so hard. I think we connected because we had similar backgrounds and both loved clothes, and he wanted to see if I had the grit needed to survive in the business world. He was as good-hearted as he was tough. I started as a stock boy, and by the time I was sixteen I was doing most of the buying for the store. At seventeen I was the manager. And when I was just nineteen, Irving offered to make me a partner. I still feel his influence on me today.

I did not realize how valuable Irving's lessons were until I lost my first business years later. Steve, who had been fired by Irving, saw his work at Dorwins as just another paycheck. That was why they did not get along. Irving had so much passion for his work that he could not tolerate anyone who was not equally committed. Every seemingly minor detail mattered to him: the cleanliness of the store, the way a customer was greeted, the quality of the merchandise, the tailoring. The employee who cares only about getting paid tends not to pay attention to all the other things that help build customer satisfaction and loyalty—something Irving never forgot.

In my first week with Irving, I realized how sloppy I had been in my previous work. At the beach hotels, I had no contact with the customer. I worked early in the morning and came back late in the afternoon when everyone was gone, so I largely worked alone. I threw the mats on the lounge chairs but never straightened them. I picked up trash but missed cigarette butts and napkins. I was not lazy, but I just did not see the connection between careful and attentive work and customer satisfaction.

But something happened to me working for Irving. For the first time, I was face-to-face with customers and saw what superior service should look like. If I had been hired on commission at a department store in young men's clothing, I might have learned these lessons the hard way over a long period. But working for Irving was like taking a crash course at business school—I saw the nuance of what it meant to give a customer a total experience. Irving was a tough boss, but I was like a sponge. Every time he spoke, it was as if everything else stopped in my brain. I was always listening and trying to learn all I could from him.

Irving was more than a business mentor; he was like Professor Henry Higgins in *My Fair Lady*—he taught me everything. He and his wife Helen would take me out to dinner. Now, my family could not afford to eat in a restaurant. Back in the 1950s, very few people had money to spend on restaurants. When we did on a special occasion, it was at a local Chinese place that was not very expensive. Irving and Helen introduced me to many of Miami's best places. They taught me how to order, what foods to eat, how to use the proper utensils, and how to display proper table manners. What might seem like trivial things actually meant a lot to me. From Irving, I learned how to present myself to the world.

Irving also taught me another lesson, a morbid but sound business practice. When an elderly man came in to buy something that needed alteration,

Irving instructed me not to do the work until the day scheduled for pickup, just in case the customer passed away. This happened fairly often, and we kept the clothes on the Dead Man's Rack in the back room. This may seem harsh, but it was the reality of the time. There were a number of elderly men in Miami Beach, and you just never knew what was going to happen. Irving would always call to remind customers the day before he promised the altered garments. If they answered the phone, he did the alterations. If they did not, he would wait until he could contact them. If he altered a garment and the person died, he did not get paid. Irving operated the store on a razor-thin margin, so every penny mattered.

Irving sensed that I was paying attention, so one day he said, "I'm going to teach you everything I can about this business, because one day you will have someone working for you who will try to take advantage of you. The only way you can know their value is to know what they do and how they do it." At first he focused on showing me how to be a tailor. Soon I could make a pattern with a pencil and piece of cardboard and do hems and other alterations. Irving's advice became really important when I was sixteen years old, during the two weeks leading up to the start of school. In the 1950s and 1960s, school shopping happened over a very compressed time period. It was not at all like it is today, spread over the summer months. Most schools began the Tuesday after Labor Day, and the major back-to-school shopping occurred on the two full weekends before the holiday. Suppliers delivered their fall merchandise in mid-July, and by the third week of August our store was packed with new clothes and customers.

While students in those days sometimes wore jeans, most young men in Miami Beach wore slacks and dress shirts to school. If you go back and watch films like *West Side Story*, you can see the kind of style that young men displayed in this era. Teenagers in Miami Beach often dressed in fashionably fitted clothes like the Puerto Rican gang made famous by the 1957 movie. As a result, many of the back-to-school purchases had to be altered. We contracted with a tailor, who had a shop inside one of the big Miami Beach hotels, to help us. We were his biggest customer, and he regularly picked up our merchandise for alterations. Throughout the weeks leading up to Labor Day, he came in to get the clothes every day to take them back to his shop. On the Friday morning before our busiest Saturday of that year, the tailor arrived before we opened.

He said to Irving, "Because there is so much merchandise to be altered, I need to double my prices so I can hire more people to finish the work." He thought he had Irving against the wall because this was our busiest season. He also knew that if there was ever a time to negotiate with Irving from a position of strength, this was it.

Irving was blindsided, but he played it cool. He knew that the tailor was not going to hire anyone else but was just trying to get more money. After a long pause, Irving looked at him and said, "I'm not paying you a nickel more." Irving was always fair, and in fact was already paying the tailor more than the going rate. Dorwins did not charge for alterations, so any extra expense had to be absorbed by Irving.

Agitated, the tailor persisted, "Irving, if you don't pay me what I'm asking, I will not do it."

Irving snapped back, "So don't. I have found another tailor who would love to have this business. Leave everything."

The tailor was dumbfounded; he never expected that reaction.

The argument escalated, and at one point Irving screamed, "I'm your biggest customer. I pay you more than anyone else in this city. I keep you in business. You drive a Cadillac because of me."

The tailor just kept saying, "I have to have more money. This is going to be a lot of work."

Irving kept saying no, and the tailor finally stormed out of the store.

I had watched this all unfold, and I knew that there was no other tailor. After he left, I asked Irving, "What are we going to do?"

Irving smiled and said, "If you have plans this weekend, cancel them."

So that Friday night when we closed the store at nine o'clock, he and I went into the back room to get to work. We had a pressing table, a 14-pound iron, a blind stitch machine for making hems, and two sewing machines. We set up an assembly line and worked until four o'clock in the morning. We finished all of the alterations, and I went upstairs to the stockroom to get a few hours of sleep. I woke up exhausted and prepared for the busiest day of the year.

That Saturday was a mob scene. We opened the store, worked all day, closed at seven o'clock, and repeated the same drill. Once again Irving and I were holed up in the back room all night. I went home and slept for a while in my own bed, only to come back on Sunday, the only day Dorwins was closed, and work all day.

On Monday the tailor walked in with his head down to tell Irving that he would take everything and do the alterations for the same price.

Irving said, "Don't worry about it. I found another tailor, and the work is all done."

The tailor was stunned. After they talked some more, Irving agreed to rehire him at the same rate. Irving knew that the tailor had no real reason to raise his prices, and the tailor realized he had erred in trying to take advantage of Irving at his busiest time.

The tailor walked out, grateful to have the business again. After he left, Irving turned to me and said, "Now do you get it? Now do you know why I wanted you to learn everything?"

"I get it," I replied. And I did.

There were usually three people working at Dorwins: Irving, an older man named Bob who had been with him for years, and me. As the holidays approached, we realized that we needed some additional sales help. I was only sixteen, but Irving left it up to me to hire someone. I turned to one of my close friends who was desperate to find some work. I didn't even interview him or really know much about his work history; I just hired him. And he turned out to be the laziest person I could have put in the store. I would tell him to do something, and he just wouldn't do it. He was a terrible salesman, so I went to Irving and said, "This guy is awful. You got to get rid of him."

Irving looked at me with a bemused smile and said, "What do you mean, I've got to get rid of him? You hired him. You fire him."

"I can't," I explained. "He's my friend."

Irving laughed and said, "That's your problem."

So he became the first person I ever had to let go. I do not know how I managed to do it, but I knew that if you were going to let someone go, you had to do it swiftly, without apologies or a long conversation. So I called my friend into the back room and said, "This is not working out. I have to let you go."

Surprised, he replied, "When?"

I said, "Right now. I'll cut you a check, but you have to go now."

And that was it. He left, and it affected our relationship for a few weeks. Then we got back to normal. It was really tough for me, just as it was for him, but the lesson I learned was something I've heard from many business leaders in the years since, from Jack Welch to Larry Bossidy (whose book *Execution: The Discipline of Getting Things Done* I would later give to my leadership team at Caribou Coffee). The biggest mistake most businesses make is keeping incompetent people far too long. If they are not working out, you have to either let them go or retrain and reassign them. I am fiercely loyal to my colleagues, but it is not good for the employee, the coworkers, or the company to keep an underperformer on the payroll without corrective action. I also learned from this experience that hiring and firing decisions in business really affect people's lives and should not be made casually.

Irving and Dorwins were respected in the business community, and our store was well known throughout the country. In the 1950s the fashion industry was situated on the East Coast. The West Coast was not even on the map, so a number of manufacturers and designers visited us to launch the latest fashions and innovations. I remember when several men who wanted to promote the use of Talon nylon zippers in clothing came to meet Irving to see if he thought customers would accept them over brass or silver. They wanted his advice before going into production. Irving had a regular stream of people pitching new concepts to him, and I became well known by association. When companies were restyling a piece of clothing, they would often come to us, especially for pants. They would bring in the prototype to the store, I would try it on, and Irving would pin it to show them how it should fit. That became their pattern for how to cut and assemble their merchandise. Irving even invented a display form for shirts and blouses and filed for a patent in 1956 that was granted in 1960. Our little store in Miami Beach helped set fashion trends throughout the nation.

In addition to tailoring, Irving taught me how to be a buyer, how to dress windows, how to merchandise effectively, how to keep a store clean and organized, how to manage other employees, and how to take care of more than one customer at a time while making each one feel as if they had my full attention. He also thought it was important for his employees to know how to do basic repairs, because you never knew when you might not have enough money to hire somebody for maintenance. My work as an apprentice electrician, carpenter, and plumber made me pretty useful, but there is no question that the most valuable part of my education as a young man came from Irving. He had become the second person to save my life.

3

It's All Sold

My life has been saved four times.

When I was five years old, we were visiting Crystal Beach in Fort Erie, Ontario. Family friends had a cottage just across the Peace Bridge from Buffalo, New York, and we had gone to the beach—a popular spot in the summer—for the day. I had just jumped off the pier into Lake Erie, and someone came off behind me and pushed me down. I was not a strong swimmer, and as I was trying to catch my breath, I swallowed a lot of water. I was drowning when Elaine Silverman, a friend of the family, jumped in to rescue me. I believe that I would not be alive today if not for Elaine.

Three other people saved me in different ways. Irving Settler saved my life by being the first person outside my family to make me feel that I had any talent or value. I was lucky enough to meet him as a teenager, and he probably had more impact on my career than any other person. My older brother, Gerry, saved my life a third time when I was eighteen. And my wife Donna saved me just when I needed it most.

In high school all I did was work; I was not involved in any sports or after-school activities.

From my three jobs—at Irving's clothing shop in Miami Beach, at a beach hotel, and as an apprentice for Lou, the landlord of my apartment building—I made $31 a week and gave my family $25, leaving me $6 for lunches and incidentals. I had little time for homework or visits to the library, and my grades really suffered. Even though he did not live with us, my brother knew how much I was missing out on being a normal teenager. In the fall of my junior year, when I was seventeen, I started talking about quitting school and joining the Air Force with one of my friends. I was an insecure kid and thought that the armed services might give me a sense of purpose. Because I was under eighteen, I asked my parents if they would cosign the application, and they agreed. I debated it throughout the year, and when I barely passed my classes, I made plans to enlist. But Gerry talked me out of it. When I told him my plans, he said, "You can always go into the military, but if you do it now, you will not give yourself a chance to see what might happen after you graduate. You will never know what kind of opportunities you passed up, and you might really regret it later." I was persuaded and dropped the idea of joining the Air Force, but I still did not have a plan.

I started my senior year without any real sense of purpose. I was not leading my life; it was leading me. I was working so hard that I barely noticed. But I had a nagging feeling that I needed to do something drastic, though I was not sure what. A month after school started, Gerry persuaded me to come live with his family in Rockport, Massachusetts. I jumped at the chance to flee that dingy apartment in Miami Beach. So I packed my 1955 Plymouth that I had bought for $150, money I had saved working for Irving. I loved that car and had spent a lot of time customizing it. I painted it pearl white, put dual Lincoln Continental headlights on the front, did my own fiberglass work, and changed the rear to look like a 1957 Thunderbird with porthole windows. No wonder that I barely had enough money to pay for gas for the trip. I knew I could not afford a hotel, so I planned to drive straight through from Miami Beach to Rockport—a total of 1,533 miles. I ran into a lot of fog and fell asleep while driving on the New Jersey Turnpike. I jolted myself awake. While looking for a rest area, I nearly ran into the back end of an 18-wheeler. I slammed on my brakes and saw the flashing lights of a state trooper behind me. He pulled me over, and I told him what had happened. He let me follow him to the next exit, where I stopped to get some sleep.

I finally arrived in Rockport at two o'clock in the morning, but I did not know where Gerry lived. This was way before cell phones, so I had to find a pay phone to call him. He came out in the middle of the night and had me follow him home. He lived on the top floor of a two-flat apartment building with his wife, Chris, and two children, three-year-old Rom and baby Terry. Gerry, after working two jobs at night to pay for college, had become a fifth-grade teacher (later an educational psychologist), and probably made less than $80 per week. Chris was an artist making very little money, so they could not afford a large apartment. They had a closet that had held the baby's crib, which is where I ended up sleeping. But we all knew that this arrangement would not work for long. My parents promised to send Gerry some money so they could find a larger place, but they never did. I would have to pay room and board. We finally settled on $25 a week, but that meant that I had to sell my beloved Plymouth for $450. It felt like I was giving away my dog Lucky all over again. I had poured so much time and money into that car; I not only did the body-work myself, I sewed the seat covers in Irving's shop and even changed out the carpeting. It was really cool, and selling it meant I lost my independence. I could no longer jump in the car and take a drive with my friends. And this was a small town, so to make it even more painful, I saw my car on the street nearly every day.

The day after I arrived and unpacked, Gerry took me to register at the high school as a new student. I was given a choice of which track to pursue. The track with basic courses was for students who were not planning to go to college; they would train for a vocation. The other track was for college-bound students. I assumed I would follow the vocational path, but Gerry insisted that I register for college preparatory courses. I finally agreed, and the English and history courses that I picked seemed pretty straightforward. But when I went to select my math class, I was baffled. I had never even heard of solid geometry, calculus, trigonometry, or advanced algebra. So I looked down the list and saw at the very bottom a course named Basic Math. That sounded like the right one for me, so I signed up. What I did not know was that it was all of those subjects crammed into one course and much harder than it sounded.

I registered and picked up all of the necessary books. When I got home, I started looking at my schedule, and I got scared. I soon found out that I was probably two years behind my peers at Rockport High School, and I was especially worried about this math class. It was so hard, and I told Gerry that I was going to go back to school and register for the vocational track. He was adamant in his reply, "No, you can do this." He made me go to the library and check out a bunch of math books so I could tutor myself. He basically threatened me to succeed—and he was a big guy, a collegiate wrestler and power lifter. I loved him, but I was scared of him, too. So I really dedicated myself to school.

Unlike in Miami Beach, I was able to act like a normal teenager, mainly because the sale of the car gave me a little cushion. I had time to go to the library and to play sports at my new high school. I became the scorekeeper for home basketball games and, later that year, made the track team. I was friends with most of the basketball players and got to travel with them to away games. I also joined the gymnastics team and became pretty good at the parallel bars. I never really had a chance to play any ball or team sports growing up, so gymnastics seemed like a good choice. Later, because of Gerry, I became involved in wrestling and weightlifting.

I eventually started working a number of odd jobs, but nothing that took up as much time as Dorwins, Irving's store where I worked in Miami Beach. Rockport was founded as an artists' colony, and because it was small, I had a hard time finding steady work. But I did discover that I could get paid to pose for art classes—up to three dollars an hour. If you posed nude, it went up to five dollars. Guess what I chose? It was the easiest money I ever made. I also raked leaves and shoveled snow like I did in Buffalo, but I really found my niche repairing cars for teachers using the tools I had brought from Miami Beach. The snow and salt in Massachusetts caused many of their cars to rust out, so I offered to cut away rust, replace it with fiberglass sheeting, and get them new paint jobs. I probably did four or five cars before I started to drive a taxi.

With a lot of help and determination, I became an honor roll student. Before my senior year, I did not know what direction my life would take. I had learned a lot from Irving, but I still had no clue what my future held. I had set my sights fairly low. After that year with Gerry, I knew I could accomplish much more. It was as if the world opened up for me. My brother had helped me prove to myself that I was more capable than I thought, and I was really looking forward to college. I graduated from high school at the age of nineteen and continued to do odd jobs and drive the taxi throughout the summer in Rockport. In mid-August, just as I was planning to leave for college, I got a call from Irving that changed my plans.

He said, "I'm getting old. I need you to come back."

I was flattered, but replied, "I really want to go to college."

He countered, "You can still go to college, but think about Dade County Junior College and then transfer to the University of Miami. You can take classes and still work for me. I'll give you one-third of my business and pay you a hundred and fifty a week if you'll come back."

Now, this was 1963, and $150 a week for a nineteen-year-old was a fortune. So I moved back to Miami Beach and worked for Irving again from August 1963 until April 1964. I saved a lot of money, met a pretty girl named Adrienne, and started a serious relationship. While I was away, Irving and his wife had separated. When they reunited, my relationship with Irving started to fall apart. Helen used to like me, but she soon became jealous when she saw how he treated me like a son. As this was all unfolding, I realized that my days at Dorwins were numbered. The one-third interest in the business that Irving promised me never materialized. Adrienne and I had planned to marry in May, but we decided instead to move to Chicago and get married on the trip. We stopped in a small town in Georgia to visit a justice of the peace, then continued north. We found a cheap apartment on the North Side of Chicago to be near her family.

Once in Chicago, I started searching for a job. At the age of twenty, I had a lot of good experience, but because I looked like I was twelve, nobody wanted to hire me. My wife's aunt Sylvia finally helped me get an interview with a man named Eddie Palay. Eddie owned three Mister Jr.

clothing shops in and around Chicago—one in the city on Devon Avenue, one in Skokie, and one in the northern suburbs, near his home. Sylvia's son, Michael, regularly shopped at the Devon Avenue store, and their family had come to know Eddie. Mister Jr. was very much like Dorwins—the same type of customers and similar merchandise. They sold clothing for boys, young men, and men, including very expensive bar mitzvah suits for teenage boys who were preparing for the initiation ceremony that Jewish youth experience at age thirteen. So I thought I had a pretty good shot at getting hired.

I went to interview with Eddie, and he told me, "Nobody is going to buy a suit from you. You look too young." His store was well known in the Midwest for selling quality merchandise, and people would travel from all around the region to buy from him.

"How old do you think I am?" I asked. He guessed, and I told him to add a few years.

I suggested he call Irving to get a reference. Eddie agreed and said I should come back the next day. Eddie and Irving knew each other and would sometimes meet at clothing shows to discuss the industry, so they had a frank conversation about me. During the call, Eddie found out that I knew sales, knew merchandise, and was honest.

I returned the next day, and Eddie and I sat in the back room for a second interview. When we were finished, he said, "I can't hire you, because you look way too young."

Determined to persuade him, I suggested an unusual arrangement: "How about if I work for you for the next month for free? You don't have to pay me. But at the end of that month, I want a hundred and seventy-five dollars per week."

His jaw dropped, and he said, "I don't pay my managers that much."

I countered, "If you don't think I'm worth seven hundred dollars at the end of the first month, you don't have to pay me anything. Irving already told you I'm honest. So I won't take advantage of the situation and steal from you. You have nothing to lose."

So Eddie agreed and sent me to his Skokie store in May of 1964. At the end of the first week, I was his top salesman. When the store was not busy, I went into the back room to help the tailor. Unlike Dorwins, all of the alterations happened on-site. Eddie had no idea when he hired me that I had these skills, but he soon came to depend on me as much as Irving had.

I also used many of the other things Irving had taught me in my new job. If a young man came in to buy a white dress shirt at Dorwins, Irving would have him try it on. Then he would pull a few ties and a sport coat off the rack so the customer could envision the whole ensemble. He would do the same thing if a customer came in for a tie or coat. The first time I saw him doing it, I asked, "Why are you doing that? Nobody bought anything more than what they asked for."

Irving replied, "Yes, but if I don't suggest other items, they'll never buy anything more."

So that's what I did at Mister Jr. I was always showing the customers more merchandise than they requested—socks, underwear, whatever I could think of at the time. We did not work on commission, but it was really an issue of pride. Irving used to joke, "Just remember that people have a pocket full of money, and they are just dying to spend it." The young manager at the Skokie store was a really nice guy. He was thrilled to see me try all of these upselling techniques and was not jealous because he knew that I was going to help him make his bonus.

On the second Friday on the job, I made the biggest sale in the store's history. Sam Pasternak, who owned a manufacturing company in Kansas City called Cake Box Bakers, came to buy his son a suit for his bar mitzvah. The boy was very small in stature, as was the father. The son wanted a suit for temple on Saturday and a sport coat for Friday night, so we spent a lot of time talking about what he liked. They were in the store for about three hours.

When working with a customer, I had a nearly obsessive habit of putting away the things that they rejected, so I could keep track of everything. Irving taught me to return the clothes and accessories to their racks quickly to keep the store clean and help other salesman find the merchandise. Anything the customer wanted to buy was placed on the counter by the cash register. Well, as the hours wore on with Sam and his son, the clothes on the counter were becoming a big pile.

While the son was trying on all of these clothes, I asked the father, "Are you all set for the bar mitzvah?"

He said, "No, and I'm really hard to fit."

I confidently replied, "Listen, I can fit you."

And I could. When other salesmen said this, they meant they had to wait for the tailor to arrive. Not me. Irving had taught me how to do alterations, so I could save the customer time and offer a better experience in the store. My skill and experience in this area helped build my credibility with the customers and with Eddie, despite my apparent youth. I had already established a relationship with Sam Pasternak and his son, and now I had an opportunity to gain Sam's trust. So I grabbed the chalk and pins and starting fitting him. I knew I had to get it right, because he lived in Kansas City and could not come in for a second fitting. I had to ship all the merchandise, so I only had one shot. I could tell he was impressed, and I wound up selling Sam and his son more than a dozen suits, sport jackets, shirts, slacks, belts, socks, underwear—close to $3,000 in merchandise. It was the biggest sale in the store's history.

Eddie was very involved in his stores, and each day he followed the same routine. He visited the store near his home first thing in the morning, then came to Skokie, and by lunch was on Devon Avenue. Then he would do the reverse on the way home. He was a tall and slender man and always seemed to be running. He came into the store like a tornado. He would look around, review the receipts, talk to the staff, and be gone in about half an hour. These visits were intense and kept all of us salesmen on edge. When he left any of the stores, we would call the next one and simply say, "Eddie Palay is on his way." Like Irving, he was really demanding.

The day of the Pasternak sale, Eddie came in and saw all the clothes draped over the counter and said loudly enough for us all to hear, "Who made this mess? Get it put away."

I looked back and said, "It's all sold."

"What? Really?" he asked, amazed.

Eddie had an incentive for his salesmen—if you sold two suits or sport coats (or one of each), you would get two dollars. If you sold three, you would get five dollars. There was nothing in the employee manual for someone who had just sold fourteen pieces. At the end of the two weeks, Eddie gladly agreed to pay me $700 a month. When Sam received the merchandise that we shipped to Kansas City, which all fit perfectly, he called me and said, "If you ever want another job, I would find a place for you."

I loved this job, but I still wanted to go to college. Before going to work for Eddie, I had befriended a couple in Miami Beach who were from Phoenix. They encouraged me to apply to Arizona State University, and with help from my high school guidance counselor, I received a partial scholarship. I was set to start in January 1965. So I planned to work at Mister Jr. for about eight months to save more money and then move to Arizona.

While at Mister Jr., I became good friends with Lenny Rosenheim, a sales representative for H.I.S. Sportswear, a line Eddie carried. H.I.S. had been founded by Henry I. Siegel in 1926. In 1949, when Henry died suddenly, his son Jesse took over the business. When Lenny heard that I was planning to leave, he told me that H.I.S. was looking for a salesman. Because Mister Jr. worked closely with H.I.S., Eddie did not begrudge me the opportunity. I was still planning to move to Arizona. In fact, I had even put in an offer on a dry cleaning store. Our plan was to have my wife run the store while I did alterations and attended college. But Lenny finally persuaded me to meet with Bob Luehrs, the regional sales manager for H.I.S.

Bob lived in the Chicago suburbs, so I drove out to his house one Sunday afternoon to talk about what might be possible. Bob covered the entire Midwest for H.I.S., and I liked him right away. After I introduced myself, Bob's first question was "How old are you?" Once again I was reminded how young I looked. Age is something you cannot ask in an interview today, but this was a different time.

I said, "I'm twenty-two." I was really twenty, but I lied because I thought he would not hire me if I couldn't even buy a customer a drink.

He replied, "We have never hired anyone that young." But he was impressed with my experience. We completed the interview, and he said, "I'm not sure we can give you a territory, but I think we can find a place for you. You're going to have to meet with our national sales manager because of your age." As I walked to my car, I turned to Bob with a guilty look on my face and said, "You know, I'm really only twenty. I thought you wouldn't even talk to me if you knew." Years later, he said that moment of candor in the driveway really endeared me to him. He knew I would be a good salesman, but now he also knew that I was honest and ethical.

Not long after the interview with Bob, H.I.S. reorganized the company and split the Midwest into two regions. They moved Bob to Cleveland and brought in Lenny Newmark to cover half of Bob's old territory. So right before Thanksgiving, I was invited to go to a formal interview with the company brass. Bob called me beforehand and said, "Look, don't go to the interview if you are not really interested in coming to work for us. We are thinking about creating a new position for you as a trainee. You won't get a territory right away, but we do not want to lose you. At the lunch, the management team will want to see if this is a good fit for everyone."

I also talked to Lenny Rosenheim, who said, "I know you want to go to college, but consider this. When you graduate, you'll be twenty-four years old, and this is the kind of job you will try to get. You might as well become a trainee for us, and see if you like it. If you don't, you can quit and move to Arizona." This was the same advice my brother had given me about the Air Force years earlier. So the week before Thanksgiving, I drove to downtown Chicago for the interview.

I met everyone in the H.I.S. showroom at the Chicago Merchandise Mart, and then we went downstairs to the private club for a lunch meeting. There were three other men at the table—Lenny Newmark, Saul Nova, the national sales manager, and Jack Uppole, a salesman in Peoria. Jack was young, maybe twenty-nine, and was one of the top producers in the company. He had come to work at H.I.S. after playing for the Chicago Bears. On the way home from training camp he was seriously injured in a head-on collision, ending his football career. It was with Jack that I would work as a trainee.

Now, remember, I was twenty years old. Dressed to the nines in my best suit, tie, dress shirt, and cuff links, I felt good about my appearance, and Irving had done a pretty good job of teaching me basic etiquette, but at that age you are still all over the map. I was really nervous and mainly concerned about what to order. I wanted to select something that was easy to eat—nothing on the bone, no pasta, and nothing that I had to eat with my hands like fried chicken or ribs. When I finally looked at the menu, I felt a great sense of relief. It was Thanksgiving week, so they had a traditional dinner of turkey, mashed potatoes, dressing, peas, and cranberry sauce. I thought to myself, "This is great, just a knife and fork. I only have to worry about getting the gravy on my tie. What could be easier?"

The meal came. When I reached across the table for the salt, one of my cuff links grabbed the edge of my plate and flipped it onto my chest. The entire meal was just sitting there. The plate did not move, because it was glued on by the mashed potatoes and gravy. All three men are looking at me, and I am mortified. This is a really fancy club, and the waiter hustles over to the table and asks, "What can I do to help?"

Without even thinking, I say, "Please remove the plate, and hand me my knife and fork?"

Everybody exhaled, and the line got a big laugh. I leaned forward and scraped the remnants of my meal off my suit, shirt, and tie, and Lenny took me upstairs to the H.I.S. showroom to find some new clothes. When we came back down, the other two men were still laughing. Saul, who had a rather dry wit, said, "Kid, that was pretty quick thinking. You need to come work for us." And that was the end of the interview. I told them I wanted to think it over, but I knew I was going to take the job. In January of 1965 I became the first trainee at H.I.S. Sportswear, with a salary of $75 per week.

4

What Strike?

*Why am I
doing this?*

On my first day of work at H.I.S. Sportswear, I left
Chicago at four a.m. to drive 167 miles to Peoria
on a blustery morning to meet Jack, who I soon
learned was a workaholic. He told me to meet him
at seven at the Pere Marquette, a historic hotel built
in 1926. It was so early that I assumed we would
go somewhere for breakfast, so I didn't eat before
leaving home. I arrived about 6:30, and it was freezing outside. I kept walking in and out of the hotel's
revolving door looking for Jack. Picture this—it's my
first day, I've had nothing to eat or drink, my new
boss is late, and it is below zero outside. Finally at
7:45 a white Chrysler New Yorker pulls up, and Jack
rolls down the window and says, "Jump in, I assume
you've had breakfast."

"Yes," I lied, because did not want him to think
that I was unprepared for the day.

"Great, so let's get right to work."

We drove to a big warehouse that I learned later
was owned by Bergner's Department Store, but Jack
never explained the reason for the trip. The warehouse is absolutely freezing, and I'm only wearing
a suit and a topcoat. There are about five thousand
pairs of pants stacked up, and Jack turns to me and

says, "Okay, we need to get this inventory of all these pants." That "we" turned out to mean me, because he left me there for four hours with inventory sheets, a pencil, and a clipboard. When he came back at noon, I jumped in the car and assumed we would go somewhere for lunch. Wrong. He drove me to Johnson's Clothing. We walked in, and there was a wall that must have been thirty feet long and ten feet high, divided by a dressing room doorway and filled with pants. There were also at least ten tables, each holding sixteen two-foot-high stacks of pants. Again Jack said, "We need to take this inventory." And again he left. By the time he returned, it was dark outside. I was starving, but we were not finished yet. We visited two or three more stores, and it was eight o'clock before he finally said, "Are you hungry? Do you want to get something to eat?"

He had spent the entire day working me like a dog without any conversation or explanation. It was horrible. He did not tell me where we were going, what we were doing, or why we were doing it. He never said, "The stores are about to have some big sales, and I need to make sure that each one is well stocked." I was just flying blind, and he just kept issuing demands that did not always make sense. I had never been treated this way in a job. I do not think he was intentionally trying to be unkind. Looking back, it appeared that he had never managed an employee before. He also seemed to be testing me—much the way junior analysts at a financial firm find themselves tested in their first few years. They are expected to work 80 to 100 hours per week to see if they can survive. If they do, they end up with a really good job. But it is a long, hard road to get there. When Jack and I finally sat down to dinner at the Steak and Shake, he talked to me for the first time all day. I was so exhausted that I could barely eat, even though I was starving, and I had no idea what he said. I was just focused on trying to get through the meal. We ate in about ten minutes and jumped back into his car.

We pulled up to the Jefferson Hotel, and he went in to register me for the night. When I got to my room, I realized what a dump it was. There was a twin-sized bed with a dingy bedspread, a desk and chair, and a tiny bathroom that you had to turn sideways to enter. Because the hotel was built before indoor plumbing was common, there were two steps up to the bathroom to hide the pipes. There was no window, and the room was so small that I could not even pull the chair out from under the desk. I sat down on the bed and thought to myself, "Why am I doing this?" I was just about to grab my suitcase and leave Jack a note at the front desk, explaining that the job was not the right fit and that I was going to college, when the phone rang.

On the other end I heard Jack say, "I forgot to tell you what time I'll pick you up in the morning." I opened my mouth to tell him that I quit, when he said, "You did a really good job today. I'll be there at seven-thirty for breakfast, and we can talk about what to do next."

Amused, I replied, "I don't need breakfast. Pick me up at seven, and we'll get started."

Early the next morning I walked back to the Pere Marquette to get my car, eat a big breakfast, and visit the sundry store to pack my briefcase full of candy—Snickers, Three Musketeers, M&M's, and Chunky bars. I was going to beat Jack at his own game. Over the next three days, Jack started helping me, and we worked a series of marathons without taking a break or stopping for a hot meal—though I would visit the bathroom and sneak a candy bar to keep myself energized. He finally threw up his hands. He had gotten the point. If you want to work hard, I will work hard, but you are not going to break me.

I think the problem was that the company hired me to help Jack stay organized, but he resented the intrusion. So he treated me like a gofer, not a partner. For the first two months, I took inventory and traveled with him to set up samples for customers, cleaned up after his meetings, and wrote up the orders. But he figured out pretty quickly that I was a hard worker and a talented salesman, so he started allowing me to call on some of his smaller customers, those who might buy less than a thousand dollars in a season. I met with them and came back with orders valued between five and ten thousand dollars. Soon I was selling to 25 percent of his customers, and we became a good team. Eight months after starting with Jack, in August of 1965, I was offered my own territory in western Michigan.

H.I.S. had seventy-five territories, and western Michigan was ranked seventy-fifth. I learned later that it had once been number five. Why else would they offer a whole territory to a now twenty-one-year-old kid? It took me a few weeks to figure out what had happened. In those early days H.I.S. was popular, and the merchandise was very much in demand. Pretty soon it became clear that the company could not keep up with the orders, so they short-shipped everyone. For major cities with larger stores, they would ship about 80 percent of the ordered merchandise; for smaller towns they might ship 40 to 60 percent. Nowhere did the stores receive all that their customers needed. After putting up with this for years, retailers throughout western Michigan started to lose faith that the company could meet their needs—so they dropped H.I.S. When I first visited those stores and introduced myself, I was often escorted out the door. If Bob Luehrs had told me why H.I.S. had lost nearly all of its customers, I probably would not have taken the job. But I was young and full of piss and vinegar, and I thought I could turn it around. So I started working my new territory, trying to repair the relationships that had been damaged by the company's failure to adequately fulfill orders.

I moved to Grand Rapids, and I was given a $150-a-week draw against commission. I had to cover my own expenses, which barely left me enough money to feed my wife and soon-to-be son, Lorin. My territory in Michigan was vast, about five hundred miles from the farthest point south to the farthest point north in the Upper Peninsula. When making sales calls, I would be gone for two weeks at a time, because it was too expensive to drive home. I also did not have enough money to stay in a motel unless I could find one for five dollars or less.

At the beginning of these trips, I went to the grocery store and bought a gallon jar of peanut butter, a gallon jar of grape jelly, and a family-sized loaf of Wonder Bread. I ate peanut-butter-and-jelly sandwiches every meal for the whole trip. I would always make my appointments with my customers after breakfast, before or after lunchtime, and never around dinner, because I could not afford to take them to a restaurant. I had a beautiful white German shepherd, Duchess, who traveled with me. We would sleep in the car, even in the winter, keeping each other warm. There were gas stations catering to truck drivers that had showers. I quickly found out where cheap motels were, and I would plan my trip around them. I held all of my orders until I checked into a motel room with a desk and then spent the evening writing them up so I could submit them.

It instantly became clear that in order for me to be successful, most of the business in western Michigan would come from the Upper Peninsula. The area had a much smaller population, but there were still good stores. Neither my predecessor nor any of the sales representatives from H.I.S. or the other clothing companies ever went that far north. They depended on the store owners and buyers coming to clothing shows to place orders. In that first year I spent a lot of time up there, because they were the only accounts that were still buying from H.I.S. in spite of the short-shipping problem. I became friends with all of the owners and buyers, and they would sometimes invite me home for dinner, especially around the holidays. I was grateful for a hot meal, and they always seemed surprised and pleased to see me.

First-year sales in my territory were lopsided. I was doing 70 percent of my business in the Upper Peninsula and 30 percent in the Lower Peninsula. I soon figured out that if I could go north four times a year, I could sustain myself until I developed more business in the lower part of the state. After the first year, I started making a little money, and I was proud that I never went into the red against my draw. I remained solvent, and then the ratio of Upper Peninsula to Lower Peninsula business started to change—from 70–30 to 60–40, 50–50, and finally 30–70.

Two years after I started at H.I.S., there was a big sales contest that ran from January to May of 1967. Each region was handicapped, so smaller markets did not have to compete head-to-head with larger ones. All the regions were judged on the percentage of their increase in sales. Since I arrived in Grand Rapids, I had been working to crack two major department stores, Herpolsheimer's and Wurzburg's. Herpolsheimer's had a lot of employee turnover, so I never really built a strong relationship with their buyer. But I had become friends with the buyer at Wurzburg's, and we used to go to lunch occasionally. I never was able to sell him much, as he was only interested in a few items, but we had been talking about featuring H.I.S. in his store. The year of the contest, he allowed me to show him the whole fall line. To my surprise, he not only loved the new line but said that he wanted to open a H.I.S. department at Wurzburg's. It was a huge order, almost a quarter of a million dollars. That represented as much business as I might do in an entire season—and half of what I might do in a full year.

Our annual sales meeting was held in August at the Concord Hotel in the Catskill Mountains of New York. The company paid for us to attend. I had no idea when I flew east that I had won the sales contest, and the $1,000 prize. Even without the handicap, I finished third overall. That moved my region from seventy-fifth place back into the top five. This was a really big deal—and I was proud to see that all my hard work had come to fruition.

After each day of meetings, a number of the salesmen would gather in the hotel to play poker, and over the weekend I won about $500 from my H.I.S. colleagues. There was always a table of older men nearby who lived at the Concord during the summer, and they played for really big money. I had been to this sales meeting before and had become friendly with them. It was fun to just sit and watch them play. When one of their players left the table at two o'clock in the morning, they asked me to join, and I bought in.

We were playing Seven Card Stud. For the first forty-five minutes I could not get a hand worth playing, and I lost $150 just putting in the ante. After about an hour I explained that I could play only one more round, because my bus was leaving at six. We played three more hands. On the fourth one, after the usual two cards down (in the hole) I was dealt a king, which turned out to be the high card on the table. I had a habit of not looking at my two hole cards until the last possible moment. But I had the high card and had to bet or get out, so I took a glance and saw that both were kings. I had three of a kind. Playing it cool, I made the minimum bet. On the fifth card, I had a pair of kings showing, but the other players of course could not see my hole cards. Now I had four of a kind, so I made the maximum bet. There were two other players left—and they each had a full house, one with aces. But that did not beat four kings, so I won an astounding $1,500. To this day, I believe those men let me win. They were all successful businessmen or retired professionals who had started as immigrants. They knew my story, and probably felt sorry for me. I am sure they fixed the cards. With the $1,000 from the sales contest, $500 from the earlier poker game, and $1,500 from this final game, I walked away with $3,000.

On the flight home from New York to Detroit, the company upgraded me to first class because I had won the contest, and I found myself sitting next to a man who worked in mergers and acquisitions. He was clearly wealthy, evidenced by his Rolex watch, a luxury item I had heard about but never seen. Today he would have been traveling on a private plane, but that was not common in the 1960s. Over the course of the flight, I learned that he bought and sold big companies and had done very well for himself. We talked about his career, and as we made our final descent into Detroit I asked him, "What advice would you give to a young guy like me starting out in the business world?" He thought for a moment and finally replied, "Life is all about taking strategic risks. If you want to be really successful, take most of them when you are young. The older you get, the more complicated your life becomes. Taking risks becomes more frightening when you have more to lose. If you take risks when you're younger, you have time to recover if things go badly. If you succeed, the risks when you're older won't be so risky." This conversation and the $3,000 in my pocket gave me the courage to take an important next step.

When I came back from the sales meeting in August, I learned that the H.I.S. salesman in Detroit had just cracked a big account, Federal Department Stores, for more than a million dollars. He was now focused on that one account, which left the rest of the state wide open. Bolstered by my recent windfall and sensing an opportunity, I decided to take a strategic risk.

I called Bob Luehrs and pitched him an idea: "Now that your salesman has only one account, Federal Department Stores, I want the rest of Michigan. I'll move to Detroit and cover the entire state. I am doing more business in western Michigan than he was doing in the eastern part of the state until he cracked this new account. I know I can get us back into the major stores. I will hire someone to work for me and will take a one-percent override." That was a pretty bold request—it meant that I was asking for a 6 percent commission instead of 5 percent. No one in the company had ever done that. Nobody had salespeople working for them. It would make me into a kind of sales manager, and he didn't think I was ready.

He laughed and said, "You are too young, just twenty-three. You can't do it. You're doing fine. Detroit is the big city, and they'll laugh at you."

Here we go again, I thought. My age seemed to be my Goliath—something I could not control but had to overcome.

"Bob," I said, "I want that territory. If you don't give it to me, I'll leave in January."

He kept laughing and said, "You are not ready. You are not going anywhere. You just started making money, and you're getting way ahead of yourself."

Disappointed, I went off and continued to work my territory, while Bob hired a new salesman to cover Eastern Michigan.

Three H.I.S. salesmen, including Jack Uppole, had left the company to work for Male Slacks and Jeans in Atlanta, and all three of them told the owner, Tad Kaminsky, about me. So Tad called me and invited me to come visit him during the Thanksgiving break in 1967. I flew to Atlanta to meet him, and he offered me the whole state of Michigan. That was what I wanted from Bob, and Tad did not care that I was twenty-three. He was only twenty-nine years old himself, and age simply was not a factor in his decision. He just cared about my sales success. He offered me the same deal that he had given the other H.I.S. salesman—a 5 percent commission against a guarantee for two years of what they had made the previous year. I had made $22,000 at H.I.S. that year, but I also had to pay all of my own expenses.

I said, "I don't want that deal."

He said, "I'm not going to pay you any more than I did for the other guys from H.I.S."

I replied, "I don't want more. I actually want less. I want a draw against commission of three hundred fifty dollars a week—which is less than I made last year—and I don't want a guarantee. But I want seven percent instead of five." It was a good deal for Tad. If I did not do well, he did not have to pay me as much. If I was successful, the whole company benefited. So I told him I would go back to Michigan and wait for his offer letter. When it arrived, I signed it and made plans to move to Detroit.

Just about that time, I called Bob to ask: "What do you want me to do with the sample line for the H.I.S. spring and summer season? Should I give it to the new salesman?"

"What do you mean? Why would you do that? I want you to go sell it," said Bob.

"Bob, I'm leaving in January. I told you in September that if you did not give me the expanded territory in Michigan, I was leaving. You're going to have to hire someone, and I need to give this line to the new guy."

He said, "Don't move. I'll be there tomorrow."

So the week after Thanksgiving he flew from Cleveland to try to persuade me to stay with H.I.S. But he could not convince me; I had already committed to leave. Though he was disappointed, we parted on very good terms. I even helped him find my replacement.

In December of 1967, I went to Detroit to meet with the salesman who had been working the territory for Male Slacks and Jeans that I was about to assume. He was a very nice guy, knew about my success at H.I.S., and did not lose any time telling me what a mistake I had made in leaving. To say that he was discouraging was an understatement. I took all of his samples back to Grand Rapids to sort through them and spent some time reviewing the customer list. By mid-January I was organized and ready to start my new job.

I began working the state of Michigan for Male in January of 1968, and Tad and I spoke, but infrequently. After about three months I had sent in only about $30,000 worth of orders. To cover my draw, I needed to ship about $20,000 worth of merchandise per month—and it looked like I was 50 percent behind to break even. One Saturday morning I got a phone call from Tad, and he was screaming at the top of his lungs.

"I took a big chance with you! You are the youngest person I ever hired," he ranted. "Everyone told me you were a hot shot—that you knew what you were doing." Suddenly my age became an issue. This went on for about a minute until, in the middle of his tirade, I hung up on him. He called back and was still yelling. So I hung up again.

He called a third time and said, "Are you going to hang up on me again?"

"Yes," I replied calmly, "if you keep yelling at me."

So he stopped yelling, but he was still really mad. "What in the hell are you doing? You haven't produced crap. I've got a good mind to just fire you right now."

I said, "Well, you certainly can do that, but I have a question for you. Do you play pool?"

"What the hell does that have to do with anything?" he snapped.

I asked again, "Do you play pool?"

He finally said, "Yes, I have a pool table in my house."

"I bet you just play eight-ball."

"Yeah," he said, somewhat confused.

"Where I come from, we call that slop pool. There is no strategy. You just try to put the balls in a pocket in no particular order. I play straight pool, where you score points with every ball you sink. But you have to make sure, when you make a shot, that you have lined up the next one. That's how I've worked this territory. For the past three months, I've been lining up all my next shots. So you can fire me if you want to, but you need to tell me what you want me to do with this four hundred thousand dollars' worth of orders that are sitting here on my desk. Do you want me to throw them out, or do you want me to write them up and send them in?"

There was dead silence on the other end of the line.

Then I heard him say, "You've got four hundred grand worth of orders? Why haven't you sent them in?"

I explained, "I just did them this week, and I haven't had time to write them up. I've been checking with the warehouse and the head of production to ensure availability. I've been calling on customers for the last three months building relationships and trying to understand their needs. Now it's all coming together. This is the way I work. This is not about a single sale. So if you want me to stay, you've got to trust me."

He agreed and hung up. In my first year, with that 7 percent commission, I earned $72,000, or $50,000 more than I made my entire time at H.I.S. I eventually did what I had promised Bob I could do—I cracked every major account in Detroit and all over the state of Michigan. Bob and I stayed good friends until he died a few years ago. Every time one of my customers ran a full-page advertisement for Male Jeans, I sent him a copy as a not-so-subtle reminder of his mistake in not giving me the state of Michigan. H.I.S. never fully recovered from their short-shipping problem, and the men's division eventually folded. They created a line for women, H.I.S. for Her, that for a number of years was very successful.

In 1970 I was living in Detroit and working my territory as well as what we called the All American Region, which was everything east of the Mississippi. For months there had been talk of a strike at General Motors, and finally the United Auto Workers walked off the job. It would eventually end after sixty-seven days, but it felt like an eternity. The strike triggered layoffs at parts suppliers and steel companies throughout the region. Detroit was a company town, and the strike had such a powerful impact that it never recovered. The real victims were the suppliers—the companies that did business with GM. Many of them shut down. And that rippled through other industries. Newspapers predicted that retail businesses throughout the state would see a downturn of between 35 and 50 percent.

Everyone in town seemed to have a connection to GM, and the prospect of a strike really put a damper on people's appetite for spending. This did not bode well for clothing stores. A week before the strike started, I was visiting one of my biggest accounts, Hughes and Hatcher. I ran into the Farah and Levi's salesmen in the break room, and I overheard them talking about where they were going to go on vacation until the strike was over. They ignored me, as they always did, but their conversation gave me an idea. While they were sitting on a beach somewhere in Florida making sand castles with their families, I was going to work the hell out of my territory to make sure all my customers were well stocked. I started calling on customers with a young man that I had hired. He helped me take inventory at all of our major accounts, and we visited stores every day, working with buyers, showing them what they were missing and filling new orders. I counted not only the fashion inventory but also the basic clothing inventory that was a big part of my competitors' business. While Farah and Levi's passively waited for the strike to end, we got more and more aggressive. By the end of the strike, I had cornered the fashion business and gained appreciable market share in the basic clothing business, much to the surprise of Farah and Levi's. At the end of the season, I had a 35 percent increase in sales, doing more business in that six-month period than anyone had done at Male anywhere in the nation. More important, I had made inroads into many accounts that would have taken years to crack had it not been for the strike and the absence of my two biggest competitors.

The strike had been my Goliath. When I discovered that all the other companies' salesmen were going to stay home, I realized how big an opportunity I truly had. What looked like a disaster turned out to be an unexpected gift. My competitors could not see past Goliath, and they were not prepared to step into the valley. Everything that I had done in business since I was eleven years old prepared me for what happened next. I realized that if the other salesmen were staying home, I might be able to reach clients who otherwise would have been out of my reach. Real opportunity comes only a few times in a career, and this was one of them. My experiences in business had taught me to look at things through a different lens. Where they saw a downturn, I saw an open door.

After posting the increase, I received a very nice telegram from Penson Kaminsky, Tad's brother, which read: "Congratulations and best wishes for the week ending August 15, 1970. After 24 selling weeks into the fall selling season, your volume of orders accepted by this company has reached 1,007,317. This is a new record for all this company, and I wanted you to know how happy all of us here in Atlanta are for you and your success. Tad joins me in sending you our warmest regards." I also received a letter from Frank Jarmin, chairman and CEO of Genesco, the company that now owned Male Jeans, which included the following paragraph: "We have many divisions of Genesco that are represented in Michigan, and the best one is only down 25 percent. How is it possible that you are up 35 percent in the midst of the worst strike in history of the state?" I copied the letter and sent it back to him with the words "What strike?" written on the bottom.

I stayed at Male Jeans for another two years, and my responsibilities continued to grow. After the strike, I moved to Atlanta, and am sad to say that my first marriage did not survive the transition. Adrienne returned to Chicago with our son Lorin, born in 1966, and daughter Jody, born in 1968.

In Atlanta I was asked to start a new division of the company, Female, which launched on August 10, 1971. Then I was promoted to national merchandise manager in September, and six months later to national sales manager for major accounts. My job was to travel the country and convince major retailers who were doing business with Male to open up entire departments showcasing our merchandise. Today most of the major clothing companies have branded sections in department stores, but back then it was a new concept. I loved traveling the country testing the new concept and putting together entire packages.

One of my first major accounts in this new role as national sales manager for major accounts was with Burdines Department Store in Miami. I was planning a fashion show and cocktail party for all the buyers, sales associates, and store managers. The event was supposed to take place in early March, but I got the flu, so we had to postpone it. We selected another date, and two weeks later we checked into the Sheraton Four Ambassadors Hotel. The team working on rebooking the event had everything planned, but while they rescheduled the male model, they forgot to rebook the female models. We needed four women—two size fives and two size sevens—to do the runway show for us. I flew in that morning and learned that we were shorthanded. Panicked, we called a few modeling agencies, but they didn't have enough time to find us anyone. So I went downstairs to the office of the hotel to see if they might have some connections.

When I walked in, I saw three well-dressed women who looked like they might be the sizes we needed. I asked the hotel manager if I could talk to them about the fashion show. With his permission, I pitched the idea and told them that they could keep all the merchandise they modeled. They agreed, but I was still short one size-seven model. I walked back upstairs, and in the lobby I saw a beautiful woman walk past me. I turned to my salesman and said, "There is our other size seven." I stopped her to explain my situation, and I am sure she thought I was just trying to use some cheesy pickup line to get her phone number. I gave her my business card and my room number and asked her to think about helping us with the show. After she checked with the hotel management and found that what I was asking was legitimate, she called and agreed to meet us that afternoon. She was on her way back from attending a wedding in Ecuador and just happened to be walking through the lobby at the exact moment that I needed her. Sometimes you simply have really good luck.

Donna modeled for me that night, and two months later, in May, I was in Houston on business. I knew that she lived there, so I gave her a call and asked if I could see her. A few months later, in the summer of 1972, I left Male Slacks and Jeans to start my first company, a chain of retail stores in Atlanta called Pant-O-Mine. Donna and I continued dating and eventually married in November of the same year. Donna would become the fourth person to save my life.

Until we met, my life had been on one big fast track. It seemed like everything I touched turned to gold, and I had gotten pretty cocky. The fashion industry was full of great opportunities, but also great temptations. Drugs and alcohol were rampant, and many beautiful people were attracted to the business. Just as I found myself being pulled into this world, Donna stepped into my life. She offered me the opportunity to put on the brakes, shift gears, and prioritize marriage and family for the first time in my life. I saw so many of my close friends who had been very successful lose everything—their families, their businesses, and their self-worth—through promiscuity or drugs, sometimes both. I had seen the underbelly of this industry, and Donna helped pull me out from under it. She saved my life when I most needed it.

Pant-O-Mine was my first full-scale business. Up until that point, I had mainly worked for other people. This time, I was responsible for everything. I originally thought I would begin a manufacturing company, but I did not have the capital, so I turned to the one thing I knew best—retail. There were a handful of low-cost pant stores that I came to know when I was at Male. But I thought I could do better, and I found an investor, a doctor in Detroit who once lived across the street from me. I also brought in a young partner who oversaw operations.

The concept for Pant-O-Mine was that all of the pants in the store were priced at five dollars; some of the belts and shirts cost a little more. We bought end lots of branded merchandise and resold them. We opened four stores on the same day, and the company took off like a rocket ship. We pioneered an advertising campaign that really did the trick. Every two weeks, we blanketed the city of Atlanta with billboards. The first one just read "SMAP" without any explanation. The second one read "SMAP— Coming to Atlanta." The third one read "SMAP" with the date we would open. The fourth billboard read "Save Money at Pant-O-Mine: The Original $5 Pant Store" and featured our logo and the addresses of the four stores in Buckhead, Clarkston, West End, and Smyrna. On opening day we had lines around the block at each store.

The company was really successful in the first two years. Then my investor ended up in financial trouble, and I had to buy him out. So I went from being well capitalized to undercapitalized almost overnight. I had to find a line of credit, in the midst of a banking crisis. Even though I paid our loans on time, our bank eventually withdrew their credit line and the company became insolvent. To complicate matters, I was paying all of my attention to gross sales and not worrying about profitability. By the time I hired a competent financial person to help with the company, it was too late. Donna and I had been married for a couple of years, and we were about to have a baby. I had many sleepless nights, worried that we were going to lose not just the business but our house. In the end, the company failed because I did not heed Irving's advice. He had taught me as a teenager to learn everything you can about your business. I was good at marketing and merchandising, but I did not pay enough attention to the bottom line, and the company had to file for Chapter 11 reorganization. For the first time in my life, I came to understand the stress my father faced with his bankruptcy, and I gained a new respect for his resilience. I learned that you have to be involved in every aspect of the company and know what is happening in every department. I also realized that you have to honestly face the role you played in a crisis. Admitting failure requires digging deep to find strength that you may be surprised you have. I left Pant-O-Mine certain of one thing. If I ever went back into business for myself, I would make mistakes—probably a lot more of them—but I would never make the same mistake twice.

Those early business ventures, from leaf and snow removal in Buffalo to starting my first company, taught me a lot. I took a lot of risks and had some successful starts and big failures. As a young man, I thought I had to be the smartest guy in the room in all facets of business. Soon I learned that this was not only impossible but foolish. A better way is to surround yourself with people who have unique and valuable expertise. Then you learn from each other, and the business prospers. There's nothing worse than someone in charge who will not listen to colleagues with more skill or experience. Leadership is about knowing when to consider other opinions, face the facts, and make the right decision. Great leaders know what they don't know.

Just about the time that Pant-O-Mine was shutting down, Tad Kaminsky from Male Slacks and Jeans called to ask me to come back to work for him. We had parted on good terms and were still friends. He wanted to start a new division named Victory, which was essentially the other side of what I was doing at Pant-O-Mine. He wanted to sell off Male's odd lots to major department stores and companies that sold clothes domestically and overseas. I was glad to have a job, but embarrassed that I had to go back to work at Male after having failed at running my own company. I stayed there for another year, but Tad left about eight months after I returned, so I started looking for other positions. While running this new division at Male, I made a number of contacts around the country and saw a real opportunity to sell young men's suits and sportswear to major retailers under either a branded name or a private label.

The 1970s was a very fashion-conscious decade, and young men were wearing really cool suits. I had plenty of design ideas and some major accounts that I thought would buy from me. So I partnered with a friend in Atlanta who had been trying to start his own company, and we eventually took on a third partner. We named it the Great American Clothing Company—this was a very patriotic time, with the upcoming 1976 bicentennial, and we wanted our customers to know that our clothes were made in the United States and not overseas. We had a good start and were doing well as we approached our first anniversary. By the following year, in 1977, I was having doubts about our future. I did not yet know that a visit to a California mall while attending a clothing show would open the door to my next opportunity.

5

Do You Know How Many Cookies?

While we're trying to figure out what we're going to do with the rest of our lives, why don't we open a cookie store?

The Original Great American Chocolate Chip Cookie Company was not a predictable success. My partner, Arthur Karp, and I had absolutely no experience selling food and only $8,000 to invest in this new enterprise. We were undercapitalized and faced several national competitors selling the same product. Interest rates were high, inflation was soaring, and new businesses were closing in 1977 almost as fast as they could open their doors. We had every reason not to do this, but we did.

I knew nothing about selling cookies, but plenty about business. At the age of thirty-three, I had been employed in the clothing industry for twenty years, working my way up from stock boy to store manager to national sales manager at companies in Miami, Chicago, Detroit, and Atlanta—which is what brought me to the city in 1970. When I left Male Slacks and Jeans to establish my first clothing company, Pant-O-Mine, in 1972, I was able to build on my skills as a merchant and marketer. I monitored profitability but never focused on it, believing that with a good margin we could make up any shortfalls with volume. I really did not have much experience overseeing profit and loss, and by the time I realized how much money we were losing, it was too late. Although my partner and I quickly reorganized the company, there was not enough money to pay both of our salaries, so I gave my interest to him. I had made plenty of mistakes, but also learned some valuable lessons about the bottom line. When I returned to Male Jeans, I changed my focus completely. At the Victory division that I was hired to create and run, selling end-lots of merchandise including jeans and jackets to major retailers, I made profitability my priority. My success over that year gave me the confidence to start a second company, with two partners, in 1976.

The Great American Clothing Company did really well in the first year because we really understood our market. Our niche was selling directly to major retailers like Federated Department Stores and multiunit retailers like J. Riggins, which meant that we could run a lean operation without a sales force. Instead of perfecting that unconventional model, my partners wanted to hire a sales team and start paying commissions to grow the company faster. They started making the same assumptions and mistakes that I did at Pant-O-Mine—believing that volume and revenue would take care of everything. I knew better but could not persuade them otherwise, so a year after founding the clothing company, I decided to start looking for new business opportunities. Having been in the clothing business since I was thirteen, I felt like I had completed a real-life MBA. I had some success as an entrepreneur, but I did not know that the next twenty years of my life would be dedicated to creating and selling the perfect cookie.

The idea to start a cookie business came from a most unlikely place. Just before leaving Great American Clothing, I was attending my last clothing show in San Diego and was planning to entertain my buyers and vendors in my hotel suite later that evening. I drove over to the local mall to buy potato chips, pretzels, and some See's Candies, a popular California brand. As I was walking through the mall, I saw a store that was packed with customers. It was the middle of the day, and at least fifty people were patiently waiting in line. Curious to see what was so popular, I got in line too. It turned out to be a cookie store. I did not know that such a thing even existed, but this one seemed to be doing really well.

When I reached the counter after about twenty minutes, I bought two dozen cookies for the reception in my hotel suite. They were expensive—thirty cents apiece—and the customers in line were buying them as fast as the employees could pull them from the two small convection ovens. I ate one and thought it was just okay. My mother had been a great baker, so I was accustomed to superior cookies. Even so, these were really selling. The man behind the counter who was waiting on me was wearing a manager's badge, so I began asking him questions. When we realized that we were holding up the line, he offered to come out and talk to me. I asked him detailed questions about how many cookies he sold each day, what his food and labor costs looked like, and his profitability. He was more than happy to share the information.

I knew nothing about the food industry, but I knew a good business when I saw one. I was fascinated by what I had learned, though still very skeptical. So I left the mall with my big bag of cookies and went next door to the grocery store. I have always had a curious streak, and I could not wait to do some hands-on research. I bought all of the ingredients to make my mother's chocolate chip cookie recipe—butter, granulated and brown sugar, vanilla, flour, salt, eggs, baking soda, and Nestlé chocolate chips. Then I went to the drugstore and bought a postage scale. I got back to my hotel suite and began to mix up a batch in the small kitchenette. I weighed each ingredient to see if the food costs were even close to what the manager of the cookie store had claimed they were, and I was dumbfounded. I could make a cookie for six cents and sell it for thirty.

In clothing manufacturing, the margins were significantly smaller. By the time you factored in the cost of the materials that comprise each piece of clothing and determine what you can sell it for, you might have a margin of 30 percent. That is before you add in warehousing and labor. Finally, you have to account for markdowns on what does not sell. Overall, you would be lucky to make 10 percent. It was sometimes closer to 8 or more likely 6. With cookies, there was no inventory, no warehousing, and nothing ever went out of style. The margins were almost unbelievable, but the best part was that you could eat all your mistakes. (A little cookie humor.)

On my flight back to Atlanta, I was flipping through a copy of *People* magazine that I found in my seat pocket and came across an article about two California brothers who had established a cookie store called the Chipyard. In 1976 Michael and Mitchell Hurwitz, aged fifteen and thirteen, were too young to get summer jobs, so they decided to rent an abandoned taco stand in Newport Beach and sell chocolate chip cookies. They opened their business on May 17, and within a week the boys were selling thousands of cookies. They made enough money to create a hefty college savings fund and then some. I was beginning to see that there was something to this cookie business.

I knew Atlanta did not have a cookie store, and I needed a plan to keep me closer to home and to my wife, Donna, and three young children, Lorin, Jody, and baby Taryn, born in 1975. With Great American Clothing, I traveled regularly to New York, to California, and around the country to meet with multiunit specialty retailers and department stores. The four selling seasons—fall, holiday, spring, and summer—ran two months each, which meant that we were on the road almost constantly. It was exhausting, and I was ready to try something new. Donna and I had looked at other businesses outside the clothing industry for several years, but we never found anything that felt right. After my California trip I sat down with her and said, "I don't want to be away from home so often, and I really miss you and the kids. I think we need to make a change. While we're figuring out what to do next, let's open a cookie store."

I met with my partners at Great American Clothing and told them that I wanted to leave the company. We had been discussing our different visions for the future for several months, so I do not think they were that surprised. I sold them my interest and called my friend Arthur Karp, who owned a sales agency, to see whether he was interested in taking over sales for my former company. Arthur was taken aback and asked, "Why would you sell your interest in the company? You guys are doing great."

I told him that I was selling the business so I could stay closer to home. When he asked what I was going to do next, I replied, "If I tell you, you are just going to laugh."

He kept prodding, and I finally confessed, "I'm going to open a store in the mall and sell chocolate chip cookies."

Arthur burst into laughter.

"You promised you wouldn't laugh," I snapped back.

He stopped and explained, "I'm not laughing at you, I'm laughing at the coincidence. Susan and I have decided to do the same thing."

I was stunned, listening to Arthur talk about all the research he had done. "How far into the business plan are you?" I asked.

"I've been working on it since my trip to San Diego when I saw this cookie store at a mall," he said.

In that short conversation, I learned that Arthur and his wife, Susan, had attended the same clothing show as I did in San Diego. They also went to a mall and visited a cookie store, though we were never able to confirm that it was the same one. Regardless, this seemed too good to be true. "Don't move," I yelled into the phone. "Donna and I are coming right over!"

When we arrived, I laid out everything I had been working on, and Arthur did the same. My research had focused on manufacturing, store design, operations, and marketing. Arthur had spent his time thinking about the recipe, real estate, and growth. There was no overlap, and if you put our two pieces together, they made a good business plan. After a few more conversations, we decided to go into business together in March of 1977.

This was not a strategic decision but an act of desperation. I had three children, no savings, and barely enough money from selling my interest in Great American Clothing to last eight months. I had no idea how I was going to support my family. But I always believed that a good salesperson could be dropped anywhere in the world and would find a way to make a living. So when I saw the margins at the cookie store in California, I reasoned that we could open one store in a mall somewhere in Atlanta and make a little money until we figured out what we might do for the rest of our lives. Worried about the uncertainty that lay ahead, we made some major changes. I was driving a Mercedes and Donna had a Jaguar, so we sold them both and bought a new Honda Civic for $2,200. We stopped going out to dinner, limited our travel by plane and started driving, and eliminated any extraneous expenses and luxuries. I knew one thing for sure: I was not going to let my lifestyle dictate how quickly I would need to grow this new business.

Our timing could not have been worse. We were trying to open a cookie store just when malls were losing faith in single-concept food stores. And we were about to try to open a store during the downward slide of the frozen yogurt business. Frozen yogurt stores first appeared in malls in 1975. They were especially popular in Los Angeles and New York but were largely rejected outside those markets. This was because the product tasted mostly like sour cream in a cone, not at all like it tastes today, like ice cream. Hundreds of malls had gambled on the concept, and the stores had recently closed. So mall managers were leery about investing in what they saw as another fad industry. But we were determined, or more accurately naïve, and pushed ahead. We had an unconventional business plan, $4,000 each to invest in the company, and a name, the Original Great American Chocolate Chip Cookie Company, but no experience and no store.

Later we learned that many people in Atlanta believed that we invented the cookie business. In reality, other companies such as Famous Amos had preceded us nationally, but none had done so in the state of Georgia. By the time we started shopping our concept to malls in Atlanta, there were already three major national cookie chains and about a hundred smaller independent stores. Now, if you were a shopping mall developer, and you were going to give a lease to someone in the cookie business—a concept about which you were skeptical anyway—was it going to be to one of the three national brands or to two guys out of the clothing business with $8,000 who had no absolutely experience in the food industry? It did not make sense to rent to us. We were too much of a gamble.

So we should not have been surprised that we had a lot of trouble finding a place to start. We tried to contact mall managers all over Atlanta from Southlake, Perimeter, and Northlake to Lenox Square, North DeKalb, South DeKalb, Cumberland, and Greenbriar. Most would not even take our calls. The ones who did dismissed our concept as a fad and flatly refused to meet with us. Arthur and I knew that our business model was better than anything else on the market, but we could not even get started. I had faced Goliath-like challenges before. As a child, it was my father's bankruptcy. When I was a manufacturer's representative, there was the major strike at General Motors. Goliath can take any number of forms. This time it was the challenge of creating a business out of thin air. We were frustrated, but we were not going to be defeated. We had even begun discussing whether we should consider opening a store outside a mall, when we found out that there was a space coming available at Perimeter Mall just one door off center court. It had been a handbag store, and we were determined to get the lease. This was our last best hope.

Opened in 1971 in the Dunwoody suburb of Atlanta, Perimeter was the fourth mall built in DeKalb County (after Columbia, North DeKalb, and South DeKalb) and the seventh to open in the Atlanta metropolitan area. It had two anchor stores, J. C. Penney and Rich's, and was suffering from competition from Cumberland, a mall that opened in 1973 in Cobb County with four anchor stores. By the time we were shopping for a lease, Perimeter was the least successful mall in the city. Sales were averaging less than $70 per square foot, while the national average was $100.

Arthur and I had already determined that Jeff Weil, the young manager who was brought in to turn the mall around, was the person we had to persuade. The mall office where he worked had several employees, and we had to find a way to reach him. We were sure that our concept—different from what other cookie companies were doing nationally—was just what he needed. But like many of the other mall managers, he would not even take our calls. That might have been a sign, but we took it as a challenge.

Not yet ready to give up, Arthur and I waited in the mall parking lot one morning, trying to figure out when he arrived. After a few minutes we saw him get out of his car at 8:30 with a big thermos of coffee. That gave us an idea. So we arrived the next day, went to the mall office a few minutes after he arrived, and told the receptionist that we were there to see Jeff Weil.

She asked, "Do you have an appointment?"

"No, but we just need him for five minutes," we said.

"He has a very busy schedule."

"We understand, but we can wait."

So we both sat down on the couch in the reception area and waited. After about twenty minutes her phone rang, and we could hear her end of the conversation.

"Yes, I told them," she said, and, after a pause, "No, I don't think they're going to leave."

She hung up and turned to us. "That was Mr. Weil. He has a very busy morning and asked if you would schedule an appointment."

We knew that he was brushing us off again; we had already tried to schedule an appointment, and he would not take any of our calls. An in-person meeting was our only chance.

We said we would like to continue to wait in the reception area and see if sometime during the day he might have a five-minute break to meet with us.

An hour passed. We had agreed that if either of us needed to go to the restroom, the other would stay on the couch to avoid missing him. We were counting on two things—if he drank the full thermos of coffee he carried in that morning, he was going to need a break, and in order to get to the bathroom, he would have to walk past us. At ten minutes to ten, his door opened. We could hear Jeff coming down the hall. When he saw us, he snapped: "What do you guys want?" We pleaded with him to give us just five minutes of his time to tell him about this new cookie concept. He finally relented, and we followed him to his office after his trip to the bathroom. As he went to sit behind his desk, Arthur and I picked up his office couch and blockaded the door. Then we turned to him and said, "You're not leaving until we make this deal."

He laughed, and we went through our presentation about why our cookie company was different from our competitors' and why he should lease to us. Now, you can tell in a conversation when people's feelings about you change. They uncross their arms, they lean back in their chair, and they start to smile and affirm what you are saying. When we finished our pitch, Jeff smiled and said, "I really like you guys."

We were starting to get excited.

"I'm going to do you the biggest favor of your life," he continued.

Now we were really excited.

"I'm not going to lease you the space," he said.

Confused, we just stared at him.

"Years from now," he told us, "you're going to look back at this and say, 'Jeff Weil really did us the biggest favor of our lives.' Let me explain this to you. If I lease you this space today, you will have to sign a personal guarantee and commit to paying us a quarter of a million dollars over ten years. I like you both, but you are probably going to fail. I don't want to be responsible for you losing everything—your homes, your cars, maybe even your families. This rent is twenty-five thousand a year. The Rouse Company owns this mall, and we are a big developer, and we really know how to tie businesses up in a leasing contract. If you think you're going to take this lease to a lawyer when your business fails and wriggle out of paying ten years of rent, forget it."

Not ready to back down, we kept pitching our concept, and he finally said, "Here." He reached into a drawer and pulled out a document that was at least an inch thick. "Take this lease to a very good lawyer. I am sure that after you meet with this lawyer, you will decide not to sign this. You will come back next week and hand me the unsigned lease and say, 'You were right. Thanks, but no thanks, Jeff. Goodbye.'"

Arthur and I looked at each other and then at Jeff and said, "Are you kidding? We're going to do so much business and sell so many cookies that this rent is going to be a slam dunk."

Jeff said, "Do you know how many thirty-cent cookies you will have to sell to pay this rent?"

We threw some huge figures around that felt more like telephone numbers than realistic sales projections, because we had no idea. Exasperated by our refusal to take his advice and worn down by our persistence, Jeff finally handed us the lease, and Arthur and I left.

This might seem brash or gutsy, but our willingness to stalk Jeff Weil in the parking lot, to move the couch in front of his door, and to insist on signing a ten-year lease worth a quarter of a million dollars was not driven by courage. It was driven by fear. Reflecting on it now reminds me of the 2005 film *Cinderella Man*. Set during the Great Depression, it recounts the true story of washed-up boxer James Braddock, who was forced to accept public relief, and even beg for money, to support his family. His former manager offers him a shot at a young contender, and, implausibly, he wins. After several more victories, he goes on to defeat heavyweight champion Max Baer, the favorite, in 1935. At a press conference before the climatic fight he is asked by a *Chicago Tribune* reporter: "What's changed,

Jimmy? You couldn't win a fight for love or money. How do you explain your comeback?" Braddock talks about a run of bad luck, breaking his hand a couple of times and recovering from a car accident. Then he says, "This time around I know what I'm fighting for—milk." Braddock is referring to the many years that he worried about scraping together enough money to feed his children. That scene resonated with me because before my father lost his business and all of our money, we owned a nice home in the suburbs where my mother cooked wonderful dinners. After the bankruptcy, we moved to smaller and smaller apartments and then to Miami Beach, and we often had only enough money to eat noodles. Braddock was fighting for milk; I was fighting never to be poor again. This was all about fear and uncertainty.

Arthur and I left Jeff's office and walked back to the empty store that we were determined to rent. Back in those days, Perimeter had big tables in the mall. Most people thought it was to make customers comfortable. But it was really to make the mall look busy and push people into the stores. We sat down at one of those tables and looked at the few people walking past what was about to become our store. Then we looked at each other and said, "Do you know how many cookies we are going to have to sell to pay this rent?" The number turned out to be about half a million cookies a year. That number did not cover all of our expenses—insurance, payroll, supplies, leased equipment, transportation, telephone, labor, or food costs. This was quickly becoming more overwhelming than we expected.

So we sat there for a while and sketched out the concept for the store on a napkin. The name we settled on, the Original Great American Chocolate Chip Cookie Company, which I always thought was too long, was intended to suggest the all-American nature of the company. The nation had just celebrated the bicentennial, and there was a patriotic wave that we wanted to ride, as I did with my clothing line. We wanted the stores to be very red, white, and blue and believed that chocolate chip cookies were the only true American confection. Most other pastry recipes were imported from Scandinavia or Holland or elsewhere in Europe. Nothing said U-S-A like a piping-hot chocolate chip cookie.

We also talked about what kind of recipe to use. When Donna and I first discussed starting the company, we thought we'd use my mother's. But Arthur's wife Susan had a better one, with a more compelling story. It had been handed down through the family from her Blackfoot Indian great-great-grandmother. The original recipe instructed the baker to prepare the chocolate by chopping it with a knife. I had eaten hundreds of these cookies over the years, because Susan often baked them for customers at clothing shows that Arthur and I attended. People who ate them would joke that if she could ever figure out a way to sell her cookies, she would make a fortune. Here was the big chance.

We signed the lease with Jeff on June 10 and went to C&S Bank to secure a loan. Since Arthur and I had only $8,000 to invest, we obviously needed some outside help. Our banker listened to our plan and said, "Do you know how many cookies you'll have to sell to pay off this rent? This will never work." We were getting pretty used to this conversation, but we finally convinced him to loan us $25,000. To get there, we had to put everything we owned up for collateral—our homes, cars, furniture, and all of our household possessions. We walked out of the bank knowing that we could not afford to make any mistakes. We had no safety net and not a single penny to spare. If we failed, both of our families would lose everything.

6

From Cookie to Counter

Is this what it's going to be like every day, guys?

Now we had a location and a loan, but the hard part was still to come. To construct a successful retail environment that would be appealing to customers and functional for employees, most businesses would hire someone to do construction drawings, but we didn't have any money. So we updated the sketch I had drawn with Arthur and submitted that single sheet of paper to Jeff. This made him even more skeptical about our chances of success.

Donna and I had just completed some construction on our house in Kennesaw, and we hired the cabinetmaker, electrician, and plumber who worked on our home to help us build the store at Perimeter Mall. We had no idea that there was any difference between residential and commercial construction, and our ignorance helped us complete the project in nineteen days. That is the fastest we ever built a store. Later we realized that high-quality commercial-grade construction for a store of this size really took a minimum of six weeks, but back then we were not experienced enough to know better. Using the skills that I had learned as an apprentice carpenter, plumber, and electrician as a teenager in Miami Beach, I served as general contractor for the construction.

Donna oversaw all of the buying. We found a wonderful man named Jack Henson who sold wholesale ingredients, so Donna called him one afternoon and told him what we needed.

He asked, "What is your business?"

Donna said, "We're opening a store at Perimeter Mall that will sell chocolate chip cookies."

"What else?" he probed.

Donna explained, "Well, we'll have six varieties of cookies." And she proceeded to talk about the various flavors.

Again he came back with "And what else?"

Donna finally said, "Nothing else. Just cookies."

Jack laughed and said, "Little lady, that will never work."

But he liked her and gave us credit to buy what we needed to open. Jack remained our supplier for years, probably longer than he should have, because we felt loyal to him for taking a chance on us. We eventually became so large that he could not handle the volume.

Prior to the June 29 opening, we distributed flyers around the mall and throughout the surrounding neighborhoods saying that from nine to noon we would be giving away free cookies. We did not have enough money to run advertisements or fund a marketing campaign, so we just hit the pavement in an effort to introduce customers to our product. We were excited about opening, especially because this would be the first cookie store anywhere in Georgia. On opening day we arrived at the mall at seven sharp, filled with anticipation. An hour and a half later, we hand-scooped three hundred cookies onto baking trays and placed them in our new oven. It had a glass window in the front that faced into the mall so that customers could watch the creamy white dough go around in this beautiful carousel—sort of like a cookie Ferris wheel. As they baked, they started to flatten, and steam started coming from the oven. Fifteen minutes later, the bell went off signaling that they were ready. The cookies had just reached the most beautiful golden brown color you have ever seen. It's a color that is unique to chocolate chip cookies. If you go to Sherwin Williams or another paint store and try to match it, it cannot be done. Only chocolate chip cookies have this distinctive color.

So picture this: Delicious, hot chocolate chip cookies were just waiting to be tasted. By this point we had a large crowd of people who had seen our flyers gathered in front of the metal gate outside the store in great anticipation. We had discussed this exact moment and decided that, as a symbolic gesture, all of us—Arthur, Susan, their son Billy, Donna, my mother Lee, and I—would place our hands on the oven door to open it and officially start the business. This was truly a family affair.

We peered into the oven and saw the trays of piping hot, golden brown chocolate chip cookies sitting on their trays at 350 degrees. And it was at that exact moment that we realized that we had forgotten the pot holders. We had nothing to take the cookies out of the oven—no napkins, no towels, no newspaper, nothing. The other stores in the mall were not open at that hour, so Arthur was running around Perimeter trying to find anything from the restrooms or housekeeping staff that might help.

Now, the people in the mall had no idea what was happening. They just kept watching the cookies go round and round in the oven. Within minutes they could see that the cookies were going from golden brown to a much darker shade of brown, then to black, to smoke, to catching fire. Pretty soon smoke was pouring out of the oven. We were on a combined air-conditioning system with Parklane Hosiery, and people were running out of the store screaming because they thought the mall was on fire.

The fire department came, and I will never forget what happened next. Standing behind the counter, looking out through the cloud of smoke, I could see this figure coming toward the gate—Jeff Weil, the mall manager. It was just like a scene out of a movie. He looked at us with dismay and asked one simple question: "Is this what it's going to be like every day, guys?" We reminded him what a great decision he made in leasing to us. He had not bought that story in his office, and he certainly was not buying it today. We were just lucky that the gate was still down and he could not get to us.

So instead of opening, we spent the day cleaning up a big cookie mess in the oven and soot in the store. This was not the start we planned. But we believed so strongly in our concept that we worked all day and into the evening. We printed new flyers with the same offer to give away free cookies and distributed them again to the neighborhoods that night. We had written a strong business plan, conducted a lot of research, invested all of our savings, created great recipes, built an inviting store, blanketed the community with flyers, and we could have been put out of business before we even opened because we forgot to buy some two-dollar pot holders.

Exhausted, we arrived early on the morning of June 30, and by the time we put the first batch of cookies in the oven, there were hundreds of people waiting outside the store. The fire the day before had sparked a lot of curiosity about this new business in the mall—everybody was talking about it. In the end, what felt like a disaster turned out to be a pretty good marketing strategy. The fire brought us four times as many customers as the flyers did. It was like a car accident. People showed up to find out what was going to happen today, and they bought a bunch of cookies.

That would not be our only fire. On the second Saturday that the store was in business, our NCR mechanical cash register caught fire. Most mechanical registers found in stores in those days were used periodically—you might have five customers in a row and then a break—so they had a fan that would come on between transactions to cool the motor. On that Saturday we had nearly three hundred customers, one after another, and the cooling fan could not work fast enough. This mistake reminded us, once again, how much we did not know. Arthur and I left to purchase two new electronic registers. We had never even considered that we would have so many customers that we needed two registers. Within two weeks we were the highest-volume cookie store in the nation. Soon mall developers all across the country were approaching us about opening Original Great American Chocolate Chip Cookie Company stores.

While starting a company might seem exciting and glamorous, I knew from my experience at Pant-O-Mine and Great American Clothing that it is a lot of hard work, late nights, and sacrifice. Today, being your own boss and starting a new company immediately evokes an image of millennials in hoodies driving million-dollar sports cars around Silicon Valley and playing Ping-Pong in the office while discussing their next big idea. Films such as *The Social Network* and *The Internship* promote that fantasy. But this image does not reflect the reality that we faced in 1977 or that almost all entrepreneurs still face. Whether you are building a cookie store or a technology start-up, you will have to tackle monumental challenges and find yourself working harder than you ever thought possible. We certainly were.

We struggled to complete each step—find a location, sign a lease, design and build the store, test recipes, hire and train a staff, market the business, and keep from burning it to the ground. This was a completely new industry for both of us, and the learning curve was huge. Somehow we managed to make it to opening day. We were ready to launch, and then we forgot the pot holders and started a fire. If I learned one lesson from those heady days of the cookie company, it was that the unexpected was our real Goliath. You cannot see it coming or plan for it, but your response is the difference between success and failure. It was for us.

In the company's earliest days, money was tight, so Arthur went back to his regular job and I was running the daily operations. While Arthur was eager to expand, I was still treating the whole thing as a temporary enterprise. I assumed that we would do this for a little while and maybe end up with two or three stores. I was not very optimistic about expansion. In those first two months before we opened, I was still looking for other business opportunities. I thought about starting a home delivery dry cleaning service and was approached by another clothing company to become their president. I was still seriously investigating possible industries, but the opening of the Perimeter Mall store was quickly consuming all of my time.

We knew at the outset that it would be difficult to succeed by selling one cookie at a time. My experiences as a teenager with my mentor, Miami Beach businessman Irving Settler, had taught me that there were two ways to attract a customer—either through an impulse buy or by making your business a destination. The first involves creating a product so appealing that a window shopper is compelled to walk inside to purchase it. But if you depend only on impulse purchases, you are going to have problems. This is where our competitors went wrong. They hoped that the smell of fresh-baked cookies would be enough to entice customers to buy their product. The second and more profitable way to make your business successful is to sell something that people specifically come to your store to purchase. The store has to be a destination. We had to open with a product that people would order and come to pick up. Our secret was the cookie cake, what someone once called an "edible greeting card."

Cookie cakes were part of our core business strategy from the beginning, and we spent the first few weeks perfecting their size and design. We finally settled on plate-sized cookies that had messages such as "Happy Birthday" and "I Love You" written in chocolate or vanilla icing. Our hope was that if customers purchased these instead of traditional cakes, we would be able to generate higher revenue. Our 12-inch cookie cake at the time cost $10, and the 16-inch cookie cake was $14. We later created a sheet-pan cookie cake and a heart-shaped cookie cake that proved to be our best seller; in fact, Valentine's Day became our biggest day of the year. These cookie cakes had a much higher margin of profit than the thirty-cent cookie, and they were really appealing.

I had made cookie cakes for my children with my mother's recipe for years. As a father of three, I had been to enough birthday parties to know that most kids do not really like cake. They love the fluffy icing, which they immediately lick off when served. But most children's birthday parties are littered with plates of half-eaten pieces of cake. Cookies are another story. If you bring a cookie cake to a kid's party, not a crumb remains. I knew that we could not depend on foot traffic alone. We needed our customers to call the store, order cookie cakes for special occasions, and drive to the mall to pick them up. This is one of the first reasons we succeeded.

The quality of our product was the second reason for our success. When we opened our business, there were three major cookie chains in malls in America and perhaps a hundred mom-and-pop stores that were not part of larger companies. The Cookie Factory had about a hundred stores, while the Original Cookie Company and the Cookie Store both had about fifty. The Original Cookie Company and the Cookie Store sold one cookie at a time. The Cookie Factory was part of a large baking company, and they sold larger cookie cakes that were frosted in all kinds of colors. They seemed to want to disguise their cookie as a cake. Unlike the others, we used chocolate and vanilla frosting because we did not want customers to expect us to do the same kind of elaborate designs that bakeries did. All three of our competitors sold cookies that were made from frozen batter, just as grocery stores and bakeries did. When they were warm, they were tolerable. But once they cooled off, they tasted like plaster. We made our cookies from scratch, always using fresh, refrigerated batter that had been hand scooped. They were delicious hot or cold, just like the cookies that your parents or grandparents made.

Temptation became the third reason for our success. We were one of the first food companies to start handing out samples outside the area right in front of our store. We had some complaints from our fellow tenants, but we persisted and gave out bite-sized pieces of our cookies to shoppers. My mother, Lee, did most of the sampling for the first store. She had moved to Atlanta in the mid-1970s, after having worked in concessions at Haulover Beach in Miami. She had a warm, engaging personality and enjoyed roaming the mall with a small silver tray urging people to take one. She was quite a character and became known as the Cookie Lady. Sharing samples of piping-hot cookies was very popular and helped us build brand awareness in the mall.

The last thing that set us apart was our staff and service. We hired bright, young, smiling employees to work in our stores. This was 1977, and there were very few food companies that made customer service a priority. McDonald's was a brand known for its innovative marketing campaigns and attentiveness to customers. They often hired cheerful cashiers who were trained to be quick and polite, as did Chick-fil-A, today's gold standard for customer service. But Atlanta had another stellar example—Rich's Department Store. At Rich's, founded in 1867, the service was legendary. The employees went out of their way to accommodate customers, going so far as to provide refunds for merchandise they did not even stock or that had been used for more than a decade. In one case, the store provided a refund for a dead canary. In another, a young boy came to Rich's to trade his baby sister for a space helmet. The salesperson declined the exchange and sent the boy home with a note "extolling the virtues of baby sisters." A decade before we opened the cookie company, Rich's distributed a press kit for the store's centennial that explained their approach to business:

"Rich's return policy isn't just merely liberal, it's lavish. Atlantans automatically expect Rich's to give something extra—a feeling of solidarity and companionship and warmth and shining trust which is so valued that it's taken for granted."

The idea of giving more than was expected was a lesson I also learned from my teenage mentor Irving Settler. At his clothing store in Miami Beach, Irving carried a Polaroid camera to take pictures of his customers sporting their new outfits. He would put them on the wall above the display of shirts such that they lined the store—almost like a neighborhood wall of fame. People used to shop there just to get their picture on the wall. This did not cost him more than twenty dollars a year, but it had a big impact on his customers and his bottom line. It was something extra, and this is what we tried to do at the cookie company. We made sure that we had an appealing product that people could sample, a lot of it on display, and a staff that was as warm as our cookies. Years later, Warren Buffet articulated this philosophy, one that I still embrace: "Your premium brand had better be delivering something special, or it's not going to get the business."

Each of these factors made us more successful than we ever could have imagined. We calculated that we needed to sell $12,000 in cookies per month to break even, and in the first thirty days we sold more than $30,000. I left the store on August 18 at 6:30 p.m. exhilarated by our newfound success. A rainy day had given way to a clear, beautiful night in Atlanta. My wife Donna had bought me a Harley-Davidson Super Glide motorcycle that year for my birthday. I had always wanted one and treated it as if it was my baby. I was cruising home, taking the back roads and breathing in the cool damp air, feeling great about the future and how much we had accomplished in just six short weeks.

I was as surprised as anyone that we had sold so many cookies in our first month. It was barely sixty days since we were fighting to secure a space, a lease, and a loan. There was nothing in our approach or timing that made our success likely. In fact, it was more likely that we were going to fail. And I knew failure—but I had started to see it from a different perspective. Most people do everything they can to avoid it, me included.

Failure hurts, humiliates, and defeats. But it also educates, pushes, and empowers. I started to wonder, why is one person motivated by failure to do better and one never tries again? It took Thomas Edison multiple attempts before he developed a successful lightbulb. He would later quip, "I have not failed. I've just found ten thousand ways that won't work." Failure might be more than a stepping-stone to success—it might be a critical ingredient. It may seem counterintuitive, but the people who have been the most successful are often the ones who have experienced the most failure—often as children or early in their careers.

There are dozens of stories of famous people who used setbacks as a training ground for success. Before becoming president, Abraham Lincoln failed twice in business, lost eight elections, and suffered a nervous breakdown that put him in bed for six months. Nearly defeated, he once wrote to his friend, "I am now the most miserable man living." Babe Ruth struck out 1,330 times in his baseball career on his way to hitting 714 home runs. Charles Schultz, of *Peanuts* fame, had every cartoon he submitted to his high school yearbook rejected, and Walt Disney refused to hire him. After Fred Astaire's first screen test, a staffer at MGM wrote: "Can't act. Can't sing. Slightly bald. Can dance a little." A casting director told Sidney Poitier after his first audition to "stop wasting people's time and go out and become a dishwasher." Each of these stories illustrates the wisdom embedded in actress Mary Pickford's axiom: "If you have made mistakes, even serious mistakes, you may have a fresh start any moment you choose, for this thing we call 'failure' is not the falling down, but the staying down." I loved history, sports, and the movies, and I grew up on these stories. They gave me hope that I could bounce back from failure and achieve more than anyone expected of me.

So on that cool August night I was feeling good. My third company was showing real promise. I was optimistic about the direction we were going and excited about the possibilities that lay ahead. Little did I know that my ride home was about to change everything.

7

The Crash

You'll never make it!

If you were going to choose a decade in the twentieth century to start a company selling cookies—a product people love but nobody needs—the 1970s would not top the list. It was an era filled with contradictions. On one hand, it was an entrepreneurial age marked by social change, new sources of capital, and the introduction of transformative technologies such as personal computers, cell phones, and VCRs. But it was also a time of corporate layoffs, labor strikes, double-digit unemployment, fuel shortages, and high inflation. Between January 1973 and December 1974, global stock markets saw one of the worst downturns in modern history. The New York Stock Exchange's Dow Jones Industrial Average lost 45 percent of its value in 694 days. It was an anxious time, and workers and business leaders were concerned about job security and economic growth. This was not an ideal time to take a big risk, but that is just what Arthur Karp and I did when we invested $8,000 to start our cookie company. Sales in our first six weeks were impressive, and our future looked bright. Then I had a nearly fatal motorcycle accident.

I was just ten minutes from home coming off the I-75 exit at about twenty-five miles per hour at the North 120 Loop in Marietta, Georgia, when I felt the rear wheel of my Harley-Davidson Super Glide lock up. I learned later that a rock had gotten stuck between the chain and the rear chain ring. All I knew in that split second was that I was in trouble. The bike slid out from under me, and I flew over the handlebars headfirst into a telephone pole. I felt my helmet crack and my nose split open. As I hit the ground, my legs went in different directions. Later I was told that I had a 95 percent dislocation of my left leg. My right leg was severely injured, and my nose was nearly torn off my face. I was knocked out for a few minutes, but I remember trying to shake myself conscious. I opened my eyes and saw a man standing over me. This being 1977, it took a while for the ambulance to arrive because someone had to find a phone, and meanwhile I was just splayed out on the side of the road, bleeding. When the paramedics finally arrived, I asked where they were taking me. They said Kennestone Hospital, which was the closest, but I told them I wanted to go to Northside Hospital where my orthopedist worked. They agreed and loaded me onto a stretcher. I was still groggy, but I could see out of the two back windows that the ambulance was making a couple of unfamiliar turns. Wherever we were not headed, it was not to Northside Hospital.

I called out to the driver, "Why are you going this way?"

Puzzled, he asked, "Isn't this the way to Northside Hospital?"

It became clear that they had no idea where they were going. It took us so long to get there that Donna, who had been at home twenty-five miles from the hospital, beat us to the emergency room. She was panicked, running all over the hospital looking for me. They finally wheeled me in, covered in blood, mostly from the injury to my nose. The paramedics transferred me to a bed and tried to take the pillow from the stretcher out of my hands. I'm clutching it because I am in so much pain, and I keep pleading, "Don't take my pillow. Don't take my pillow." But they insist, until I finally make one of the paramedics lean down and I say, "Look, if you take this pillow from me, I'll tell the ambulance company that you got lost." Needless to say, I kept the pillow.

The emergency room doctors took one look at me and immediately called the plastic surgeon on duty, who was just about to leave for a dinner party. I was incredibly lucky, for he came in, numbed my face, and repaired my nose on the spot. I was kept sedated overnight, and the next morning I faced four and half hours of surgery on my legs. I awoke to a full-length cast on my left leg and a brace on my right. The doctors who did the surgery told me that my legs were so badly damaged that, although I would recover, I would not walk again without a cane or crutches. My ability to run, play golf, or do karate was at an end. This was a lot to absorb, but when I came to understand how bad the accident was and the real possibility that I might not have woken up at all, I tried to put everything in perspective. The only thing I was sure about was that my future and the business were both in doubt.

The idea that I was going to stay in the cookie business for a short time before moving on to something else flew out the window. I was now facing a very painful and prolonged period of rehabilitation. During the months following my accident, I slowly moved from using a walker to crutches, and eventually to walking with the aid of two canes. Because I was so immobile, I had a lot of time to focus on the business. Arthur was still working full time at his other business while overseeing the legal issues related to new leases for the cookie company. He had to take a week off to manage the operations while I was in the hospital, but once I was discharged, he went back to his other company, and I resumed the daily management. It could not have been a more critical time.

In September, about a month after my accident, we opened our second cookie store in a mall in south Atlanta called Greenbriar. This was a big decision, because we had just faced an unexpected expense at Perimeter. The residential-grade construction that we used because we did not know any better could not sustain the heavy commercial use. After just two months, the counters were literally falling apart. We could not afford to lose a single day's worth of sales, so when we closed Perimeter one night, we had a construction crew come in to install the new counters and were ready to open the next morning. Under these circumstances, even considering opening another store was a big gamble.

Perimeter was 532 square feet and cost us $25,000 per year in rent. Greenbriar was three times the size but rented for $10,000 per year. Mall traffic at Greenbriar was much heavier than at Perimeter, so we were sure that we would strike gold with this new location. Greenbriar, which opened in 1965, was a good mall whose sales averaged $100 per square foot. It was next to Delta Air Lines' world headquarters, so many of the airline employees regularly shopped there, especially around lunchtime.

The addition of a larger store allowed us to make some changes in manufacturing. When we first opened at Perimeter, we made the cookie batter in Arthur's garage. We hired a person to mix the dough in a commercial-grade mixer and store it in a commercial refrigerator. He then brought large drums of batter to the store, carrying the empty drums back to the garage to be commercially washed. But we knew that we needed a better system. So we used 500 square feet of the Greenbriar store for retail and the additional 1,000 square feet to build a small batter facility. In the back of the store there was an existing walk-in cooler left by the previous tenant. We brought our mixer from Arthur's garage, which could handle the capacity as long as we were an Atlanta company. We also started lining the batter drums with industrial-grade food service bags to help keep them clean and the product fresh. This new system worked a lot better, and we were poised to thrive.

Chick-fil-A had opened its first mall location at Greenbriar ten years earlier, it was doing well, and we were right next door. What could be better? But in our first week we did only $2,000 worth of business. We gave away samples beyond our lease line just as we did at Perimeter Mall. We had cookie cakes in the glass showcase. There was three times the foot traffic, but we had far fewer customers. What was happening? I had to find out fast, because we were doing the one thing a new business cannot afford—bleed money. I was reeling in pain from the accident, Arthur was still working for his other company, and we were both in a panic about the $75,000 we had just spent on opening this new store. This was not a nine-to-five problem; I couldn't just go home and not think about it until the next morning. This was a twenty-four-hour-a-day problem. I often woke up in a cold sweat and had many sleepless nights worrying about how I would care for my family and recover if the company failed. Days felt like months; weeks felt like years. We were in big trouble.

The crisis at Greenbriar forced me to turn all of my attention to that store. I was still doing physical therapy every day and had limited mobility, so someone had to drive me. I first had to face the fact that Arthur and I had overlooked a critical piece of information about the shoppers at Greenbriar. They had much less disposable income than those at Perimeter. A thirty-cent cookie was still a luxury item. This was a pretty big oversight, but customer income did not entirely explain the low sales volume. Because I was overseeing operations, I had to cut costs, find a way to attract more customers and encourage them to buy more of our products, and put a tourniquet on the bleeding to just try to break even. People had to eat lunch and dinner, which explained why Chick-fil-A did so well. But we were an indulgence. Perimeter Mall had been too easy. Customers fell into our lap at our first store; not so at Greenbriar. So I had to look at every aspect of our business and ask tough questions to find out what was working and what was not. If we could not turn Greenbriar around, we would be out of business within a few months.

I realized that part of my problem was that I always approached my work as an entrepreneur—from my leaf- and snow-removal business as a child in Buffalo, through my time at Mister Jr. and Male Slacks and Jeans, to the founding of Pant-O-Mine and Great American Clothing. I was great at getting things started and then moving on to the next challenge. Now I was going to have to manage the daily operations of a company—build a brand, increase revenue, introduce new products, develop a training program—without losing my entrepreneurial spirit. Not only was I physically disabled, but I also had to change my whole approach to business and really focus on the numbers, something I had learned the hard way at Pant-O-Mine. Everything I thought I knew about the cookie business was now in question.

Efficiency became my top priority. In order to lower our food costs from 28 percent to below 20 and our labor costs from 35 percent to 20, we needed to generate higher sales while running a lean operation. Training and customer service became my most powerful tools. When we opened

Perimeter, I created a basic two-week training program for staff, but it never dawned on me that we needed an operations handbook that detailed our policies and procedures. Now I developed a much more thorough training program and manual that helped prevent our employees from burning and dropping cookies, as well as controls that would keep them from giving away cookies to their friends. Better training and operational controls helped reduce staff turnover; it also meant that we could function with fewer employees while still delivering excellent customer service. I also heeded the old expression "Fish where there are fish." I studied customer shopping patterns at Greenbriar and adjusted the staffing needs accordingly. Perimeter was consistently busy, so I hired people for specific jobs: work the counter, operate the register, scoop and bake the cookies. At Greenbriar, I cross-trained every employee. This made it possible to operate with a leaner staff, thus cutting back on overhead. Each store had its own needs, and differentiating made a huge difference.

Customer service was my second major focus. Cheerful, well-trained employees helped attract more customers and encouraged them to buy more of our products. We tried to teach our front-line staff that cookies are fun, and customers should want to take some home to their friends and family. This was not just about upselling, it was about creating an experience that could be shared, which was a big part of our brand. We had talented employees, but I knew I needed to change our Greenbriar store manager. I interviewed a number of applicants and hired a very personable young man who was also a talented artist. He helped us transform our cookie cake business by creating beautiful designs with clever messages, which we soon adopted at Perimeter Mall. People who came to buy a cookie were awed by his cookie cakes and often added one to their order. When we opened Greenbriar, barely 10 percent of our business came from the cookie cakes. Within a couple of months, he had grown it to 40 percent.

Taken together, these changes helped cut costs, attract more customers, and increase sales. In seventy-five days we turned the store around. There are moments in every business when the company's trajectory is altered. Most of those go unnoticed or only become obvious years later. Businesses are complicated, and there are a number of factors that affect whether you are going to grow and thrive. Few executives can point to a specific decision or event that determines their company's future. We could, and this was that moment. Everything that happened after Greenbriar was based on the lessons I learned there, and they changed everything. Today I am convinced that the crisis at Greenbriar was the key ingredient to our success. We were able to deliver a great product and incredible customer service, all with a better-trained staff that could function in a lean and efficient manner.

In October, several months after my motorcycle accident, Rouse, the company that owned Perimeter Mall, approached us about opening a store in Columbia Mall in Maryland. We found ourselves at a turning point. This would be a really big decision. Columbia Mall had opened in 1971 as a planned community. It was huge and attracted an affluent clientele. Rouse offered us a location on the second floor of the mall. Arthur was excited, but I was hesitant to make such a big move and investment. Because I had been running the day-to-day part of the business, I knew that it would be difficult. Transporting food across state lines required that we conform to all of the regulations set forth by the United States Department of Agriculture and the Food and Drug Administration. We were not even close to meeting these strict guidelines. I knew we had to make some drastic changes in a very short time if we were going to take this new space in Maryland.

The most important one was creating a real manufacturing facility. I hired a food safety engineer who designed warehouses and manufacturing facilities, and we paid him several thousand dollars to draw some plans for the company. This engineer came to my house in Kennesaw, because I still could not walk very well. He explained what we would need to conform to food safety rules, and we sat down to review his suggestions. A new facility had to have a space to hold ingredients, a space to mix the batter, and a walk-in cooler to store it. He went into great detail about the kind of climate-controlled areas we needed: how they had to be constructed of cinder block with epoxy-covered walls to restrict moisture, and how they had to have very precise controls for humidity and temperature.

He also detailed what size office and warehouse spaces would be required. I listened patiently and then asked:

"Can you estimate how much this new facility might cost?"

He replied, "To do it right, between a hundred fifty and two hundred fifty thousand dollars."

When I heard that number, I sucked in my breath and tried to say as calmly as I could, "Thanks. This is good information."

As soon as he left, I called Arthur to recount our conversation. I ended by saying, "We cannot afford a batter facility that costs this much. We might be able to do something in between, so let me start thinking and looking around at some locations and try to come up with something we can afford."

We were at a crossroads. This was not just about opening a third store; it was about becoming a national company. We needed a new facility if we were going to grow the company and go to Columbia, but we had no money to build one. I had no salary, and I could barely walk. Arthur was still running his successful sales agency and was not engaged in the cookie company's daily operations. What we needed was a miracle.

On my way from Perimeter to Greenbriar one day, I saw a billboard with Mitchell Brannen's name on it. Today, Mitchell is a successful commercial real estate broker in Atlanta. Back then, he was in his early twenties and had a billboard advertising warehouse space. I wrote his number down and called to tell him that I was looking to rent inexpensive warehouse space. He was patient and explained, "You really only have two choices in Atlanta for inexpensive warehouse space—either Fulton Industrial Boulevard or Chattahoochee Industrial Boulevard." Mitchell did not know much about our specific requirements, but he told me he had a client who was having trouble renting a space that had been subdivided in an awkward manner and would be willing to make a great deal if we would consider taking it in its current form.

We did not have a lot of options, so I asked Mitchell to pick me up to take a look because I could still not drive. As we toured the warehouse, I could not believe what I was seeing. The space had been rented by a printing company and was about 8,500 square feet. It had two climate-controlled rooms—one where they stored the ink and supplies and the other where the printing was done—both constructed of cinder block. It looked a lot like the facility the food engineer had designed for us. If we rented the space, we would end up with most of what we needed. The only thing missing was a walk-in cooler, and we could lease that. This was almost too good to believe.

When Mitchell asked what I thought, I tried to contain my excitement. In my head, I'm thinking, "This is incredible." But I said as casually as I could:

"Well, I don't know. It's not a great space. The demolition could cost a lot of money, which we don't have. If we keep the two cinder-block rooms, do you think the owner would build out the offices, epoxy the walls, and install new floors?"

Mitchell thought he would, so all we had to do was lease two larger mixers and a walk-in cooler; we moved the other ancillary manufacturing equipment from our Greenbriar Mall store. I used the furniture that I had taken with me from Great American Clothing to outfit my office, and Arthur and I shopped at a bargain store for two couches and a coffee table to put in the lobby. I found an old desk to put behind the reception window. So, at the end of November, we opened our first real batter facility without any significant cash outlay.

Was it luck, a miracle, or really just meant to be? As I think back on it now, I am not even sure why I went to look at the space with Mitchell. We did not have the money and had no prospect of borrowing or raising it. We would not be able to open the store in Columbia without the batter facility, and we had no money to build one. But, somehow, all the pieces just fell into place.

The facility was mostly empty except for the three employees who manufactured and shipped the batter, and me. I took the front office and situated my desk in such a way that I could see through the window who was approaching the building. We put a bell on the door, so it was easy to hear. Every time it rang, I would push myself up from my desk and limp to the front to greet the visitor in the lobby. We could not afford to hire a receptionist, but I wanted to give the impression that we were a bigger operation than we were, so I would always say, "Our receptionist is out, may I help you?"

The new manufacturing facility changed the focus and the future of the company. We were no longer going to be just an Atlanta company, so we had to change how we packaged and shipped the batter. It would be impossible to continue using the plastic tubs, because we had no way to transport them back. I started experimenting with cardboard boxes. The twelve-inch-square industry standard could not hold the weight of the cookie batter without breaking. Through trial and error, I settled on a ten-inch-square box lined with commercial-grade plastic. This format was more durable but also maximized what each retail location could store in its walk-in cooler. Columbia would become the testing ground for all future shipping and operational issues.

I also had to change my own focus. When our stores were located in metro Atlanta, I could stay close to home. I had left the clothing business because I was traveling so much, and now we were about to take our concept to Maryland. This was a big decision, and once we agreed to open the Columbia store, Arthur had to commit to the company full time. We were no longer able to operate as a mom-and-pop company. We were on the cusp of becoming a national one.

8

Inch by Inch

Okay, Coles, you wanted a new challenge. Well, here's your chance.

Growth costs money, and we still did not have the resources necessary to open Original Great American Chocolate Chip Cookie Company stores all over the country. It seemed we had three options. We could bring in investors and give up part of our ownership. We could bring in a partner and, again, give up part of what we owned. Or we could consider franchising the business. While these were all reasonable solutions, we did not want to give up our control over the company, so the most logical one was to franchise. But franchising was a new concept for us, and we needed to research what would be involved. We had plenty of people trying to buy franchises from us in our first month, yet we knew little about how the system worked on any scale, large or small. I remember sitting at one of the tables in front of the store at Perimeter Mall with a franchise attorney, posing questions about growing the company.

"If franchising is such a great way to build and grow a business," I asked, "why do so many franchisors go out of business?" Arthur Treacher's Fish and Chips, a fast-food seafood restaurant that started as a franchise in 1969, was closing stores all over the country. They were not the only one failing in this economic climate, and we could not afford to follow that path. The attorney gave us books about franchising to address some of our questions. The biggest lesson I gleaned from that reading list was that the relationship between franchisor and franchisee is usually cast in David and Goliath terms. The franchisor is the giant and has the right to dictate everything that the franchisee does. Yet if the franchisee does not make money, the franchisor will fail. From talking to other franchisors, I learned that you have to support the franchisee in order for the venture to be successful. All good franchise companies know this. If we were going to franchise, we could not treat the franchisee as someone who must obey us, but rather as a partner who could help grow the business. This would become the most important decision we made as a company.

We wanted to test the waters with a franchise for the Columbia store, so we signed the lease knowing that we did not have the money yet. It was a big risk, but we did not want to lose the opportunity. I had been meeting with a possible investor regularly to discuss our dilemma. Our cookie concept was really working, and we needed to grow, but we did not have enough resources to make that a reality. After we agreed to go to Columbia, I asked him if he knew anyone who might want to help. He finally said that he would like to be a financial partner in the store, and that we would continue to run the operations. We formed a separate company that bought the first franchise; the cookie company owned 60 percent and the new company owned 40 percent. So in reality we became both franchisor and franchisee. If the concept did not work, we would buy the franchisee out and convert Columbia to a company store. While the Perimeter Mall store had cost $30,000 to build and Greenbriar cost $75,000, Columbia was going to cost nearly $175,000. The costs were expanding exponentially because everything we did had to be built on a commercial sales platform. It had to withstand the constant flow of repeated transactions. We knew it would be more expensive, and not just because of the higher-grade construction. We now needed a professional set of drawings and plans that included both design and engineering. The drawings would have to be reviewed and approved by mall management, who would not accept the hand-drawn plans that Jeff Weil so graciously did at Perimeter.

Just about this time, Maryland passed a franchise disclosure act that would go into effect on January 1, 1978. Other states had similar laws, many based on the 1971 California Franchise Investment Law, often called the grandfather of state disclosure laws. The increasing popularity of franchising resulted in substantial regulation aimed at safeguarding existing and potential franchisees. Maryland's law was directed at full disclosure of relevant facts by the franchisor at the beginning of the franchise relationship. According to the new law, in order to open a franchise, the company had to be in business for a certain number of years. It was a good law, but the timing was terrible for us. Our company had only been operating for six months, so we had to open before January first. If we failed, we would not be able to move forward.

We worked to move heaven and earth and were set to open on December 10, 1977, but Rouse, the mall's owner, was locked in a battle with the health department over a central grease trap shared by all the restaurants. The health department held us hostage and would not issue us a certificate of occupancy until the issue with Rouse was resolved. After trying to address the problem on the phone, I flew to Maryland to meet with the health department, explaining that if we were unable to open the store before the end of the year, we would be out of business. They were unmoved, so I went to Rouse and pleaded with them to resolve the grease trap issue. They promised that they would, and we opened on December 30. But we had to close the next day because the health department, feeling they had the upper hand, kept pushing Rouse. The mall management refused to give in to the new demands, so the health department closed us down for three weeks. We had already hired and started training our employees two weeks before the opening day, so we had to pay them for a total of five weeks without any sales. Now we had three stores, and Columbia was bleeding money. This was not an auspicious beginning.

When we finally opened at the end of January, the Columbia Mall store did not do as well as we expected. We sent one of our managers from Atlanta to run it, and I visited every week. I started doing an informal traffic study and quickly realized that our location was part of the problem.

Numerous variables make a store successful. Perimeter had low sales per square foot ($70, when most malls in the nation were averaging $100), yet it was our most successful store because of its location and a reasonably well-off clientele. It was one store off center court, what was called a "95 percent location." That meant that 95 percent of the mall's visitors were going to walk past the store. Greenbriar had the most foot traffic of the three stores, but the customers were less affluent and did not have thirty-five cents (we had raised the price in November) to spend on a cookie. At Columbia, even with its large and more affluent clientele, we did 30 percent less business than the first-floor stores.

Second-floor mall locations are never as good as those on the main floor because you simply do not have as much foot traffic. Most mall entrances are on the main floor, and shoppers tend to stay on that level unless they have a compelling reason to go upstairs. A first-floor location on or off center court has more traffic than a center court location on the second floor. But we did not know that when we signed the lease at Columbia, even though we asked some questions of the mall management about shoppers' income and education and mall traffic. It was obvious that we were still pretty green and had a lot to learn about real estate. In the 1970s, few malls engaged in detailed research about these topics, so they would often reply with generalizations that did not give us much information. The Columbia store was profitable, but never as strong as Perimeter.

After we opened the Columbia store, an opportunity came available at Southlake Mall in Morrow, about twenty miles south of Atlanta. Southlake was a good mall, but we particularly wanted the location because the same company owned Cumberland Mall, which was the second most successful mall in Atlanta. We opened our Southlake store using the same partnership arrangement with our investor that we had at Columbia. Jim Bebe, an employee of Carter & Associates, the mall owner, oversaw the architectural review process for both malls and was instrumental in helping us change the look of our stores. He rejected the first drawings we submitted for Southlake, gave us a sample set of plans to show us what he was after, and sent us to Gary Aldridge, a store designer. The plans eventually cost us $25,000, almost as much as we spent to open the Perimeter store. At the time it seemed like a huge investment. But Gary and Jim made a persuasive point—this design would help us become a national brand; it would be an investment in our future. And they were right. Gary created a beautiful store that would cost close to $200,000. It changed our company's whole look. We also came up with special promotions and tried to drum up excitement. The stores were fun, and that was part of our appeal. We brought our store manager from Greenbriar over to run it, and at one time Southlake was our highest-revenue store, with sales over $700,000.

I knew from my time in the clothing business that all companies had their ups and downs, and we were no different. Our first year was nothing short of a roller coaster ride. But we also knew that we had to expand. We had tested the waters with franchising at Columbia and Southlake, but we needed to focus on it as a recipe for growth. Franchising allows people to go into business for themselves but not by themselves. Franchisees benefit from brand awareness, marketing and public relations support, proven recipes, supply discounts, and management expertise from the franchisor. Without this kind of support, about 90 percent of new businesses fail in the first five years, while only 30 percent of franchise businesses fail. It is a safer pathway to the American Dream.

Bolstered by our experience with our new investor, Arthur and I began a process to qualify potential franchisees. It takes a while to find the right kind of franchise partner. In the early years, companies often take on franchisees like themselves, but it is almost never the right formula. Unfortunately, we made that mistake and brought in people who were very entrepreneurial, just like us. By this time we had created a comprehensive six-week training program that detailed every aspect of the store's operations, from food preparation to customer service to marketing. Some of the original franchisees completed the program, but their entrepreneurial background became a liability. After ninety days they thought they knew more about the cookie business than we did and tried to run the stores their own way. This was a very scary moment for us. Defiant franchisees can ruin a company, and we were still young in this business. We did everything in our power to show them why our system worked, but they ignored us and eventually defaulted. We ended up taking back several stores in Florida, Texas, and Ohio, and implemented all of our standard operating procedures that had been proven to work. In almost every case we turned the store around, made it profitable, and resold the franchise.

To be a franchisee, you have to be a special kind of person. You have to embrace that you are buying into a system of strict operating standards. We had some notable successes, like Larry "Doc" Cohen, a former pharmacist. Doc wanted a store in California, but the franchise laws there held that a business had to have been in operation for five years. We offered him a store in Louisiana, and he turned out to be a rock star. He was a terrific operator and retailer because of his drugstore background. He was entrepreneurial enough to be creative, but he also knew how to hire well and follow our advice regarding operations. He was absolutely committed to running a great business, and we worked very closely together and often tested new ideas and products in his stores. At one point he had more than twenty stores. He is still in the cookie business with a few stores in Atlanta and Texas. Doc is like Al Pacino in *The Godfather*: he keeps trying to get out of the business, but it keeps pulling him back.

The cookie company was growing and making money, and our future looked bright. The batter facility was humming along, and we were expanding. But I was frustrated and stalled. My recovery from the accident was progressing, but not very fast. I was starting to doubt that I was going to get any better.

This was made worse by an episode with my younger daughter, Taryn. She was three years old, and we were outside at the bottom of our very steep driveway. She asked if I wanted to race her up the hill to the mailbox. Though I was still using two canes to move around clumsily, I readily agreed to her challenge. But when I took off to run, I realized that I could not do it. The pain in my legs was simply excruciating. I began to make excuses, and she tried to reassure me, saying, "It's okay, Daddy. I really don't feel like racing anyway. I'm too tired."

When we got back to the house, I was devastated. It was not the physical limitation that so frustrated me, but rather that my daughter and I had completely accepted it as a permanent condition. This was the first time since my accident that I realized that I was disabled—not so much in my legs, but in my mind. Growing up as a poor kid, I was used to people telling me what I was not capable of, and I always stubbornly tried to prove them wrong. But this time was different. The doctors' prognosis that I would never walk again without help became a safety zone—something I just accepted. This was partly because learning to walk again really hurts; it was also because I was afraid of what would happen if I failed. So instead of fighting, I had surrendered to my fate.

This incident in the driveway would turn out to be a defining moment in my life. When I got back to the house, I found my wife Donna to tell her what happened. We made the decision right there in our kitchen that, regardless of the outcome, I had to work harder to try to get better. There was no way I could spend the rest of my life like this. I simply could not allow my daughter to grow up with a father who could not run with her to the mailbox.

For months I had been spending so much time just reading about how to recover that I was not making much progress. I was finally ready to get down to business. I wanted to walk without help and maybe even become an athlete again. But those were huge, seemingly insurmountable goals, according to my doctors, and I realized that I had to set smaller, intermediate milestones. If your goal is too big, you will never reach it. The magnitude of it will defeat you, and each day it will seem further and further away. Without small successes, you will have no incentive to continue. Anyone who has ever been on a diet knows what I'm talking about.

So I had to change my attitude, my approach, and my expectations. I was still determined to defy my prognosis, but I had to create a more realistic timeline. With that, I started a slow and difficult period and came up with my own rehabilitation program. I had to stop hiding behind the acceptance of my new circumstance and fight back. I knew that my response to the accident was going to determine my physical well-being; it took me longer to realize that it could also shape the future of my family and the company. After talking with Donna, I sat down at the kitchen table and saw that my calendar and day planner was open to May 6, 1978. In the space provided, I wrote: "Today, it begins. It's not going to be easy, but I'm going to do it inch by inch." That was how I began to take my life back.

The goal at the beginning of my program was simple. I wanted to restore some flexibility, range of motion, and strength to my legs, all while learning to walk without help. I knew that every inch mattered; I was determined to get better.

The physical therapy regimen prescribed by my doctors was very thorough and time consuming, and the round-trip commute between my house in Kennesaw and Northside Hospital was about fifty miles. To be more efficient, I tried to do as much as I could at home in support of their efforts. Water therapy was part of the hospital's program, so Donna and I bought a wooden hot tub and installed it in our bedroom. She would get in the tub with me and massage and bend my legs to help break up the scar tissue. Each movement felt like a bone breaking; you could actually hear this eerie cracking sound even under the water. Every day, I would try to put one foot in front of the other, which is much harder than it sounds. Because I had become so sedentary, strength was also an issue. The physical therapist had me lift light weights with high repetitions at the hospital, but the progress was slow. This was the 1970s, and the physical fitness craze was not yet in full swing. Most thirty-four-year-olds were not athletic, so the physical therapy was much less rigorous than it is today. In my twenties I had started running, weightlifting, and doing martial arts, so I was used to pushing my physical limits.

At the small gym in our house, I used much heavier weights to work on my quadriceps. At first I could bend my legs only an inch or two, but I discovered that heavy weights forced me to go further. I also started with 50-pound leg presses; within a month I could press 200 pounds. After three months, I could press 450 pounds, and in nine months I was up to 600.

To further increase my range of motion and increase my aerobic capacity, I began riding a stationary bicycle. I had to put the seat up as high as it would go, because I could barely bend my legs to make a full revolution.

At first I could barely do two minutes before exhausting myself. I tried to extend it by a minute or two each day. After a month I could do half an hour, increasing the speed as well. After about three months, I could lower the seat and completely bend my legs.

By October of 1978, I was tired of being indoors and looked for a way to get some fresh air and enjoy the cool fall weather. I went to our garage to find my old yellow Schwinn Continental that had been collecting dust for years. I hoped it would provide me with a change of scenery. Donna and I had bought bicycles when we moved into our home in 1973, but we had ridden them only a few times. Prior to that, I probably had not ridden a bicycle since I was thirteen years old in Miami Beach.

I cleaned up the Schwinn, replaced the chain, and slowly walked it from the garage up the steep driveway to our mailbox. I had to lean on the bike for support the whole way, because I still could not walk well. When I reached the top of the hill, I slowly climbed on and began pedaling. It was easier than I remembered, mostly because I was pedaling downhill. I made it to the end of my street and felt great. Turning left on New Salem Road, I kept pedaling. I flew down another steep hill, and it felt as if nothing could stop me. Then I faced my first uphill climb.

Momentum from the downhill helped me get about halfway up the hill. But I did not have enough strength to get to the top. So I found myself stuck in the middle of the road, having to get off the bike to keep from falling over. I remember saying out loud to myself, "Okay, Coles, you wanted a new challenge. Well, here's your chance."

I turned the bike around and rode back down the hill that I had been trying to climb and went about an equal distance up the other side. I got off the bike and turned around and tried again. I was worried that I would fall over, so I pulled my feet out of the toe clips to help with my balance. After half a dozen tries, I realized that I was not going to make it. Exhausted and sweaty, I got off and pushed the bike back home up those steep hills toward the house, leaning on it for support.

But I was not going to be defeated, so I set a new goal. I wanted to make it to Stilesboro Road, which was about three-quarters of a mile from the turn onto New Salem Road, which had two steep hills. Every day, I took out that old Schwinn and tried again. After two weeks, I finally made it.

My next milestone was to reach the base of Kennesaw Mountain, the site of the famous Civil War battle in 1864, about seven miles away. It took me three months to conquer that short distance. Donna would have to come and pick me up because I did not have enough strength to make it home. By January of 1979, I was able to ride to and from the battlefield. I remember pedaling each day up the hill, the very same ground that had nearly defeated me months before. Now I could do it.

The walk with Taryn was the catalyst for my rehabilitation. She got me into the valley to face Goliath. But I knew I still had something to prove. I had often faced him, and he had stepped into my path one more time on that damp summer evening in 1977 and wrecked my motorcycle and me. I was now David, and I had to find a way to conquer this mighty giant. For all my progress, movement remained a big hurdle. My first step was to learn to walk normally again with the help of my doctors and physical therapists—which is more difficult and painful in your thirties than you might imagine. I had to dig really deep every day to retrain myself to do a movement that comes to most people naturally. Then I had to build my strength. On the bicycle, I had to find out how far I could go.

I remained dedicated to my rehabilitation program, and by happenstance one night as Donna and I saw a man named John Marino being interviewed on television about riding his bicycle across the continental United States. I didn't even know there was such a thing, but I was intrigued that John completed this amazing feat despite not having been a cyclist. He had played baseball and football at Hollywood High School in California and then at San Diego State University. While a student there, he was drafted twice by the Dodgers. Both times, he turned them down so he could finish his teaching degree. But the part of the story that most resonated with me was that he suffered a severe injury to his back while lifting weights, ending his baseball prospects.

In the fall of 1976, John was thumbing through the *Guinness Book of World Records* looking to pick up another sport. He ultimately chose cycling and the U.S. coast-to-coast record because it seemed like a huge adventure. He explained, "After setting the record, I realized that the endeavor was more than a race. It was an expedition. It was more than merely pedaling a bicycle fast and long. It was incredibly interesting. There was so much about the challenge that could pique one's interest. It also has an 'off the wall' quality. It's just so 'out there.' This is really living life to the max. It's not for everyone, but definitely a huge attraction to some." John trained for the ride for two years, and in 1978 when he broke the world record, he called that moment "the greatest thrill of my life."

After watching the interview, I began to wonder if I could do the same thing. After all, we were a lot alike. When he started planning for his ride, John was not a competitive cyclist but an average guy. He had been a successful athlete in other sports; so had I. He overcame a serious injury; that was what I was trying to do. Maybe I could do this. Maybe this would be a way to prove that I could take control of my life again.

In September 1979, I rode from Dunwoody to Helen, Georgia, a total of ninety-one miles. It took about twelve and a half hours and was the hardest thing I had done up to then. I had to finish the last five miles with one leg, because my right leg had cramped so severely that I could not use it. As I rode across the Chattahoochee River into Helen, I thought to myself, "I am so lucky." I thought about all the people who faced similar challenges, and I felt I needed to get a message out there about determination, about the importance of not quitting, never giving up. It was at that moment that I decided that I wanted to ride my bicycle across America. Looking back, this was one of the craziest decisions of my life.

John's story had piqued my interest, and the fact that I could complete the ride to Helen motivated me. So I started to do some research, which was not easy back then with no Internet, no Google. I made some calls to people I knew in cycling. I read some books and articles and tried to learn what would be involved in a cross-country ride. I finally decided that I was going to ride from Savannah to San Diego and try to set a world record. My bicycle was going to be a symbol—my slingshot. I believed that if I could just finish this ride after such a terrible accident, I might inspire others to persevere in their struggles against their own Goliaths. What might have been the end of my story actually became the beginning.

Over the next two years I gradually increased the length of my rides, often with Taryn in a child's seat strapped on the back. I rode that Schwinn Continental until I bought a lightweight Trek bicycle. The difference between a 42-pound bike (with Taryn in tow) and a 20-pound bike was amazing. During spring break in 1980, my friend Dave Johnson and I rode from Atlanta to Panama City, Florida, over a three-day period—a total of 286 miles. The first day, we faced a torrential downpour and had to stop at a convenience store to buy black trash bags. We each used one to cover our gear and another to make an improvised poncho. Sixty-five miles into the trip, we stopped at the Pine Mountain General Store in Callaway Gardens to dry off and use the restroom. I was leaning under the hand dryer to dry my hair when the door opened and a man came in. When I looked up, I saw that it was the Reverend Billy Graham. I smiled and said, "They told me that this ride could be a religious experience, but this is ridiculous." He laughed, and we talked for a few minutes about the ride, and then Dave and I got back on the bikes and headed to Florida. When we finished, Dave rented a car to drive the bikes back to Atlanta. I flew to Orlando to meet Donna, daughter Taryn, and son Lorin at Disney World. A year later, in 1981, I repeated the Dunwoody-to-Helen route and covered the same ground in 4 hours 41 minutes, about eight hours faster than my time in 1979.

John Marino had crossed the United States along the northern route from Santa Monica Pier to New York; I decided to go the southern route. I wanted to end in San Diego, where in 1977 in a mall I first saw the cookie store that inspired me to start the Original Great American Chocolate Chip Cookie Company. It was an important place in my life, and I thought it would motivate me to head west. I did not stop to consider that the prevailing winds were more forgiving west to east. I was determined to get to the Pacific Ocean. Speed did not really matter; I just wanted to cover the distance. I calculated that I could do the ride in about twenty days, averaging about 140 miles to cover the 2,800 miles. I really had no idea what to expect. I knew that I would need a place to sleep and would have to figure out how to eat efficiently without getting off the bike, which Donna embraced as a challenge. I do not recall if Marino had a crew, but

I assumed that I would need some support. We owned a motor home, so on my first ride in 1982 my crew was my wife Donna and seven-year-old Taryn. We packed food and clothes. I took only one bike, a Cinelli, on this first trip, along with some extra tires and tools.

We started on June 14 at the courthouse in Savannah. Before we left, I contacted the *Guinness Book of World Records* to determine how to verify the ride. They told me that I needed to keep a signed log to document my progress. Each time we passed a major milestone, we had to find a someone over the age of eighteen who was a resident of the town and have the person sign and time-stamp the log. We tried out our system on the first morning, as we planned to leave Savannah at four. But it was really hard to find someone at 3:45 a.m. to verify the start. We finally saw a guy wobbling near the courthouse who was coherent enough to confirm his residency. We explained what we were doing and what we needed, and he signed the log quite willingly. He became our one-man cheering section and kept asking over and over again, "Where are you going?"

"San Diego!" I shouted as I put my leg over the bike, ready to start.

When the clock tower reached four a.m., I began to pedal. As I pulled away, he asked one more time, "Where are you going?"

I shouted, "San Diego?"

He yelled out, "On a bicycle?"

I screamed back, "Yes."

He screamed, "You'll never make it!" That was the last thing I heard as I rolled past the courthouse steps.

9

Exit 666

*On a good day,
Goliath is a
tough adversary.
Imagine battling
him when he
wakes up on the
wrong side of
the bed.*

Looking back now to June 14, 1982, when I pulled away from the courthouse in Savannah for my first bicycle race across America, it is hard to quantify how much I did not know. I projected that I could complete the race in fourteen days, faster than I originally planned. We mapped out the 2,800-mile route from east to west, not realizing how unconventional this approach really was. Most ultramarathon cyclists ride from west to east to take into account the prevailing winds, but we planned to start in Savannah and go west through Georgia (Columbus), Alabama (Montgomery, Selma, Demopolis), Mississippi (Meridian, Jackson, Vicksburg), Louisiana (Monroe, Shreveport), Texas (Marshall, Dallas, Hobbs), New Mexico (Roswell, Lincoln, Cloudcroft), Arizona (Show Low, Globe, Phoenix), and California (Blythe, El Centro, ending in San Diego). My daughter Taryn decided that she was going to keep a log of everything that happened every day on the journey, recording all the major highlights. She was excited. So we bought her a small notebook, and she wrote on the front cover: "Savannah to San Diego, Michael Coles." The first entry in her book read: "We left Savannah at four a.m." It turned out to be her only entry—it was as if she could predict what was going to happen.

We were woefully unprepared, and that became clear immediately. Donna had to do all the driving, because Taryn was seven and obviously could not help. We slept in the motor home or a hotel on the road, and Donna was not getting much rest. The stress was intense. She had to take care of Taryn, who was great but still only a second-grader, and also worry about me. I was on the bike for sixteen hours a day. Taryn could sleep while Donna was driving, but Donna did not have any support. Taryn had her own job to do—she had to feed me and monitor my progress. We taught her to make peanut butter and jelly sandwiches, shakes, and other high-calorie foods to keep me going. She turned out to be a very competent chef and cheerful delivery person, hanging out the window to pass me food and drink.

I knew that boredom would be a constant issue, so before the race in 1982 I bought two Sony Walkmans and headphones. I made two cassette tapes for the whole trip. One was a mixtape that had music I listened to when I was working out at the gym. The second had the soundtrack for *Rocky III*, the Sylvester Stallone movie that had been released in theaters a few weeks before. On the flip side of the second tape, I copied Survivor's "Eye of the Tiger" over and over again. Taryn would hand me a new Walkman when I waved my hand. How did I know that 180 minutes of music would not be enough to cover 2,800 miles? I must have listened to that song two thousand times.

Everything about the 1982 race would have been perfect had I been better prepared, trained harder, and had a larger crew. My longest training ride without resting was to Helen, Georgia, and back—150 miles in under nine hours. That was not enough by a long shot. By the time I reached Columbus, Georgia, on the first day, I already knew we were in trouble.

As I crossed into Alabama, I seriously considered turning around and going back to Atlanta. But I made the decision to keep going. I had been preparing for this for four years, and I just could not quit even if things were not going as planned. The race was partly about me trying to get my life back, but it was also about setting an example for other people who were trying to overcome a big challenge. It was also about family. This was a big adventure for the three of us, and it was important to savor our time together. I had been working hard growing the cookie company and trying to recover from the accident, and I needed some time to recharge. I not only had to be an endurance cyclist, mechanic, and nutritionist on this race, I also had to be a father and a husband. When we did stop at a hotel, I swam and played at the pool with Taryn, who had been cooped up in the motor home all day, and gave Donna a chance to rest. If I quit, I was going to let everyone down.

We pushed on and, despite everything, soon found ourselves on the next phase of the trip. That is when the heat really became an issue. As we went through Roswell, New Mexico, to connect to Interstate 10 through Phoenix, the temperature started to rise. Blythe, California, was the hottest place I had ever been. At midnight the temperature was still over 100 degrees. During the day the temperature rose to 114, and the road would heat up to 140 degrees. The extreme heat melted the asphalt—so much so that my tires kept sticking. It was like riding in sand. California brought other challenges as well. Though we tried to leave early in the morning to beat the heat, we had to deal with extreme temperature swings with the elevation changes. It was more than 70 degrees when we started, but at the bottom of the hills, which were below sea level, the temperature dropped to less than 40 degrees. I would climb half a mile up a hill, then ride half a mile down. By the time I reached the top, sweat was pouring off me. On the way down, the wind froze me. This happened over and over again for a very long, brutal stretch.

We limped across the country in fifteen and a half days. It was a very amateurish attempt, but I had to finish. When I finally got to the Pacific Ocean, I held my bike in the air, but I felt nothing. There was no sense of accomplishment. I knew that I had not given it my best effort. I could have done a lot better—I could have planned better, I could have had a larger crew, I could have gone faster. But it was over, and I was not going to do it again. I would go back to Atlanta, get back to the cookie business, and put this chapter behind me.

Still, I remained interested in cycling. Before the 1982 race, I had invested in a Schwinn bicycle shop in the Dunwoody suburb of Atlanta with Dave Johnson. Dave was a former Marine and seasoned marathoner, and we had met when he owned a running store in Cumberland Mall. During my rehabilitation he had helped me select my first lightweight performance bicycle, the Trek. We became friends and then business partners.

I regularly read *Bicycling Magazine* and remember coming across a story about the Great American Bike Race (later renamed the Race Across America or RAAM). At nine o'clock in the morning on August 4, 1982, John Marino started what has become one of the hardest endurance races in the world. The 2,968 miles from Santa Monica Pier in Los Angeles to the Empire State Building in New York City involved four racers: John Marino, John Howard, Michael Shermer, and the eventual race winner, Lon Haldeman. ABC's Wide World of Sports covered the event. Reading about it later, I saw that three of the four riders finished five days faster than I did.

In the early spring of 1983, I attended my first bicycle show in New York with Dave, and there I met Michael, John Marino, and Lon. They had formed the UltraMarathon Cycling Association (UMCA) in 1980, and I told them the story of my 1982 race. Bob Hustwit, who was also involved in the UMCA and would later direct RAAM, asked me to send him the logs that Donna had signed each day. Bob certified them and confirmed that I held the world record of fifteen and a half days for the southern route. A number of people had been asking me since I finished if I was going to do it again. I always answered with an emphatic "No!" But as I talked to more people at that bicycle show, I found myself saying, "I'm thinking about it."

That 1982 race had been nagging at me for months, because I could not shake the feeling that I could have done much better. I had not slain Goliath. Actually, I had barely faced him. I simply limped past him on my way across the country. On the flight home from the New York show, I told Dave that I was going to do more research to find a better route that avoided the heat in Phoenix. He wanted to help, so a week later we rented a car and drove to Savannah. With a map and notebook, we worked our way toward San Diego trying to figure out the best route.

One night we were in Alamogordo, New Mexico, eating dinner at a Chinese restaurant. When we finished, the waitress brought us the check and two fortune cookies. I broke mine open, and it read, "Your goal is near. Go for it." I looked at Dave and said, "Well, I guess my decision is made." I put the fortune in my wallet, and we drove on to San Diego.

Energized by my goal to do the race again in ten days or less, I carefully crafted a new training regimen. My rides in 1982 were not long enough to prepare me for the sheer endurance required to get across the country. This time I trained smarter and better, doing 250-mile rides to build up my stamina and strength so I could shave five days off my record. I also became good friends with Michael Shermer. I served as his judge on his record-breaking race from Miami to Maine in 1983, accompanying him on my bike for countless miles. We had numerous conversations about how to assemble an effective crew, and I heeded his advice as I planned for my 1983 race.

Dave and I now owned two Schwinn bicycle shops, and I knew I could recruit two mechanics to join the crew and help drive. Dave agreed to become my crew captain. My longtime chiropractor helped recruit a massage therapist. Michael agreed to serve as the judge from the UltraMarathon Cycling Association to ensure that the race was certified from the beginning. Donna and a chef rounded out the team. After assembling the group, I started using these longer rides to see how well they worked together and to see if they could build a shared sense of purpose.

We also enlarged our operation in significant ways. We still had the motor home that served as a mobile kitchen, place to sleep, and restroom in 1982, but we added a black truck nicknamed Little Pepe and a motorcycle. When the truck had to peel off to find food or supplies, the motorcycle supported me. In 1983 I also had sponsors, including Bianchi, Campagnolo, Gatorade, Kucharik, and Specialized. I took along three bikes and enough equipment to build two more. And I had the good sense to bring more music—no more "Eye of the Tiger." I created about thirty mixtapes and would rotate them throughout the race. This time I studied temperature and wind patterns in the *Farmer's Almanac*, and August looked like the most desirable month. This turned out to be the right decision. We had really good weather—40 percent tailwinds, 40 percent headwinds, and no wind for about 20 percent of the race. We also changed the route in 1983 to avoid the heat in Phoenix. We mapped out essentially the same route until we reached New Mexico, then we planned to drop down from Alamogordo to Las Cruces and take the interstate through Tucson. Once entering California at El Centro, we would pick up the interstate on the way into San Diego. In total, we predicted that we could shave nearly two hundred miles off the previous attempt and avoid the high heat.

Just as in 1982, in 1983 we had a strong management team in place at the cookie company, and I had things well organized before I left for the race. I tried to adhere to Dunkin' Donuts founder William Rosenberg's mantra, "A person builds a team, and a team builds a business." Arthur and I had been working to build the company for six years, and we had become a great team. We approached the business, at first, with very different objectives. Arthur saw it as a nationwide company from the start; I thought it would be a small Atlanta-based chain with half a dozen stores. My accident changed my perspective, and I became focused on slow and strategic growth. In retrospect, we provided a good counterbalance for each other. Arthur was aggressive, I was conservative, and that helped us meet in the middle.

Our different approaches also influenced our franchising plan, which was somewhat unconventional. We found the locations and then sold them to the best franchisee. Many companies do the reverse: they sign up a franchisee, then search for a location and depend on that person to build the store and the business. We did both. We were also successful because we did not approach the stores as if they were bakeries; we thought of them as retail outlets. I believe we could have sold jewelry or hardware just as effectively. The company kept growing, and we were particularly successful in the Southeast and Southwest. Confident in my team and my training, I was ready to take off a few weeks to try to beat my transcontinental cycling record.

We had a great start, leaving Savannah at high noon on August 26, 1983. We sped through Georgia, Alabama, and Mississippi in the first few days, on track to beat my own record.

In Vicksburg, just as we were approaching the city's historic bridge to cross the Mississippi River, the bridge keeper stopped us. Dave, my crew captain, pulled out a letter from Mississippi governor Cliff Finch, giving us permission to cross, to which the bridge keeper said, "Do you see the governor here?"

Dave replied, "No."

The bridge keeper continued, "Well, this here is my bridge, and you're not going across."

So we had to get onto the interstate and ride an extra five miles to cross the new bridge. While that may not seem like a lot, the clock was ticking and every mile mattered.

By the time I reached Texas around Day 4, it looked like I might make it in less than ten days. The weather could not have been better; the winds were moderate and I enjoyed headwinds and tailwinds in equal measure. Entering New Mexico, I thought I might beat my old record by six days. I sped across the state and was feeling great.

During my preparations, I had worried about the wind and weather, but the problems on the 1983 race came from my own team. There was a lot of turmoil on that trip. I had tried to prepare them to work seamlessly together, to stay motivated, and to remain focused on a single goal. I also hammered home one cardinal rule: Once the race started, they should hide any problems from me. I was to be kept in a bubble so I could focus on the race. I had my own drama and demons to confront—Goliath in the form of 2,600 miles of open road. I could not manage a bickering team of adults.

Problems with the crew were the last thing I needed, but that's exactly what I got. The chiropractor and the massage therapist were good friends when the ride started. A few days in, they stopped speaking to each other. Though not the crew captain, the chiropractor started acting like General George S. Patton, bossing everyone around. Nobody was getting much sleep. To complicate matters further, the chef veered away from the menu we had selected, so I got sick. My stomach was constantly upset—which was miserable and affected everything.

Ironically, I was riding as fast as I ever had amid complete chaos. Every time I came in for a massage, adjustment, or bathroom break, everybody would unload all of their gripes and complaints on me. I would get back on the bike and try to work out how to solve the crew's problems. I was sick and had a hard enough time concentrating on the road ahead of me. Finally I pulled the chiropractor, massage therapist, and crew captain aside and insisted that they stop complaining and focus on the race. But it never got any better.

On Day 8 in Arizona, 488 miles from San Diego, at the exit for Route 666 in Cochise, I crashed on the highway. Maybe it was an omen, but Goliath appeared in the form of a dust devil. These compact whirlwinds form on flat surfaces in extreme heat. The one that got me was twelve feet tall and six feet wide and came up from behind. The crew saw it but did not have time to warn me. It hit me first, because I was riding on the outside. Two of my crew members were riding with me, and they went down too. One minute I was pedaling, and a split second later I was going over the handlebars in what felt like slow motion. I could feel my body turning, and when I hit the asphalt, I heard and felt my collarbone break. In that moment I knew I was not going to be able to get back on the bike.

The crew helped me get into the motor home, and we drove back one exit to Northern Cochise Community Hospital in Wilcox, Arizona. The crew members were not seriously hurt, but when they x-rayed me, they saw that my right collarbone was completely broken. Sometimes you just end up with a partial fracture, but this was a clean, hard break. In the hospital, they put me in a figure-eight brace, and we talked about finishing the race. That was the thing I most wanted to do. It wasn't that far, and I still might have finished in less than ten days. But it was simply too painful. Using the handlebars put too much pressure on my shoulders, which meant that I could no longer control the bike. So I had to quit.

Everybody was devastated. It had been an incredibly hard trip, and we were so close to the end. Crew members were crying, and we were all sort of numb. But unlike the 1982 race, I really felt I had given it my best shot. I went to sleep in a hotel that night and got up the next morning to meet the whole team for breakfast. I said, "I'm going to do this one more time." I heard Donna gasp, "Oh my God!" Everyone else was stunned into silence.

We drove to Tucson and stayed for a few days. While there, I met Richard DeBernardis, who later founded the Perimeter Bicycling Association. He would go on to coordinate a number of distance races, and he held two perimeter bicycling world records, at home (around the perimeter of the United States, covering 12,092 miles in 180 days) and in Japan (around the perimeter of the island of Honshu, covering 6,235 miles in 77 days). We became good friends, and he would play an important role in my 1984 race. Then Donna and I flew home. The crew drove the motor home and the support vehicles back to Atlanta. I met with my orthopedist and asked him how soon I could begin training again. He replied that as long as I did not put pressure on my shoulders, I could start that afternoon. And I was off. I just could not give up. I had done my best, and the dust devil knocked me down. I was going to get back on the bike and beat the wind, my Goliath at that moment, inch by inch.

Michael Coles at the age of two on a pony, 1946

Michael Coles (front center) with his family in New York, 1948

Michael Coles
at Miami Beach
Junior High
School, 1958

Michael Coles
(right) working
as a salesman at
Dorwins Ivy Shop
in Miami Beach,
1961

Telegram from Penson Kaminsky congratulating Michael on his sales record, 1970

Advertisement for Michael Coles's first company, Pant-O-Mine, 1972

Lorin, Donna, Michael, Taryn, and Jody Coles, 1979

Dave Johnson and
Michael Coles after the 1981
ride to Helen, Georgia

AUGUST

WEDNESDAY	THURSDAY	FRIDAY	SATURDAY
3 215/150 ~~25~~ 120	4 216/149 ~~25~~ 100 ~~25~~	5 217/148 ~~75~~ 250	6 218/147 ~~X~~ 200
10 222/143 ~~100~~ Rest	11 223/142 100 ~~100~~ ~~25~~	12 224/141 ~~250~~ 100 ~~250~~ 50	13 225/140 ~~200~~ ~~200~~ 50
17 229/138 25	18 230/135 50	19 231/134 50	20 232/133 50
24 236/129 Rest	25 237/128 Rest	26 START 238/127 Go for it!!	27 239/126
31 243/122	NOTES:		

Training calendar for
the 1983 Savannah to San
Diego Ride.

Site of the dust devil crash, exit for Route 666 in Arizona, 1983

TTGT (Time to Get Tough) sign that Coles created to motivate him while training for the 1984 Spirit of America Ride (SOAR)

Michael "Caffeine" Coles during the 1984 Spirit of America Ride (SOAR)

The support vehicle, fondly named the Mothership, for the 1984 Spirit of America Ride (SOAR)

Patches made to celebrate the World Record, 1984

Arthur Karp, Larry "Doc" Cohen, and Michael Coles, 1988

The Diet Coke Lightning team that won the HPV four-man relay division
of the Race Across America, 1989

Michael Coles in front of the Great American Cookie Company store at Lenox Mall in Atlanta, 1994

Hank Aaron, Donna Coles, Michael Coles, and Mickey Mantle at a 1994 fundraiser for Zell Miller's gubernatorial campaign

Michael Coles announcing his candidacy for Congress at the Coles College of Business at Kennesaw State University, 1996

Michael Coles announcing his candidacy for the U.S. Senate at the Coles College of Business at Kennesaw State University, 1998

Arthur S. Karp
Founder
Chairman Emeritus

October 23, 1998

Dear Michael,

As we get to the last days of your election campaign, I am sure that your schedule is crowded. There are some things I wanted to say to you so I thought I would write. I have known you for over twenty five years and we functioned as business partners for over twenty of those years. I know that you are a man of principles, that you live your life based on a code of ethics. I have been there when you made decisions that were "the right thing to do" even if not the most profitable. There are few people that I trust completely, you are one.

When Susan and I attended the fund raiser in July, I heard you endorsed by the Mayor of Atlanta, the Governor of Georgia and the President of the United States. I was proud of you. The family looked great and I am sure they also were excited and proud.

I believe you have added another page to the history of the American dream. A young man from humble beginnings who through hard work and focus became a success in business, gave back to the community in numerous ways, and then at a point in your life when you could relax and enjoy the fruits of your labor you offer yourself for elected office.

The people of Georgia will be well served if they elect you their next Senator. If not you can still have a powerful voice that speaks for the people. Jeb Bush lost a close race for Governor of Florida four years ago. This year he is running a large lead over his opposition. During the period between elections he continued to run. He spoke out about things people cared about and made many friends.

I recently spoke with a young man who is twenty years old and is trying to decide what to do with his life. He is now in college but wants to finish so he can begin the rest of his life. I told him about you and your belief that there are no limits except those that are self imposed.

Good luck in the election, but win or lose you've won in my opinion.

Warmest Regards,

Great American Cookie Company, Inc.
4685 Frederick Drive, S.W., Atlanta, Georgia 30336, USA
Telephone (404) 696-1700   Fax (404) 505-2841

Letter from Arthur Karp to Michael Coles regarding his 1998 Senate race

Kennesaw State University president Betty L. Siegel with Michael and
Donna Coles on the occasion of Michael's honorary doctorate from KSU, 1999

Georgia film industry shoots for Hollywood comeback

**Coles leading effort
to spur more
movie-making**

By Matt Monroe
STAFF WRITER

and Yla Eason
CONTRIBUTING WRITER

The Peach State's long affair with the
silver screen may soon be rekindled.

Michael Coles, the governor-appointed
chairman of the Georgia Film & Video-
tape Advisory Commission, is ramping up
state efforts this year to once again make
Georgia a prime motion picture filming
location.

Coles is no stranger to ambitious ventures. He is founder of the Great American Cookie Co., a two-time
transcontinental biking champion and a
1996 candidate for Georgia's 6th Congressional District. He won 44 percent of
the vote against Rep. Newt Gingrich —
then Speaker of the House.

Now, he hopes to do for film production
in Georgia what he did for cookie shops in
the mall: make it visible and expansive.

The film industry "is a nonpolluting
industry that brings a lot of high-paying
jobs to the state," Coles said.

Last year, six productions were filmed
in Georgia. They included two from
Steven Spielberg's Dreamworks SKG:
"Road Trip," which shot primarily in

Homemade: www.gafilm.org

SPECIAL

Atlanta and Athens, had a budget
around $14 million; and "The Legend of
Bagger Vance" was filmed in Savannah
with a $70 million budget. The Walt Dis-

ney Studios production "Remember the
Titans," starring Denzel Washington,
was shot in Atlanta at the same time.

The six big 1999 productions generated
around $203.5 million for the state econo-
my, according to the Georgia Department
of Industry, Trade and Tourism.

Officials estimate that film companies
drop more than half of their budget in
the states they film in, said Greg Torre,
director of the Georgia Film and Video-
tape Office.

To continue attracting film companies,
Torre and Coles are trying to establish a
strong foothold at international film festivals by marketing Georgia on its temper-
ate weather, diverse scenery and

➤ See **MOVIES**, Page **35A**

The *Atlanta Business Chronicle* celebrating Michael Coles's role in
revitalizing the film industry in Georgia, February 2000

R.K. Sehgal, Michael Coles and other members of
The Georgia Film and Video Commission
along with
Governor and Mrs. Roy Barnes
and
Jane Fonda and Ted Turner

Lt. Gov. Mark Taylor   Mr. and Mrs. Henry Aaron
Evander Holyfield   Rep. and Mrs. Larry Walker
Martin Luther King, III   Dexter King
U.S. Sen. Paul Coverdell   Cong. Johnny Isakson

invite you and your guest to
A Private Champagne Brunch
to salute the Film and Video Industry in Georgia
at the home of
The Hon. and Mrs. Matt Towery
1430 North Harris Ridge, Atlanta

Saturday, January 29, 2000
11:00 a.m. to 2:00 p.m.

R.s.v.p. 1-800-357-6549   Business Casual Attire
**This invitation is non-transferable

An invitation from the Georgia Film and Video Commission saluting the film and video industry in Georgia, 2000

Greg Torre, Governor Roy Barnes, and Michael Coles celebrating the passage of House Bill 610, the first tax incentive bill for the film industry in Georgia, which transformed the industry, 2001

Colin Powell and Michael Coles at an Arcapita dinner
at the Four Seasons in Atlanta, 2004

Caribou Boot Camp, Minneapolis, 2006

Donna and Michael Coles in New York after Michael's opening of NASDAQ on behalf of Caribou Coffee, 2006

Michael Coles with Mary Stuart Masterson when Caribou Coffee was honored for being the first coffee company in America to be 100 percent certified by the Rainforest Alliance, 2007

Michael Coles and George Foreman, speakers at the Think Big Day presented by the Learning Annex, which drew an audience of ten thousand at the Minneapolis Convention Center, 2007

Michael Coles in front of the Coles College of Business at Kennesaw State University, 2018

10

TTGT

Here I go again.
The ocean had
never seemed so
far away.

In contrast to my 1982 bicycle race from Savannah to San Diego, in 1983 I felt a tremendous sense of success, even though I came up short. DNF is a designation given to someone who did not finish a race. In this case, it stood for Did Not Fail. I reached every goalpost that I had set for myself, and I was on track to cross the country in ten days or less. The year before, I knew it was not my best effort. This time, I really pushed myself to the point that I could not have done any better. I gave it everything I had, and I was stopped by something over which I had no control.

That became an analogy for my business. When you are in business, you try to anticipate everything that can go wrong and address those issues one at a time. But it is never the things you prepare for that test you. It is how you deal with the unexpected that really matters.

When the race was over, I went back to Atlanta and got right back to work at the Original Great American Chocolate Chip Cookie Company. We were growing and doing pretty well. We had built a new batter facility that was five times the size of the one we opened in 1977. It was in the Fulton

Industrial area of Atlanta on Frederick Drive, and it backed up to Six Flags. On warm summer days, we could hear people screaming while riding the roller coasters. This 35,000-square-foot facility cost us about a million and a half dollars and was designed in such a way that we could add an additional floor if needed. We never thought we would fill the building, but in less than two years we started planning to build a second floor. Once that opened, I began to get a glimpse of how big the company might become.

I started planning for the 1984 race immediately and completely changed my training regimen. In 1983, the most I rode in a twenty-four-hour period was 250 miles. This time, I did four round-the-clock training rides. My longest one was from Kennesaw south to Columbus, Georgia, and then across the state to Hilton Head, South Carolina, covering about 420 miles. On an average Saturday, I would ride from Kennesaw to Chattanooga, Tennessee, and back—about 200 miles. I had bought a new car before my 1982 race, and by the time I was ready for the 1984 one, I had just 6,000 miles on the odometer, because I rode my bike everywhere. From the 1983 crew I kept only four people: my wife Donna, Michael Shermer as the judge, and two mechanics from my cycling shops. I changed the role of one of the mechanics to crew captain, and I added four new members: a chiropractor/nutritionist, a massage therapist, a medical student, and an additional driver. This time I felt like I needed a slogan to keep me motivated. While recovering from my broken collarbone, I had small cardboard signs with "TTGT" printed on them and put them on all of my bikes, all over my office, and all over my house. I also gave them to the crew. Every time I faced an obstacle in my training, the abbreviation for "Time to Get Tough" was there staring me in the face. Once again I pored over the *Farmer's Almanac* and studied the weather, and that research revealed that May typically had the least wind of any month. So the calendar was set.

A documentary film crew came along to film this third attempt, what I was now calling the Spirit of America Ride (SOAR). I had enjoyed good coverage of the 1983 race; *PM Magazine* did a feature that was picked up by their affiliates as I worked my way west. Channel 11 (WXIA) in Atlanta covered the entire race. There were pictures of me all along the route, and even one of me in a wheelchair coming out of the hospital. Gary Whittaker, a producer at Channel 11, and I had become friends during the 1983 race, so when I made the decision to go again, I called to let him know. He thought it was a crazy story—a guy in the cookie business tries for a third time to race his bicycle across the country after being knocked off by a whirlwind less than five hundred miles from the finish. So he hired a crew, including cameramen Willis Boyd and David Brooks, and started filming my training; he even photographed me riding the stationary bike with my collarbone still broken.

As the May departure date approached, Gary decided to take vacation time to lead the documentary crew. His wife, Joan, coordinated all of the public relations related to the ride to help draw attention to it. I welcomed the publicity, because I wanted to use the race to show others that they could accomplish their goals. I hoped that my story would be a source of inspiration, proving that you could go from being on crutches to riding a bicycle across the country. I wanted to prove the truth of the famous utterance by Winston Churchill, "If you are going through hell, keep going."

To prepare for the 1984 race, I packed twelve changes of clothes, three bikes, and enough parts to build three more bikes. I had rain gear and winter gear, which I became especially thankful for in Texas. It got so cold at night that I could barely open and close my hands. I also had three helmets, ten sets of gloves, and four pairs of shoes. I had three new Bianchi bikes with Campagnolo components, and all of the same sponsors. We added a red, white, and blue banner on the back of the motor home with a picture of a bicycle that read "Michael 'Caffeine' Coles, Savannah–San Diego, World Record, Go for It!" Michael Shermer had given me the nickname Caffeine Coles when I served as a judge on his race up the east coast from Miami to Maine. He teased me because I seemed to have a boundless amount of energy and never need much sleep. Our support truck Little Pepe had a yellow and black banner that read: "Bicyclist Ahead."

To help stave off boredom, I asked each member of my crew and the documentary film crew to make me a mixtape. I would then spend the day trying to guess who made each one. I thought that would help keep me occupied, but I never could figure it out.

The new chiropractor/nutritionist put me on a semi-liquid diet to keep food from sitting in my stomach. This allowed me to absorb more calories in a much shorter period. Everything I ate was the consistency of blood—potato soup, banana shakes, anything with a high caloric content. It was really hard to manage after a few days. I couldn't get enough calories, even though we added high-energy and high-protein tablets to all my food. To survive an ultramarathon bicycle race, you have to eat constantly. An average person consumes about 2,000 calories a day. Serious athletes take in about 5,000, but an ultramarathoner needs 15,000 calories per day to fuel such a feat. During this ten-day period I would eat enough food to feed seventy-five people. Doing a race on this scale was the equivalent of doing three-quarters of a million consecutive push-ups, running twenty-six marathons back to back, or swimming the English Channel thirteen times without stopping. But one thing was certain—I made sure the crew had plenty of cookies.

On May 4, 1984, the whole crew rolled out of Savannah at high noon. We had a huge sendoff. In 1982, Donna and Taryn and I started without any fanfare. By 1983, interest in the race had grown so that local television stations and the mayor of Savannah came down to wish us well. In 1984, we had the documentary film crew, five television stations, many of our friends, and hundreds of strangers lining the streets. It was easy to get caught up in the excitement with all that adrenaline pumping. The film shows me leaving the courthouse with one of my mechanics singing Willie Nelson's "On the Road Again."

But I wasn't a block into the race when it hit me what lay ahead. Another song, Bob Seger's "Against the Wind," started playing in my head. There's a line in the song, "Wish I didn't know now what I didn't know then," that seemed apropos of the moment. It is one of those lines that sounds nice but does not get much thought. At that moment it really resonated. Sometimes it's a lot easier to face the unknown—you do not have time to worry. I had already completed two coast-to-coast races. In those first few miles, I started thinking about how many revolutions my legs were going to have to make to reach the Pacific Ocean. As a thirty-mile-an-hour wind blew across my face, I recalled the last words that I heard in 1982, "You'll never make it." With that, all the excitement of the start was gone in a split second. I thought: Here I go again. The ocean had never seemed so far away.

Just outside Savannah, I saw a scene that would haunt me the entire race. A tornado had recently torn through the community, uprooting trees and destroying buildings. It looked like a war zone, foreshadowing what was to come. We covered the same route in 1984 as we had the year before, so I knew what lay ahead. The work had really begun, and I did not know yet what shape Goliath would take. But I knew I would have to face him. On that first day, even with a strong headwind, I streaked across Georgia way ahead of record pace.

My prediction about May's weather would turn out to be completely wrong. For only the second time in history, the year's tornado count in 1984 exceeded 1,000. The 1,047 tally was 42 percent above normal, with 329 tornadoes logged in May alone. They were especially bad in the Southeast. There were days upon days of tornadoes, and we learned that when a tornado goes through, the wind behind it can last for days. Had I looked at the tornado patterns for the whole year, I might have delayed the race. But we had too many people committed to it—my crew, the UMCA judge, the film crew, sponsors—and the planning was just too far along to stop it.

On May 5, it was clear that once again Goliath was going to be the wind. As I crossed into Alabama, I was still battling constant thirty-mile-per-hour headwinds. But I was moving at a new record pace. I arrived in Selma, and my training was really paying off, though I was not sure that I could sustain the pace with this kind of constant wind in my face. When we crossed into Mississippi, I was twelve hours ahead of schedule, and the team was working well together. We were feeling optimistic and strong. But as the sun went down, instead of the wind dying as it typically does in the evening, it gathered strength.

Into the evening of May 6, the wind had reached forty miles per hour. It was piercing and relentless. That night we passed Jackson on the way to the Mississippi River, a major milestone in the journey, but I almost did not make it out of town. On the interstate where I-20 and I-55 split, the motor home was behind me signaling for me to move over. I thought I was riding in its headlights, but they turned out to be the lights of an 18-wheeler on the right-hand side of the road. I don't know what made me not change lanes, but I didn't, and the truck flew past me. Had I moved into the other lane, I would have been killed.

I had three states behind me and five ahead. But my body was showing the effects of the struggle against the wind. The pressure I had to put on the pedals made my feet swell so much that I had to cut open my shoes. My neck hurt, and my hands were so numb that I had to shake them every few minutes to get the blood flowing again. By this point, I looked forward to only two things: eating and sleeping. Because this was a race against the clock, I could only afford to get about two hours of sleep a day, and I was exhausted. After three days on the bike in that wind, everything became painful—I felt every bump, every piece of gravel, every stick in the road. Riding at night was especially brutal, as the headlights from cars and trucks hypnotized me. Boredom was a constant companion. I listened to the tapes and tried to do anything to keep from getting drowsy. My goal was just to make it through the night. I could hardly wait for the dawn, because I knew that as the sun came up, I would wake up. The sunrise energized me.

My crew members prepared high-energy meals in the motor home, put them in plastic cups, and passed them to the crew in the truck, who handed them to me through the passenger window. Unlike in my first two races, this time I had plenty of company. A number of cyclists had learned about my journey through their cycling clubs or bicycle stores, and they came out to join me for part of the race to offer moral support. It was gratifying to feel like everyone was pulling for me. I was ahead of schedule to beat my old time. I now had four states behind me and four to go.

But Goliath was not going to let me get through Texas without a fight. In Marshall we faced a serious setback in the form of severe thunderstorms that brought lightning, flooding, and high winds. We had to sit out the bad weather in a motel. As the rain poured down, I slept for ninety minutes, the longest stretch so far. I found that the longer I slept, the harder it was to get back on the bike. While in the room, I got a boost from a local television station that did a story on the Spirit of America Ride (SOAR). The story focused on my goal and on how it might help others reach theirs.

Sensing my frustration over the relentless wind and the delay caused by the heavy storms, my support team decided to play a practical joke on me. They salvaged a red child's bicycle from a Dumpster, and as I emerged from the motel they presented it to me. It was one of the best moments of the race. Chuck Ritz, my crew captain, joked, "We've lightened it up for you. We took off the chain." We all laughed, and I sat down and rode it for a few yards in the dark. Humor was an essential component of the race—as it was in my business. We made plenty of mistakes with the cookie company and with the first two races, but laughter became a necessary safety valve. My 1984 team was not afraid to laugh. The training rides revealed a lot, helping me see how well the group could handle pressure, take a joke, and pull together when it really mattered. Before and during the race, we played jokes at each other's expense, which really helped bind us together in a common purpose. Running a business was a lot like doing the race. It was tough, and you had to commit to the long haul. If you can use humor to energize yourself, you have found a great tool. So with a smile on my face, I got back on the bike to continue the race. But the high winds remained.

I approached Dallas–Fort Worth on May 8 on a crisp clear morning with fifty-mile-per-hour headwinds beating down on me. After days of nearly constant pressure, my neck and knees ached. I was in so much pain that I barely noticed the police escort shutting down traffic as we passed the gleaming skyscrapers. West of Fort Worth, as we approached the halfway point, I was sure that the wind would finally abate. Instead it persisted, and the temperature started to climb in West Texas. Soon it topped 100 degrees. With the wind and heat, I had to do more rest breaks. My muscle massages became longer and deeper. Donna started to get really worried. Prentiss Stefan, the medical student who signed on to help drive as well as monitor my condition, was also concerned about sleep deprivation. I had barely slept six hours in four days. Sandstorms became another problem that contributed to my deteriorating physical condition. I was falling behind: it took me as long to cross Texas as it did to cross Georgia, Alabama, Mississippi, and Louisiana combined. Those endless hours in the Lone Star State really wore the team down both physically and psychologically. When we finally crossed into New Mexico on the afternoon of May 10, it felt as if a barrier had been shattered.

The incessant headwinds, which felt like being hit in the face with boxing gloves, were Goliath trying to force me to quit. At first, a state line was a big goal. As the race wore on, I lowered my sights from state lines to county lines to city limits to exit signs. I was determined to keep moving forward, inch by inch. The wind made me ride the bike differently, and the constant pressure fatigued my muscles and put my nerves on edge. My chest hurt, my knees were worn out from pushing into the wind, and I could barely hold my head up because I was bearing down so hard. The wind, the heat, and the added climb of the southern tip of the Rockies were really taking a toll. In New Mexico, I started hallucinating to the point that the crew forced me off the road and into an emergency room. A doctor diagnosed me with severe fatigue and recommended bed rest. I refused. I was not going to quit. The hospital staff warned me about the risks of continuing, but they sensed that I was not going to listen.

We pushed on, not knowing that the worst conditions were yet to come. On the way to the ski village of Cloudcroft, New Mexico, I faced an uphill 106-mile climb that was difficult in the best of circumstances. With forty-mile-an-hour headwinds, it was nearly impossible. But I kept telling myself that once I crested the mountain, I could coast thirty miles down to Alamogordo. It took hours—but I never got off the bike. Not to rest, not to get a massage, not to go to the bathroom. At the crest, I straddled the bike for a few minutes, ate a quick snack, and prepared for the long, relaxing ride down. But the winds just increased, and I faced a fifty-mile-an-hour headwind forcing me to pedal the whole way down the mountain. When I got to White Sands, home of the Trinity Atomic Test Site in 1945, the landscape was completely desolate—no bugs, no trees, everything dead. That was exactly how I felt. I felt like I had nothing left.

Sick of my semi-liquid diet, near Lordsburg, New Mexico, I mutinied against the crew and insisted that they get me a Big Mac and chocolate shake. The chiropractor/nutritionist was asleep, so a few crew members took Little Pepe and went searching for a McDonald's. I ate the burger with relish. Big mistake. Within an hour came the aftermath—I was horribly sick to my stomach for hours. This was made much worse by the fact that I had to ride past farms that had just spread manure, and you could smell it for miles. I had learned my lesson, to follow my nutritionist's advice.

I turned my attention to the two states I had left to cross. With Cloudcroft behind me and Arizona ahead, my team worked hard to keep me fit and motivated. The crew pushed me along—I think because they now became convinced that we were going to break my old record.

We crossed into Arizona after sundown on May 12. It was dark, but I had plenty of reason to celebrate. When I reached Cochise, where the dust devil had ended my 1983 race, my crew had painted TTGT (for "Time to Get Tough") on the highway. Richard DeBernardis had a whole group of supporters holding a huge banner on the bridge overpass that read "TTGT." This was a major milestone, and I stopped to take a thirty-minute nap and get a massage. When I emerged, I was wearing a pink and black one-piece cycling suit. Everyone on the crew knew what the pink suit meant—this was the blitz. We were not going to sleep until we got to San Diego. We had 488 miles to go. This was it. I was completely motivated to go all the way.

11 The Reckoning

Has it come to this? Am I really going to walk to San Diego?

Most companies ask the same question over and over again: Why don't more customers buy our products? In my years selling clothing, cookies, and coffee, I have discovered that this is the wrong question. Invert it, and instead ask: Why does anyone buy our product? If you are willing to take a hard look at every aspect of your business, you will see the necessity for innovation. Then you have to go one step further to implement those changes in such a way that they become part of your company's culture. Execution is the key to everything. How will you persuade your team that change is necessary? What kinds of activities will you undertake to turn innovation and strategy into commercial success? Asked another way: How do you finish the last five miles in a three-thousand-mile race, but also plan for the next three thousand?

My focus on innovation and execution can be traced back to my 1984 Spirit of America Ride (SOAR). It was my third attempt, and I battled Goliath in the form of relentless headwinds for all but twelve of the 2,600 miles across the country. Facing that kind of challenge changed my perspective on everything. State by state, city by city, mile by mile, and inch by inch, I had to fight my way toward California. That focused intensity gave me a kind of clarity that I had never experienced before. I remember the exact moment when I realized that good enough was neither good nor enough—either for me or for the cookie company. It all started at ten o'clock at night on May 13 in Arizona.

About a hundred miles west of Tucson, on the way to Yuma, my body finally gave in to exhaustion. A muscle spasm wrenched my neck, and I collapsed. Every movement sent extreme pain coursing through my shoulders and into my head. I knew it was bad because my support crew was completely silent. The therapist massaged my muscles, and then the chiropractor hooked me up to a Galvanic Stimulator, a machine that uses electric impulses to bring spasms under control. The temporary clinic set up on the side of the road must have been an eerie sight for passing motorists. But nobody cared. They were just trying to help me manage the excruciating pain. When they finally put me in the motor home to sleep an hour later, everyone thought this was the end. We were 260 miles from San Diego, and again I was going to be beaten by the wind.

When I awoke at dawn on May 14, my neck was still wrenching in pain. In the dim light I somehow managed to put on a neck brace to take off some of the pressure, thinking I could manage it. My knees were still throbbing, but I could bear that as well. I was determined to continue. While the crew was sleeping, I put on my shoes and slipped out of the motor home. The night before, Donna had begged me to get undressed, but I refused because that small, seemingly insignificant act would have meant that I had quit. Instead, I insisted on sleeping in my cycling clothes, so when I woke up six hours later—the longest sleep of the race—it took me only a few minutes to get back on the bike. I was completely alone for the first time since leaving Savannah: me, my bike, and two water bottles. There was no support team, no documentary crew, no vehicles, no friends, no family, nobody. I saw my life spread out in front of me in the dawn on that Arizona highway. It was an out-of-body experience. I was managing to pedal, but I had no awareness of how. My mind was drifting. I saw my parents, my childhood mentor Irving Settler, and my early years in business. I saw the Original Great American Chocolate Chip Cookie Company.

I saw the motorcycle accident that nearly killed me seven years earlier. I saw my wife and children. I saw every single mile that I had covered to get to this moment in the past nine days.

This was my whole world, and I had to step into the valley alone to face Goliath. If I was not going to be able to finish this race in this relentless wind, I did not want anyone to witness it. There was nothing else except me and the 260 miles to San Diego. At that moment, that distance was the only thing in my life that mattered. I knew that if I quit, I would end up in a motel in some sleepy California town, awaken the next morning, and have to start over. That seemed impossible; I never wanted to do this again. I knew that success was just on the other side of determination, and I had to meet the challenge right in front of me or face repeating it. Even with each obstacle—the rain, the heat, and above all the wind—somehow I had managed to get back on the bike. I knew I would not quit unless I was physically unable to continue. And as bad as it was, somehow I just kept going. It was so absurd that I started laughing, and in that moment I realized how determined I really was. I had no idea that I had that kind of strength. On that lonely highway watching the sun come up, my race took on new meaning. I had to beat the wind.

I learned later that Donna woke up a few minutes after I left, looked around, and started screaming, "Michael's gone!" The whole crew jolted awake and started scrambling. They finally caught up with me, and we all had to dig deep to keep pushing toward San Diego. The wind was still fighting me, pushing me back and making the Pacific Ocean seem beyond reach. At sunset on the tenth day, I finally reached one of the race's last major milestones—the California border. I knew it had to end here in either triumph or defeat. As I pressed into the wind and crossed that final state line, my sense of humor or desperation got the better of me, and I yelled out, "Inch by inch!"

I rode all night, and May 15 dawned full of promise. I knew I had to face one last major obstacle—the trailing edge of the Sierra Nevada Mountains on the way to the Pacific Ocean. But Goliath saved his biggest test for last. As I climbed the first of a series of about ten 4,000-foot California peaks, the ocean winds swirled up over the mountains and came crashing down on me at seventy miles per hour. In the canyons between the peaks, cars and trucks were struggling to stay on the road. For a cyclist it was impossible, so I made the decision to get off my bike, not to quit, but to walk. If I could not ride, I was going to push my bike all the way to San Diego. I would not quit. I remember laughing about it and saying to myself: "Has it come to this? Am I really going to walk to San Diego?"

The wind had become this incredible force in the race and in my life. If I could beat the wind—which at that moment seemed an impossible challenge—I would never look at things the same way again. While I was struggling to simply stay upright, my thoughts came into clear focus, and I realized how committed I was not just to this race but also to my company. As an entrepreneur, I had been involved in numerous businesses and founded three companies. I would do a job for a while and then move to another venture. But I had never had the opportunity to see something come completely to fruition. I assumed that once the cookie company started to grow, I would sell it and move on to something else. That slow and torturous walk against the wind while pushing my bicycle changed my mind. Now I was determined to build a national brand.

Just as I made my final push over the last California peak, in the last twelve miles of the race, the wind stopped. It simply disappeared. It had plagued me state by state, county by county, town by town, hour by hour, and inch by inch for the whole race. Then it was as if Goliath finally surrendered, saying, "Okay, you win." When I got to that crest of that final climb, my father, David, his second wife, Millie, my sister, Elaine, and my daughter Taryn were waiting to surprise me, hoping to boost my spirits, which they did. But it was not over yet.

We had planned to send the documentary film crew and support vehicles ahead to the courthouse in the final five miles of the race so they could film the finish. My friend Dave Johnson would meet me as we turned off the highway to escort me for those final five miles into San Diego. We were unable to get a police escort to lead me to the finish line, so Dave agreed to help. Suddenly we found ourselves weaving in and out of heavy, rush-hour traffic and halting at each traffic light. Until now, nothing had stopped us; we had been unimpeded for the entire race. The only time I ever stopped was for a restroom break and whatever little sleep I was able to get. We had enjoyed police escorts through every major city in the trip except for this one, and I had been in full control of when I stopped until now. In these last few miles, we had to wait at intersection after intersection, and I realized that I was in trouble.

I had already ridden from Savannah to San Diego, so I knew what to expect as we approached the finish. But I had no idea what the long-term effect of the wind would be on my body. Throughout the race, I had pushed to overcome all kinds of pain, but this was different. When I stopped at each traffic light, fatigue washed over me, and it became worse with each stop. It was as if my whole body had become one giant charleyhorse, every muscle seizing up each time I stopped. When I pushed off to start riding again, I could not get my legs going. I could not feel them anymore, just all this pain. It was as if I had never ridden a bicycle before. I could not be assured that my legs could remember how to pedal, and I was afraid I might not be able to work up enough momentum to stay upright. The pain was only part of the problem. For the first time during the race, I was scared that my body was breaking down. It felt like I was dying. I remember saying to myself as I crossed into California that I would not stop unless I simply could not continue. I was now only three miles from the courthouse and that seemed to be what was happening.

I turned to Dave and said, "I can't go on. I just can't do it. I have nothing left." I could not feel my hands or legs. I felt like I did not have any control over what I was saying, and those words just poured out of my mouth. I was completely spent, numb, and exhausted.

He looked at me as if I were speaking a foreign language that he could not understand. He simply said, "But you're only three miles from the finish."

It might as well have been three thousand miles. I paused for a few minutes with my bike between my legs, unsure what to do. All I could think was: I never want to do this again. The same motivation that got me on my bike after my neck went out swept over me once again. My desire to finish overwhelmed the extreme pain and fatigue and helped me get back onto the bike seat. I finally said aloud, "Okay, let me try to go a few blocks."

So we rode from traffic light to traffic light. I kept saying, "Let me try to do two more blocks, four more, six more." I had no idea how exhausted I was until I was forced to stop. As long as I was moving, I could not feel the full extent of the pain. I lost seven pounds in the last three hours of the race, because my body was just breaking down.

We finally made a right turn onto West Broadway, and I could see that the street was lined with people. The stop-and-go traffic was horrible, but once I saw all these supporters cheering me to the finish, my adrenaline started pumping. This was the best, if also the most painful, part of the race. Spectators were cheering and honking their horns, and the documentary film crew was there to capture the final miles.

My mind was racing in those last minutes. I started thinking about everything that it took to get to this moment—the walk with Taryn in 1978 after the accident, the doctor's visits, the rehabilitation, the weightlifting, the training, the two previous races—and now it was finally here. I also thought about how often I had faced failure, pain, and uncertainty in the past. When you are caught by the unexpected—the missing pot holders when opening the cookie company, the motorcycle accident just weeks later, the wind—you have to find a way through. I now knew several things with absolute certainty. I would finish this race. Being forced to dig deeper than I ever had before, I discovered who I really was. No situation that I would face from here forward would ever look as difficult. And the last five miles is what really counts. It is not the thousands of miles you have to cover. It is not about the big idea. It is all about execution—step by step, inch by inch. That is the difference between success and failure. The last five miles will define you and prepare you for the next five miles.

It did not matter that it took me more than an hour to complete those last five miles. I probably could have walked faster. When I finally reached the courthouse steps in San Diego and saw a huge crowd waiting for me—my family, my crew, the documentary team, dozens of spectators, and local television and newspaper reporters—suddenly it was all worth it. I had finally reclaimed my physical health and had become an athlete again. They poured bottles of champagne over my head, and we jubilantly celebrated near the courthouse steps for about an hour.

I arrived in San Diego on May 15 at 5:15 p.m. Pacific Standard Time—eleven days, eight hours, and fifteen minutes after leaving Savannah. I had slept a total of twenty-two hours, or less than two hours a day. At the age of forty, I broke my own record by more than four days and again became the fastest person to cross the southern United States on a bicycle. As I lifted my bike into the air on the courthouse steps, it started to sink in. I had beaten the wind, vanquished Goliath, and nothing would ever be the same.

After the celebration was over, Donna and I hosted a big dinner at our hotel to thank everyone for their help. It was the first real meal that I had had in more than eleven days. I ordered my favorite dish, abalone, a real California delicacy. It was delicious, but I was so tired that I actually fell asleep in my food; I could not muster enough energy to keep my head up and eat. After saying goodbye to everyone, Donna and I went up to our room to get our first good night's sleep. On the nightstand before climbing into bed, I lined up half a dozen unwrapped Snickers bars so I could just grab them and eat them anytime I awakened. That night, even with the candy bars, I lost an additional five pounds because my body was still breaking down and burning so many calories from the exertion.

The next day, Donna and Taryn and the crew flew home from San Diego. We left the truck in California, and I stayed behind for a few days to get the motor home repaired. It had taken quite a beating in the wind, and it finally broke down as well. I flew home three days later and did a week of press interviews. When I finally went back to work, I thought I would slip back into my old routine. But something had changed, and that became clear to me on the first day back.

The most surprising thing about my race from Savannah to San Diego in 1984 was how, once I arrived at the courthouse, it was over. Three attempts and two world records were enough. I was finished, and it became part of my past in an instant. Cycling was now a permanent part of my life, but I did not want to revel in the accomplishment or spend much time recounting what happened. I just wanted to focus on my future. In business, that is the real key to success. It is wonderful to celebrate your company's milestones and accomplishments, but you have to move on to other things to remain nimble in an ever-changing marketplace. It would take me a while to realize how important this perspective was.

Quality always came first at the cookie company. Each day, we mixed industrial-size batches of cookie batter in the batter facility. From each batch, we scooped a tray of cookies, baked them, and brought them into the offices to sample. Three or four staff members regularly participated in this quality control effort. The batter facility staff would bring up the hot cookies, and if there was something wrong, we discarded the whole batch.

The first day I was back at the office after returning from California, the sample cookies were brought up, and I ate them as usual. I took one bite of the first cookie and thought it was fine. It was okay. It was good. These were the same cookies we always had. And that was the problem. There was no excitement. No thrill. Cookies should be extraordinary, even extravagant, and these were just fine. What, I wondered, had changed? For seven years we had tasted and served the same cookies. As we built the company, I had also listened to many of my friends and associates say repeatedly, "Your business is so simple." To which I would always reply, "Oh, yeah? Think about what I do. I sell a product that costs more than the most expensive steak you can buy in a grocery store per pound. And I sell a product that nobody needs. Wake up every morning with that as your value proposition."

Though I knew these cookies were not irresistible, I had little choice but to approve and ship the batch. But something kept nagging at me; we were missing something. I felt as if Goliath was close by, but I could not yet see him. The ground had shifted beneath our feet, and we were not paying enough attention to notice. Our customers had tasted our cookies for years, but we also knew their palates had become more sophisticated since 1977 because of increased competition. I was experienced enough at retail to know that our customers expected more than we were currently giving them. If we kept being just good, we were not going to survive.

After that tasting session, I decided to visit our stores with a new set of eyes. It was as if someone had removed my blinders. I tasted our product and evaluated our suppliers. I looked at our store design. I thought about the name of our company. I scrutinized hiring, training, and customer service. I also visited our competitors' stores to see what they were doing. Then I came back and brought my executive team together—the people who knew our operations, our monthly sales, and our financials. We sat in my office and I said, "We are seven years into this, and we are really good. There is no doubt that we have done well. But if we are going to take this company to the next level, we have to start thinking differently. If we are going to define our future, we have to change our thinking about everything we have done in the past. Everything is on the table. Here's how I want you to think about this. If we were starting a cookie company today, how would we compete against us—the Original Great American Chocolate Chip Cookie Company? What would we do to differentiate ourselves from them? How could we become the clear choice for a new customer? I challenge each of you to come back in a week with some ideas that will make us better."

The team reconvened the following week and discussed what needed to be done. At first they suggested small changes. I sat, listened, and digested everyone's feedback. Then I stood up and said, "What we need is a revolution. We are going to create a new product, shorten our name, develop a new look and customer experience, and implement a new training program."

In this moment, change became our Goliath, and everyone was nervous, because the company was doing well. That is when I recounted a story from my mentor Irving.

One Saturday when I was working at Irving's clothing shop Dorwins in Miami Beach, we were closing after a particularly successful day. I turned to Irving and said, "These customers love us. We own them."

He shot back, "Kid, the minute you think you own any customer is the day you lose your business. Remember, there are fifty companies standing in the wings waiting to take your business from you. Never get cocky and think that you have a contract with a customer. They can always shop somewhere else if you don't give them the product and the price and the customer service they deserve."

Irving's warning has always hung in the back of my head. I was fourteen years old, and that story became a kind of reckoning that would guide the cookie company's revolution.

I returned from the bike race in the middle of May 1984, and by June we had started the company's transformation. We had to do everything simultaneously—shorten our name, develop a new store design, create and test new products, rewrite our operations manual, and establish a new training program and manual. All of this had to be completed at the same time. We realized that we needed the new plan fully designed to roll out at our annual franchise convention in the spring of 1985.

This was a huge undertaking that should take at least eighteen months, maybe two years. But we did not have that kind of time. I told my team that we had ten months. I felt like I was sixteen years old again with Irving in the back of Dorwins scrambling to alter all the clothes we had just sold before school started in a single weekend. I told my team, "If you have any big plans or vacations in the next ten months, cancel them. There are forty hours in a workweek; we are going to have to work eighty, maybe more. Nine-to-five is gone; this is now a twenty-four-hour job." And they all agreed because they now believed this was transformational. It was not uncommon for Richard Gully, who oversaw our manufacturing, to call me in at ten o'clock at night to come taste new samples.

The product was our first priority. In the company's early years, we used the same base recipe passed down through my partner's wife's family. It was delicious, but all of the cookies started to taste the same even when we added different ingredients—chocolate chips, peanut butter, M&Ms, various nuts. So we started experimenting with new recipes to reformulate each cookie. We finally realized that each cookie had to have its own base and unique taste. As you can imagine, a lot of batter found its way into the Dumpster, but we finally found success. If I had not still been riding my bike to and from work, I would have gained fifty pounds, because we were sampling dozens of batches every day, often late into the evening. Once we settled on the new recipes, Richard hired someone from the American Baking Association to help us scale them for our industrial-size mixers.

With the new products in place, we began testing our new retail model. We started with ten of our company-owned stores in the fall of 1984, and then partnered with a few franchisees after the first of the year. We needed them on board to help us work out any kinks before we rolled out the revamped system to the rest of the company at the spring convention. Our entire approach was new: instead of marketing piece by piece, we would now sell cookies by the pound.

To complement the revised recipes and pricing structure, we refashioned our branding. Our name—the Original Great American Chocolate Chip Cookie Company—was cute at first, but it had become a liability. What might work for a small, local company did not have national cachet. So in 1985 we shortened it to the Great American Cookie Company, with a plan to shorten it further to Great American Cookies.

The last two components of the revolution involved training and store design. Training became a critical component of the new brand. For years we had trained our associates from behind the counter—showing them all the mechanics of how to make the cookies, handle the food safely, clean the store, ring up purchases. But something was missing. We realized that if you are only showing your employees the experience from one vantage point, you have a missed opportunity to serve your customer. So we put them on the other side of the counter as well, to let them understand the shopper's viewpoint. We wanted them to see what a good cookie looked like and what it was like to encounter a welcoming employee. We had each employee and trainee bake a batch of cookies, and we lined them up on the counter. Then we asked them all to pick the best batch—so they could see what was overbaked, underbaked, or, like in "Goldilocks and the Three Bears," just right. This, the training emphasized, was the cardinal rule: If you burn a batch of cookies, you throw them away. You do not worry more about food cost than about quality. No customer has a contract to come back—you have to make sure you sell the very best product you can.

Finally, we focused our attention on store design. We moved away from the original store concept from our early years and worked on creating stores that were colorful, engaging, and fun. Our first concept, modeled on a jewelry store, used elegant cases to showcase the product—much the way retailers display expensive watches or diamond rings. This revised design still showcased the product, but we added bolder colors and back-lit photographs of people enjoying our cookies. We featured big, dynamic images of cookie cakes and parties, which could be changed on a regular basis to keep the store looking fresh and new. After we completed the five major changes—recipes, marketing, name, training, and store design—we interviewed two consulting firms to help guide the launch. Both suggested that we operate the old and new concepts at the same time. I thought that was a bad idea, as it would have been confusing for the customer. They also suggested that we host focus groups to test the new products. But I refused. That decision was later validated by Steve Jobs, the founder of Apple, who once observed: "It's really hard to design products by focus groups. A lot of times, people don't know what they want until you show it to them." Another pioneering computer scientist, Alan Curtis Kay, made a similar point: "The best way to predict the future is to invent it." I knew in my gut that we had to roll the dice, so we planned to present the whole package to our franchisees at the May 1985 convention.

We had started hosting conventions in the early 1980s at the Marriott Hotel in Marietta, Georgia, about ten miles from my home, and that was where we rolled out the new plans. Over the next two days, our leadership team made presentations on the upcoming changes. But this alone would never make the franchisees willing or excited to adopt them. Our secret weapon was the franchisees who had been working with us since the first of the year. We invited these franchisees—notably our largest, Doc Cohen—to present at the conference. They talked about what was coming and gave all the changes their blessing, which built credibility in the eyes of the other franchisees.

We could tell that the other franchisees were nervous, but we had confidence borne out from the testing we had done, and we wanted to share that confidence. We also drew upon the data. A careful analysis of our operations revealed that in our first two years the company grew by 30 percent. By 1984, growth had slowed to less than 6 percent. The stores were doing fine, but they were capable of doing much more. When we started in Atlanta in 1977, most of our consumers were from Georgia and had never seen a cookie store in a mall. Seven years later, we had more than eighty stores in twenty states and were operating in a competitive national marketplace. The consumer now had more choices, so we had to change. And this revolution was the ticket to increased sales and long-term viability.

As you can imagine, the franchisees at the 1985 convention were concerned about timeline and cost. These were big changes that were going to really impact their operations. The new product, company name, and selling strategies were to be implemented within thirty days. The new training program would be rolled out immediately, and the new store design would be fully in place as soon as possible. Franchisees whose mall leases were up in the next two years could wait to complete the redesign; the others would make the change in the next year. In May 1985 we closed down all of the stores. We went to sleep one night as the Original Great American Chocolate Chip Cookie Company and woke up the next day as the Great American Cookie Company. The revolution worked, the company soared, and Goliath crawled away defeated.

If we had not made that transformation, the Great American Cookie Company's growth rate would likely have continued to decline over the next several years. All businesses have to evolve, and sometimes one reinvention is not enough. You have to constantly test yourself and be sure you are doing everything you can. If you are in the cookie business, and an Auntie Anne's Pretzels opens next door, you do not suddenly start selling pretzels. That is not the way to compete. You have to make your product more relevant—whether it is cookies, cars, or computers. You have to promote a clear brand message that resonates with customers.

A revolution in any business is stressful, and I wanted to avoid going through that process again. I only wanted an evolution. So I began hosting weekly meetings in my office to review our operations. We discussed new training initiatives, point of purchase strategies, ingredient quality, and new product launches. To keep tabs on our competition, we brought samples of their products on a regular basis and made adjustments to our recipes to reflect what we learned. Because we were no longer a small company, we contracted with manufacturers to make our chocolate chips and mill all of our flour. We went from using three vertical mixers that could produce 200 pounds of batter to a horizontal mixer that made 1,500 pounds. All of the ingredients were programmed into a computer, which preserved our secret recipes and prevented variation among batches. We were also big enough that we could buy truckloads of sugar and flour to be placed in silos. These ongoing adjustments helped keep our price down, ensure consistency, and continually improve our product. All of this helped our bottom line, but more important, it gave customers a great product at a competitive price.

Throughout this transformation, I read a number of business and history books, looking for new approaches and ideas. The most influential one turned out to be David Halberstam's *The Reckoning*, which argues that the shortsightedness of the Detroit automakers paved the way for Japanese domination of the market. You might be wondering what a book about manufacturing cars has to do with selling cookies. The answer is, everything.

Halberstam's focus on Nissan and their Z car was particularly illuminating. In the 1960s, ten engineers at Nissan (then still called Datsun) built a clay prototype of what would become a revolutionary new sports car. In 2001, Nissan president Carlos Ghosn summed up the power of the Z: "In the fall of 1969, Nissan introduced a two-seat sports car that revolutionized the automotive world at the time. It had European styling, American muscle, Japanese quality and global desirability." Nissan did not just add the Z to their existing line of cars; they used it to change the whole company. While they continued to sell the Datsun 2000 for another year, they used the Z car to elevate customers' expectations and helped Nissan replicate the Z's quality and advanced technology in future models. Reading about how Nissan used the Z to change their entire operations affirmed that we had acted wisely in refusing to operate two different concepts at the same time. We were not going to compete with ourselves by selling old and new cookies; we were going to make sure that everything we sold was great.

Halberstam's book also drew attention to a problem that I never even thought about. Most American businesses at the time were structured as rigid hierarchies. The top leadership are mainly isolated from the hourly workforce. They function like a king or queen with everybody below them. A few top managers have access to the royal family, but nobody else. After I read that, I realized that our business was based on this antiquated model. We had hundreds of people in the field—franchisees, store managers, district managers, regional managers, and store employees—and I wanted each of them to know that they could call me with an idea or a complaint. I had to break down the employer-employee barrier. I printed business cards with my private phone number and later my email address, and people called me. If they had an idea that could improve the business, I wanted to hear about it. I received dozens of calls and letters with suggestions, and to reinforce that we were listening, I set up a program whereby if we adopted your idea, the company would give you $200. My daughter Taryn, who was now in high school, even got into the act and suggested creating a cookie cake that was sold in a tie box for Father's Day. It was really popular, especially because customers connected with our marketing slogan: "Fathers Hate Ugly Ties. Give Them Something They Really Want." Encouraging our management to listen to the people on the front lines of the company was a game changer.

For the next decade, the company continued to grow and thrive. Of course, not everything we tried worked. One discussion that I remember involved coming up with a clever new name for the large decorated cookies we sold. We hired a marketing firm to help us develop a new name and engaged in an extensive and complicated branding process, with a number of possible options including the Jumbo Cookie, the Edible Greeting Card, and the Extra Large Cookie. After entertaining these and other unappealing choices, I finally asked my leadership team, "What do our customers call them?"

They replied, "Cookie Cakes."

"So why are we trying to change it?" I wondered.

Sometimes the solution is defined by your customer and is right in front of you.

12

That Was Pretty Fast

I don't think this is going to work.

Growing and refining the Great American Cookie Company occupied most of my time, but I continued to be active in the cycling community. I still commuted to work on my bicycle, enjoyed long rides, and competed in a few tandem races with Donna and with my friend and fellow cyclist Michael Shermer. I was not trying to prove anything; I was just enjoying the sport and trying to stay in shape. Then an invitation came, and I felt like I was in *The Godfather* with an "offer I can't refuse."

Pete Penseyres is probably the greatest long-distance cyclist in the history of the sport. He holds more than ten records, including two Race Across America first-place solo rides from the West to the East Coast, in 1984 and 1986. He was inducted into the Ultracycling Hall of Fame in 2003. We were friends, and we were both training to participate in the Assault on Mt. Mitchell. This is quite a race— 102.7 miles from Spartanburg, South Carolina, up to and along the Blue Ridge Parkway, to the summit in Mount Mitchell State Park in North Carolina. The combined vertical ascent is more than 10,000 feet. As we had been training for the same event,

I invited Pete and his wife, Joanne, to stay with us on their drive from San Diego to the start. While they were with us in Kennesaw, he and I did a tandem ride covering sixty-five miles at close to twenty-five miles per hour. When we got back, Pete said, "Great ride. That was pretty fast." And then we did not talk about it again. We both packed our bikes and left for Spartanburg. The next day, while removing my bike from the roof of our car, I threw out my back, making it impossible for me to participate. So we went to the start of the race to deliver banners and cookies to the organizers, because the Great American Cookie Company was a race sponsor, and Donna and I drove back to Atlanta. We were frustrated, after all of my training, that I would not be able to compete with Pete.

The next week, I was surprised to get a call from Pete, who started by saying, "I want to talk to you about the HPV four-man relay that is now part of the Race Across America."

I knew that HPV meant human-powered vehicle—a category that embraced regular bicycles and a range of other contraptions including tandem and recumbent bikes. I thought I also knew what Pete wanted. So I interrupted:

"Pete, before you go any further, let me tell you that I already talked to Michael Shermer when he was joining a team. I told him that the cookie company was not interested in being a sponsor."

Pete laughed and said, "I'm not interested in a sponsor, I want you to be on our team."

"What? Why me?" I asked.

He said, "Because you are one of the strongest people I've ridden with on a tandem."

Now I'm thinking to myself: Pete rode across the country with Lon Haldeman in 1987 on a tandem bicycle in a world-record pace of 7 days, 14 hours, and 55 minutes, and he is telling me that I'm one of the strongest people he's ridden with? I was flattered. No, I was amazed.

But I felt I had to confess, "Pete, I'm still having some back trouble, and I don't know if I can do it."

He reassured me, "Look, you just start training, and go at your own pace. The HPV will be great for you."

So he sent me a recumbent bike frame without the aerodynamic skin that would comprise the outer shell. I started training and was averaging about 17 miles per hour. On my regular racing bike, I could travel about 20 to 22 miles per hour. I had never ridden a recumbent bike, so I did not realize how much slower it would be. The major difference is on hills, where you cannot stand up and really push. While the recumbent was good for my back, the slow speed was bad for my ego. At the end of the first week, I called Pete and confessed, "I don't think this is going to work. I'm really slow."

He laughed and said, "Just wait until you get the outer shell, you'll be flying at twenty-five to thirty miles per hour."

And he was right; the skin made the bike so much faster. So I kept training and got stronger and stronger. The team—Pete, Bob Fourney, Pete's brother James, and me—did one twenty-four-hour ride and estimated that we could complete the race in six days, covering five hundred miles per day. When I finished the 1984 race, I thought I was done with that chapter of my life. But here I was back at the starting line. Our recumbent bike, called the Diet Coke Lightning, was built by Tim Brummer and had a nose cone on the front, a lightweight aluminum shell on the back, and adjustable Lycra wrapped around the entire body. The rider's head projected out the top and was protected by a clear windshield that allowed the aerodynamic helmet to fit perfectly inside without any wind drag. Numerous teams considered entering, but only four left Los Angeles on the way to New York. All four of the bikes competing were vastly different. They shared only one feature—they were powered by humans.

We had an eighteen-person crew to help support what is the fastest four-person bicycle race in the sport's history. The twenty-four-hour relay race began at three p.m., and the four teams immediately had to face the Mojave Desert. We fell into a steady pattern: each person rode for two hours and then took a six-hour break. In sum, the four riders each rode six hours a day. Our fiercest competitors—Gold Rush, composed of Michael Shermer, Dan Tout, Greg Miller, and "Fast Freddy" Markham riding their Easy Racer—took an early lead and kept it for the next 2,500 miles. We were averaging 600 miles per day—100 more than we expected—and we were still in second place. But we were consistent.

By the third day, Gold Rush had a nearly four-hour lead. They were at least 100 miles ahead of us. That distance became our Goliath—seemingly impossible to overcome. I remember sitting in the motor home with Jim Penseyres and talking about how frustrated we were. Pete, who had just gotten off the bike to hand it over to Bob Fourney, came in to eat and get a massage. Now, you have to picture this scene. Here was the best long-distance cyclist in the world; he was like a god in the sport. He opened the door to the motor home. The sun was behind him, so you could not see his face, only his silhouette. And here we were—his teammates griping about our second-place status. Pete saw our faces and said, "What's wrong?"

I grumbled, "We're doing better than we ever thought we could do, and we're falling farther and farther behind."

He looked at Jim and me and said, "They're going to slow down."

It was as if the world had stopped, as if David had just stepped into the motor home with a slingshot in his hand.

My next question was, "How do you know that?" It wasn't that we doubted him; we just didn't understand how he knew.

Pete said, "If they don't slow down, we won't win."

We laughed, but he was right. They were disorganized and were racing as if it was a 2,000-mile race instead of a 3,000-mile one. We started rotating riders every hour instead of every two hours to increase our speed. We had another advantage—wisdom. Our team had made plenty of transcontinental crossings, and our average age was about forty. Gold Rush's average age was in the mid-twenties. They were younger, but in this case experience trumped age. Our ultimate weapon, though, was Joanne Penseyres. Pete's wife (who has since passed away) was the glue that held our team together. She had helped coordinate every transcontinental race that Pete did, was a seasoned veteran, and one of the major reasons we won this race. In the last thousand miles, just as Pete predicted, Gold Rush fell apart. One writer described them as "a group of drowning rats in a whirlpool." Their team was competing without sleep, with not a single cooked meal, no showers, and barely a change of clothes. Once again, Pete's wisdom bolstered us. He said, "This race doesn't begin until the Mississippi River." And once again, Pete was right. We passed them 171 miles from the finish, and 15 miles later the Gold Rush team dropped out. They had been in first place for more than 2,500 miles, and they just quit.

Once we knew we were going to win, Pete had to decide who would ride the last miles into Battery Park in New York City. He gave the honor to me, even though I thought that he should do it. He was the best long-distance racer in the sport, and this whole team was his idea. He kept us together, motivated us, and was largely responsible for our win. When I protested that he should represent us all in those final miles, he insisted that I take it. So I rode the last leg of this incredible journey—my fourth race across the United States on a bicycle. As I neared Battery Park, I found myself at the top of the George Washington Bridge looking down on the Statue of Liberty, overwhelmed with emotion. Just think—five days earlier, we were all standing at the Pacific Ocean. Twelve years earlier, if I had stood in the same place, I would have been using a walker. It was hard to fathom how much had changed.

Even though we were trying to beat the clock, I stopped in my tracks, and the power of that American symbol flooded over me. My grandparents came through Ellis Island, and here I was completing this incredible journey in the shadow of the statue that would have meant so much to them. For a brief moment, I reflected on how lucky I was, and it was really emotional. But it also cost us an extra five minutes in the race. In the end, three teams completed the race, and we averaged 24.02 miles per hour. Our winning time was five days, one hour, and eight minutes. Our record, which still stands, is the fastest crossing of America by a four-person team on a bicycle.

My first three transcontinental races were about proving to myself that I was physically whole. The 1989 race was all about teamwork and opening a chapter that would become part of the rest of my life. I was a cyclist. The motorcycle accident in 1977 was horrible, but it was also a gift. It transformed me back into an athlete and made me a better businessman. The previous races changed the way I saw the company and helped us get from good to great. The 1989 race was all about fearlessness. Once I realized what a great company we had become, my eyes opened wider to new opportunities.

By the 1990s, we had hundreds of stores and annual sales around $100 million. Through the success of Great American Cookies, I was able to involve myself in numerous community activities, and the 1989 race helped me decide to take my next big step. In 1994, I campaigned for my friend Zell Miller and helped him win Cobb County on his way to securing a second term as governor. Miller had been involved in Georgia politics for years, serving as lieutenant governor from 1975 to 1991, and then as governor from 1991 to 1999. In this first term, he started one of the most popular and enduring programs related to education in any state in the nation—the HOPE Scholarship, an acronym for Helping Others Pursue Education. The lottery-funded program offered free tuition to thousands of Georgia students who maintained a B– average through high school and college, thus improving their access to the state's public colleges and universities. Watching that program grow and thrive, I saw how much public service could do to change people's lives. I also saw that not every Georgia politician was as effective.

I remained engaged in politics after the governor's race and was working to help recruit someone to run for Congress in 1996 against Newt Gingrich. Gingrich had become a contentious figure in Cobb County, especially because of an incident at Kennesaw State College that garnered national attention. The episode involved Gingrich teaching a course titled "Renewing American Civilization" as a part-time adjunct in the School of Business Administration. Controversial from the outset, the class had an overtly political agenda, and Gingrich embroiled the Kennesaw State College Foundation, where I served as a board member, in a controversy that threatened its tax-exempt status. He ultimately was investigated and fined by the House Ethics Committee, and the national and local press coverage left a stain on the college, the county, and the state.

Many community leaders in the Sixth Congressional District lost confidence in Gingrich, and I had been beating the bushes looking for the perfect person to run against him—either Democrat or Republican. We needed someone who lived in the district, someone who cared about improving our community and its institutions, and someone who was not a career politician. Each time I described what I was looking for, the person I was trying to persuade would say to me, "You should do it." I had never even considered running for public office; I was a businessman and had my hands full growing the cookie company. After a few days of this, I came home and recounted the conversations to Donna. She listened intently and finally said, "They're right. You *should* do it."

"Did you hear what I said?" I asked.

Without missing a beat, she again said, "You should do it. You care about this. You're immersed in this community, and you would do a great job."

That got my attention. I really trusted her judgment and started thinking about it more seriously. I was not sure, with only seven months before the election, that I could learn everything I needed to know to defeat the Speaker of the House. I did know that it would be too hard to make such a big decision while working full time, so I took an unplanned two-week break from work and locked myself up with two boxes filled with the federal budget, all the bills that were pending, and books written by or about Newt Gingrich. I posted a simple message on my computer, "Why do you want to run for Congress?" Every day when I walked into my home office, I knew that I did not yet have a good answer. And until I figured that out, I was going to immerse myself in the issues. I read and studied and wrote about the things that I cared about—balancing the budget, veterans' benefits, saving Medicare, and education reform. At the end of the second week, I walked to the computer and wrote: "I want to run for Congress because I want someone to represent the issues that are important to our community who does not care about being re-elected. I want to be a congressman who simply does the right thing."

When I announced that I was a candidate, I was immediately besieged by requests from the press. Most congressional races do not attract much national attention, but this one did. Gingrich was a political Goliath, albeit a troubled one. He enjoyed a 20-percentage-point lead at the start of the race, and few people predicted that I would make a respectable showing. Russell K. Paul, Georgia's Republican chairman, remarked in a September 18, 1996, article in the *New York Times* that he was not worried about me as an opponent and wondered how much of my "children's inheritance" I wanted to "waste on this endeavor." Georgia state representative Roy Barnes countered, "He's got a shot, No. 1 because he's got money, No. 2 because he's articulate, and he's got a success story to tell, No. 3 because he's got a history of accomplishing things, and No. 4 because he's running against Newt Gingrich."

There was no doubt that I was an unusual opponent. I remember in particular one headline that ran in *Time* magazine: "Newt's Cookie Monster." The day I announced my candidacy at the Coles College of Business at the renamed Kennesaw State University, some Gingrich supporters staged a counterdemonstration outside the building. They dressed somebody up as *Sesame Street*'s Cookie Monster to belittle me, but it backfired, and everyone thought the stunt indicated that Newt was in for the fight of his career.

It was a baptism by fire, and I decided that if I was going to do it, I had to be prepared to fight. I could not forget the pot holders, as we did on the opening day of the cookie company. The eyes of the district and, in fact, the nation were on this race, and I had to step into the valley and face the giant.

This was Gingrich's tenth race for the congressional seat, coming just two years after he launched his Contract with America. I was fifty-three years old, and this was going to be an uphill battle. The Sixth District, which includes Cobb County north of Atlanta, has historically been one of the country's most reliably Republican areas. In 1994, Gingrich won with 64 percent of the vote. To further complicate matters, only twice in the history of our nation have voters failed to reelect the Speaker of the House (in 1862 and 1994). But I was not one to shy away from a tough race, and I thought I had much to offer. I was more interested in listening to constituents' voices than in hearing my own—something you could not say about Gingrich. I made a strong showing, but in the end he won. Yet even in defeat, I felt that had I brought many important issues into the local and national conversation.

The day after the election, I woke up, called my campaign manager Kate Head, and asked, "So, what do we do now?"

She replied, "We pack up the office and go home."

Not satisfied, I pressed, "Well, what about all these issues we were fighting for?"

Kate replied, "Well, you lost, and it's over."

I kept pressing her. "What about all these people I met? What about all the veterans?"

She said, "You'll just have to learn to live with it."

It was really hard. As a businessman, I never thought of things as being over. In business, there was always something else I could try. Not so in politics—the voters had spoken.

But it was not over for me. I had the same feeling in 1996 that I did in 1982 when I completed my first race from Savannah to San Diego. There was more to be done, and over the next year, while I continued to expand the cookie company, it really nagged at me. So in 1997 I announced that I would run for the U.S. Senate in Georgia against Republican incumbent Paul Coverdell and Libertarian Bert Loftman. I focused my campaign on six issues: ensuring that all Georgians had clean drinking water, improving education by hiring 100,000 new public school teachers, repealing the marriage tax penalty, strengthening medical care benefits for veterans, reforming health care to give patients more rights, and strengthening Social Security. I enjoyed broad support throughout the state and endorsements from former president Jimmy Carter, the International Brotherhood of Police Officers, the Georgia Association of Educators, the American Nurses Association Political Action Committee, and the Sierra Club.

If the 1996 race was a sprint, 1998 was a marathon. It lasted fifteen months instead of seven. If 1996 cost three million dollars, 1998 required more than twice that. I had learned a great deal from my first campaign, especially about the power of the incumbent. I also quickly discovered how grueling a statewide political campaign could be. At the cookie company I had a terrific executive team that oversaw the daily operations. In 1996 I promoted David Barr, our former chief financial officer, to president. When I entered the Senate race, he took over as chief executive officer. But I remained very active as chairman of the board, and it felt like I was juggling two full-time jobs—one keeping the company going and one traveling around the state meeting with thousands of Georgians and trying to earn their support.

I was really gaining traction against Coverdell, and all of the polling indicated that I was going to win. So I began to prepare for a new job in November. I could not serve in the Senate and run a multimillion-dollar company at the same time. When the opportunity presented itself that year to sell the company, it seemed as if the stars had aligned. In August 1998 we sold Great American Cookies to a group that was purchasing other snack food companies. It was a good decision, but I learned a valuable lesson. In a statewide race, time is your Goliath. You can always find more supporters, and you can always find more places to visit, but you cannot manufacture time. Time often determines who wins and who loses. The more time you have, the more voters you can engage. I worked hard, but eventually I ran out of time. In spite of all of the predictions, I lost the election to Coverdell by a margin of seven percentage points, 52–45. And, just like in 1996, it was over. I woke up the morning after the election without a company to run or a job.

13 Building a Brand Religion

*Friends don't
let friends drink
Starbucks.*

In the last year and a half before we sold Great
American Cookies, we introduced gourmet coffee
in our stores. We had sold soft drinks for years, but
we thought we should accommodate our customers'
more sophisticated palates. What could possibly go
better with a warm, freshly baked chocolate chip
cookie than a really good cup of coffee?

I had always loved coffee, ever since I was a child.
My parents used to give me a cup of coffee brim-
ming with milk when I was as young as six. Then
we moved to Florida when the beatnik era was in
full swing, and coffee shops were opening up all
over Miami Beach. That's where I first tasted Cuban
coffee and espresso and began developing a taste for
good-quality coffee.

When I moved to Atlanta in 1970, I used to order
gourmet coffee beans from a mail order company
out of New York. I was grinding my own freshly
roasted beans, which was almost unheard of back
then. In 1973 I brought a small espresso machine
back from Italy. It was impossible to find one in
the United States. When I got it home, I remember
being thankful for all I had learned as an apprentice
electrician under Lou, the landlord of our building,

when I was a teenager. The machine was made for a European market, so I had to rewire it for American outlets. I'll never forget how, when making my first cappuccino in our kitchen, I removed the coffee holder too soon. Hot water and coffee shot up in the air, all the way to our twenty-foot ceiling. I clearly had a lot to learn. I started studying the different kinds of beans and roasting techniques, but I never expected that this casual hobby would lead me into the world of coffee.

Selling coffee at the cookie company proved to be a real challenge. Our research showed that the growth in coffee sales was after lunch, and we wanted to capitalize on the old adage "Fish where there are fish." The bulk of our business already came after noon, so we thought that we could offer our customers added convenience, becoming a one-stop shop. They would no longer have to go somewhere else in the mall to buy a good cup of coffee. However, we misjudged how willing customers would be to purchase two luxury products. Pairing cookies with gourmet coffee required a hefty financial commitment.

Another big challenge we faced involved freshness. Coffee back in the 1980s and 1990s was not what it is today. The big brands—Folgers and Maxwell House—were dominant, and their brewed products could sit in a pot for three or four hours because the beans they used did not have much flavor to begin with. The rich, complex taste of gourmet coffee lasts about two hours before it starts to lose its flavor.

Timing was also an issue. Our store opened about an hour before most of the other stores in the mall, but most people do not even think about buying a cookie until lunchtime. Consequently, we did little business in the mornings. We made all this gourmet coffee that become stale in the thermal pots during those slow opening hours. Because we did not use frozen dough like many of our competitors, our cookies stayed fresh all day. But the coffee did not last and had to be thrown away. We also tried to lure customers to our stores in the morning by testing new products, but we were not successful in capturing the breakfast crowd.

While we were experimenting with new concepts, I remember a friend telling me that it is hard for a single-concept food store to get credit for doing two things well. Customers accepted that we had really good cookies, brownies, and cookie cakes, but if there was a Starbucks or Barnie's in the mall, we could not compete, because our competition was just too well established in the coffee business. We finally pulled the plug on serving gourmet coffee after three months. I thought that would be my last foray into the coffee sector. I was wrong.

In November of 1998, for the first time in my life, I had the luxury of weighing my options. I had just lost the campaign for U.S. Senate and was exhausted. I found myself without a job or a company to run and was at a crossroads. I had made enough money from the sale of Great American Cookies to reach an important goal—to secure the future for my family. For once, I was not pressured to rush to decide what to do next. On the board of Charter Bank, where I had served since 1987, I was about to become the chairman. I stayed active in politics, supporting candidates who were concerned with issues that were also a focus of my two campaigns. I was also doing some work with Atlanta-area nonprofits, which was fulfilling, if not the same as building a team and running a business. I was fifty-four years old and considered retiring and dedicating myself to cycling, fly-fishing, and golf—three sports I loved. It did not dawn on me that when you start working at the age of eleven and never stop, you feel a tremendous void when the work ends. I had faced Goliath all my life, and I was energized by those battles. Now I had no big challenge. I had always thought of myself as a transformational leader, and I needed something new to transform.

Looking into other food concepts for possible ideas, once again I started thinking about coffee. I quickly discovered the huge gap between the largest player in the business, Starbucks, and the closest challenger. I tried to buy a coffee company in 2000 and 2001. When that proved unsuccessful, I decided to start my own company, which I was going to call PerQs, a play on words blending "perk" (to brew coffee) and "perquisite" (a special advantage or benefit). The store would offer great coffee, freshly made food, and something extra—Internet access before that was really common, as well as fax machines and copiers. It would be more like a business center that also sold gourmet coffee. I toyed with creating memberships that would give customers a portable office—with food.

While I was still developing my business plan, in 2002, my friend Larry Stevens, head of mergers and acquisitions for PriceWaterhouseCoopers in Atlanta, introduced me to Charlie Ogburn, executive director of Crescent Capital Investments, Inc. Crescent owned a number of companies, including Cirrus Aircraft, and they were looking for someone to help with sales and marketing. Larry thought I might be a good fit as consultant, so we scheduled a lunch at Charlie Brown Airport in Atlanta. Larry had not told me much about what to expect at the meeting, so I started doing some research on Crescent Capital and found that they also owned about an 80 percent stake in Caribou Coffee, a company headquartered in Minneapolis. I thought, well, this is fortuitous. I had a personal connection to the company—there was a Caribou near my home. Atlanta was the company's second market after Minneapolis, and I had been going there for some time. I even had my own white ceramic Caribou mug that I had bought and carried for years. It was pretty chipped and worn, and I repaired it with Super Glue when the handle broke off. But I still have it to this day.

Caribou was the second largest non-franchised coffee-house chain in the nation, with 207 stores in nine states and the District of Columbia. The company was founded by John and Kim Puckett. John had been a management consultant with Bain & Company, while Kim worked for General Mills, and they were regular customers at Coffee Connection in Boston and interested in opening their own coffee shop. They researched for more than a year, looking for ways to improve on the concept. While sitting on the summit of Sable Mountain in Denali National Park during a backpacking trip to Alaska, they were talking about their new company. On the descent down the mountain, they saw a herd of wild caribou— which became the inspiration behind the name. The Pucketts moved to Minneapolis in the summer of 1992 and opened the first Caribou Coffee in Edina, a suburb, in December. The Caribou concept was warm and welcoming, evoking a mountain lodge with fireplaces, exposed wooden beams, earth tones, and oversized leather sofas and chairs. Each store had a children's corner that appealed to harried parents looking for a safe, quiet place to relax. Walking into a Caribou Coffee was like escaping to the mountains, and several coffee chains, including Starbucks, later adopted similar designs. From the moment Caribou opened in Minnesota, it became the coffee café of choice. When the Pucketts sold Caribou to Crescent in 2000, the company headquarters remained in Minneapolis.

So I went to the meeting with Charlie prepared to talk about coffee. He came expecting to discuss Cirrus airplanes. We hit it off immediately, and once Charlie realized I wasn't too interested in Cirrus, we turned our attention to Caribou.

Charlie was surprised by how much I knew about the company. He told me that in the two years since they bought their stake, the company was not growing in the way they expected. I asked if they had any interest in selling Caribou; they didn't. As we continued to talk, I learned that they were hoping it could be franchised to spur growth, but were uncertain about how to proceed. Since I had a lot of experience with franchising from my time at Great American Cookies, Charlie asked me if I would study the company as a consultant and see what might be a good way forward. So that fall I traveled to a number of Caribou stores in Atlanta, Washington, D.C., Chicago, and Minneapolis. The stores were inconsistent in quality of product, speed of service, and customer experience. But at peak times they were still filled with customers. On my last few visits, the reason why they were so busy suddenly became obvious.

Whenever I was in a Caribou store, at some point someone would come in wearing a Caribou hat or T-shirt, often carrying a mug with the logo that featured Caribou's tagline: "Life is short. Stay awake for it." I was also visiting Starbucks stores while doing this research, and I never saw anyone there with any logoed merchandise beyond a coffee cup. Starbucks is like McDonald's. It is ubiquitous; it is a brand of convenience. If you want a gourmet cup of coffee or an inexpensive lunch, Starbucks and McDonald's can satisfy you. They are fast, easy, and convenient. I knew that customers would likely select an alternative if it offered a better product and, more important, a better customer experience. I also knew Caribou had something that Starbucks did not—a real connection to its customers.

The answer to whether or not Caribou was a brand that could be expanded was crystal clear. It could. Caribou was the best alternative to

Starbucks in the market, and its stores were beloved in the communities they served. Their customers were evangelists. While in Minnesota, I saw a bumper sticker that read: "Friends don't let friends drink Starbucks." The company did not produce these. A customer had gone to the trouble to design and give away the stickers.

This was quite different from Great American Cookies. The cookie company did not generate the same kind of followers that Caribou did; nobody made a bumper sticker touting our cookies. It was a great company, but it was not iconic. This was partly because Arthur and I, for the twenty-one years we worked together, put most of our energy into operating and growing the company, not on building the brand. The better-known brand in the cookie industry was Mrs. Fields. We had a superior product, but they understood how to market their story. Their name evoked warm cookies coming out of your grandmother's kitchen, but the founder was a young, photogenic woman, so she got all the publicity. We always felt like the Rodney Dangerfield of the cookie business—we "got no respect." This was mostly our fault: our name was too generic. In retrospect, we should have named the company Art and Mike's Cookies to give it a more personal connection. And we never effectively told our story about how the company was started, about the recipe that was four generations old, and about how two guys built the most successful cookie company in the nation.

But Caribou was different; it had something special. This fledgling chain was up against Goliath in the form of Starbucks. If it was going to compete, I had to find out how. The key turned out to be that Caribou was not just a coffee shop—it was a "brand religion."

Why do some brands create a cultlike following and others just sell products? What makes customers camp outside a store to buy the latest iPhone or try the new In-N-Out Burger that just opened? Business leaders have searched for this perfect recipe like the Holy Grail for centuries. What is the secret? In the January 29, 2014, issue of the *Harvard Business Review*, Ron Faris tried to tease out some answers. Surprisingly, his most illuminating source was not found in the world of business but in the history of religion. He cites Malcolm Gladwell's book *The Tipping*

Point, which argues that religions take hold when a charismatic leader creates dogmatic followers. The key ingredient seems to be emotion. Transferring this logic to the world of business, Faris explains that when a fanatic becomes emotional about a product, "he or she is apt to pay more, wait longer, and share louder" than other customers. The key to developing a brand religion is finding a way to create both physical and virtual opportunities for fanatics to share their experiences, all while offering them scarce products or experiences that are not available to the wider public. Ironically, value and price rarely figure into the equation.

Over the past century, numerous companies have made their brands not just popular but iconic. There are dozens of examples, but three companies offer powerful lessons on how to create and maintain an effective brand religion.

No company in American history has come to better represent the spirit of freedom, independence, and self-reliance than Harley-Davidson Motorcycles. The sheer loyalty of the fan base is evidenced by the fact that its logo is one of the most popular tattoos in the world. What better way to measure a brand religion than to find customers who permanently ink its logo on their bodies? Founded in 1903 by William S. Harley and brothers Walter and Arthur Davidson in Milwaukee, Harley-Davidson is one of the nation's most celebrated brands. Its history is inextricably linked with popular culture, and even casual fans who have never ridden a motorcycle understand the power of the brand. Most closely associated with the famous 1969 film *Easy Rider*, the Harley has been featured in dozens of movies and television programs, from *The Rocky Horror Picture Show* (1975) to *Animal House* (1978) and *Rocky III* (1982) to *Ghost Rider* (2007). In the 2015 film *The Meddler*, J. K. Simmons offers Susan Sarandon a ride home, and she says she can't ride on a motorcycle, to which he replies, "Oh, this isn't a motorcycle, this is a Harley-Davidson, world of difference." It is an American icon.

For years Harley had the majority of the big bike market. Harleys were so beloved that if you parked one, you had to chain it up to keep it from being stolen. Urban legend holds that someone secured his Harley Sportster to a tree. When he came back a few hours later, the tree had been cut down and the bike was gone. But Harley's dominance would be tested beginning in the 1960s. In 1969, two things happened—American Machine and Foundry bought Harley-Davidson, and Honda released the CL350. AMF reduced Harley's workforce and struggled with quality control issues, resulting in a dramatic decrease in sales. In fairly short order, the once prized brand was referred to disparagingly as "Hardly Drivable." In contrast, Honda, like other Japanese manufacturers in the postwar period, adhered to a philosophy of *kaizen*, or beneficial change. While Harley was struggling, *kaizen* became the key to quality and innovative design that enabled the Japanese to penetrate, expand, and quickly dominate the American market. Honda was not the first manufacturer to market a high-pipe, two-cylinder scrambler, but the CL350 was likely the most successful. This affordable and reliable bike appealed to casual riders. To counter the negative biker image, Honda introduced an advertising slogan, "You meet the nicest people on a Honda." Honda also featured women in its advertisements. Along with the other Japanese manufacturers such as Suzuki, Kawasaki, and Yamaha, they transformed the industry. From 1900 to 1960, about 50,000 motorcycles were sold annually in the United States. The Japanese manufacturers' expansion of the market drove that number to 1.5 million in 1974.

As Japan's star was rising, Harley's was fading, and the company found itself at a crossroads. In 1981 a group of thirteen investors bought back the company and made some important changes. The company retooled and installed a rubber-mounted engine to reduce the vibration for which the company had been widely criticized. They also started offering customized motorcycles for the first time to the general consumer, giving the sense that every bike was a reflection of the rider's unique personality. These changes protected the brand's cachet and helped it rebound and become a major player again.

Unlike "hipster" brands such as Under Armour, Zappos, or Apple, Harley-Davidson's customer base is over fifty. AARP members are not the ones you associate with rebellion, but throughout this transformation, the company brilliantly appealed to customers who were still lured by the romance of the open road. Brock Yates, author of *Outlaw Machine:*

Harley-Davidson and the Search for the American Soul, explained: "The classic Hells Angels rider can't afford a Harley anymore. It's the 45-year-old, divorced orthodontist that is buying them by the tons now." Despite the fact that Harley-Davidsons are heavier, slower, and more expensive than their Japanese counterparts, they remain extremely popular, and their riders are evangelists. While motorcycles have remained their main product, the company today sells more than $75 million in clothing and accessories—often to customers who do not own a bike. As Owen Edwards, coauthor of *Quintessence: The Quality of Having "It,"* puts it, "The 'real thing' is not necessarily the best thing. . . . The Harley guys don't want something that looks like a Harley—they want a Harley." Today Harley is facing new challenges appealing to millennials, but the brand's religion remains strong.

Unlike Harley-Davidson, Apple's followers did not just follow the company, they followed its founder Steve Jobs. The cult of personality that he created was essential to the brand's success. Jobs was removed from Apple in 1985 and established a rival firm, NeXT. For the next twelve years, that company focused on building computer workstations for higher education and business. Jobs would return in 1996, when NeXT was purchased by Apple. This time around, he brought with him a philosophy of creating products with sleek and simple designs, typified by the iMac unveiled in 1998.

The launch of Mac osx in 2001 would be a game changer, as would the opening of the first sleek, futuristic Apple Stores in Virginia and California. On May 19, more than a thousand people lined up at Tysons Corner Center, a mall near McLean, to visit the new store. The mall is situated in Fairfax County, Virginia, a suburb of Washington, D.C., that in 2001 was named the richest county in the United States. More than two thousand miles away, a second store opened in the Glendale Galleria, a mall in the affluent Los Angeles suburb of Glendale, with a similar demographic profile. In a 2011 article in *Macworld*, Benj Edwards reported that more than 7,700 people visited Apple's two stores that first weekend and bought almost $600,000 of Apple products. But this was not an ordinary shopping experience. It was a chance to buy into the hip Apple lifestyle that appealed to creative consumers such as graphic designers and archi-tects. As with Harley-Davidson, the shopping experience was much more about building community than it was about a retail transaction. Both of these companies tapped into the deep emotional strain that Ron Faris identified in his *Harvard Business Review* article on building a brand religion.

Apple's rise was bumpy, and Kirk McElhearn wrote in *Macworld* that the "iPod helped turn Apple Computer into Apple, Inc., from a computer company into one of the most recognizable brands in the world." Apple premiered the new product in 2001 and faced plenty of competition. There were other MP3 players available, but they were clunky and required cus-tomers to download music onto memory cards that were inserted into the device. The iPod was different. Steve Jobs understood that a sleek, elegant player was not enough. You had to support it with a platform that made it easy for customers to download music. That platform was iTunes, launched on January 9, 2001, well in advance of the iPod. This transformed the customer experience and completely disrupted the MP3 market. Six years later, Apple dropped the name "computer" from the company's name to reflect its dominance of the market.

More recent products such as the iPhone (2007) and iPad (2010) fur-ther transformed Apple from a niche company into a brand religion gone wild. My experience with the Apple Watch explains how. When it first came out in 2015, I thought to myself: This is the dumbest thing Apple has ever done. I had a Garmin watch that served as a GPS and alerted me when I had new emails and text messages at half the cost. I wondered why anyone would waste their money on Apple—until I got one. Now I wear my Apple Watch 3 everywhere and often travel without my phone. With each of these products, Apple changed the way we listen to music, watch television, use our telephone, and think about technology. They invented products that customers did not even know they wanted, but now cannot live without, thus creating a long line of evangelists. They also changed packaging in the industry, using sleek, beautiful designs. Long after cus-tomers opened their product, they kept the packaging because it was too beautiful to throw away. Apple is now the gold standard in this arena.

Apple understood all of the touch points that were important to a consumer, and the brand religion can be found in those small details. It was not about just selling a product; it was about giving customers something that made their life better. And it felt like a gift.

Today it's hard to walk on a city street, ride a bus, or board an airplane without seeing people hunched over their iPhones or playing games on their iPads. There is some competition for these products from Samsung, Nokia, Amazon, and Microsoft, but as with Harley-Davidson, these are often seen as substitutes for the real thing. The entire industry measures itself against Apple, much the way the motorcycle industry looks to Harley-Davidson. The brand with the religion becomes the barometer. No surprise, then, that by June 30, 2015, Apple was the largest publicly traded corporation in the world by market capitalization.

Tesla is a third, more recent example. Like Steve Jobs, Elon Musk understood that a good product is not enough; you have to provide the infrastructure to make it a mass-market success. That is why the company has committed so many resources to building supercharging stations across the globe, and why *Consumer Reports* published an "Owner Satisfaction Survey" in January 2017 that showed that 91 percent of owners would buy a Tesla again. As the author of the article, Matthew DeBord, noted: "That's an astounding figure in a highly competitive industry. It's like a Major League Baseball player batting .900." I am one of those owners, having recently completed a two-thousand-mile trip from Jackson Hole, Wyoming, to Atlanta, Georgia. Every time I stopped to recharge, I plugged the car in, grabbed a cup of coffee or lunch, and after about forty-five minutes was back in the car. I am more than a customer; I am an evangelist.

I have been fascinated by brand religion during my entire business career. The companies that achieve it build a loyal base of customers and rarely follow conventional marketing practices such as running television commercials or investing in print advertisements. Instead they depend on a whole slew of evangelists to promote their product. This was Caribou Coffee—but the company had not yet reached its potential. The employees knew they had a great product, but they did not yet understand how deeply committed their customers were to it. They were a brand religion, and if we could tap into that evangelical spirit, the company could soar. We could not undermine the core business proposition—sell a great cup of coffee in a welcoming environment. We had to enhance it.

14

Fifty Percent to Go

Who the hell is
this guy?

I knew from my years in business that times change, but success does not. A lot of companies lose sight of what brought them to the dance in the first place. They become different companies from what made them successful, which ultimately means they won't grow. I believe in expanding only as quickly as a company can maintain the quality of its brand. This sounds so simple. It is, but that is not what companies tend to do as new CEOs and bright young executives come on board and want to make their marks by changing things. Successful companies know what they do really well, so they do more of it. But they also know what they do not do well. So they simply stop entertaining the distractions.

While I was preparing my report for Charlie Ogburn, I realized that I had made the consultant's fatal mistake—I fell in love with the company. I knew there was something special about Caribou, and I also knew that their success could not depend on just selling a good cup of coffee. From my early days with Irving through my time running Great American Cookies, if there was one thing I knew about, it was customer experience.

The company had to figure out how to perfect that experience and implement it in every store during every single transaction.

In September 2002 I came back to Charlie and said, "This is a really good company. I am amazed by the brand loyalty, and I think it can do incredible things. I feel so strongly about this that I want to buy into Caribou and go to Minneapolis to run it." Charlie was really taken aback. He said, "Let's talk about it." Over the next few months we discussed the terms of my involvement, and in January 2003 I walked into Caribou Coffee as the new interim CEO. My children were grown, so it was easier for Donna and me to think about commuting between Atlanta and Minneapolis while I turned my attention to coffee.

I signed a contract for a hundred-day commitment and agreed that at some point during that time we would decide whether the move would be permanent. When I left Atlanta, it was 65 degrees. The following morning, when I walked out of the Marriott in downtown Minneapolis, it was two below zero. It felt like twenty below. Just as I pushed out of the revolving door, my cell phone rang. One of my golfing buddies from Atlanta was calling to say, "Hey, we've got three, do you want to be the fourth for golf today?" Standing outside the hotel freezing even in my overcoat, hat, and gloves, I said, "I told you a couple of days ago that I was going to Minneapolis." He laughed and said, "Yeah, we know." They had looked up the temperature that morning and called just to make me a little crazy.

I knew before I even started at Caribou that my Goliath was Starbucks. We had 207 stores; they had more than 6,500 locations around the world. Founded in 1971 in Seattle, they had experienced explosive growth without much challenge. But we had a better product. We saw ourselves as a Wendy's who came into the marketplace behind McDonald's and Burger King. Wendy's would put their restaurants close to other fast-food outlets and then offer different, fresher, or healthier fare, like a salad bar or baked potato. I did not fear Starbucks, and we were not trying to slay the company. On the contrary, we needed Starbucks to do well. When we built the cookie business in 1977, one of the toughest things that we had to do was start selling cookies in the mall when customers had no experience with the concept. These are called pioneer markets. For the first ten years of the Great American Cookie Company, a lot of communities had never seen a cookie store. That was not the case with coffee because Starbucks had paved the way. As journalist Bruce Horovitz noted in a May 19, 2006, article in *USA Today*, "Starbucks changed what we eat. It's altering where and when we work and play. It's shaping how we spend time and money." I got into the coffee business because of the market that they created. We just wanted to give customers a better product and a much different experience.

When I arrived at Caribou, the company was stalled. For more than two years, same-store sales had declined. I mistakenly thought that upon my arrival the management team were going to carry me around on their shoulders like an Olympic god. I would be the white knight, here to save the day. I could not have been more wrong. It was like the pot holder story from the cookie company all over again. I was totally unprepared for how I was received—and it is always the unexpected that gets you in the end. I knew that Caribou was a very good company, but good was keeping it from being great. The management team feared that I would come in and change their culture. My mission was to protect and enhance the culture of the company and capitalize on Caribou's brand religion, but they did not know that. And I did not do myself any favors on my first day.

In the week leading up to my move to Minneapolis to take the helm at Caribou, I prepared what I was going to say to my leadership team. During my short visit in the fall, I was shown around the building and saw that they had no dress code. Most employees were dressed pretty casually— not business casual but softball casual. (I used to joke, "If you could wear what you have on to play softball, it is too casual.") This was casual Friday gone off the rails. I knew that one of the things I had to accomplish was to create a more business-oriented attitude. So I made the decision to show up in a three-piece suit. I deliberately wore something disruptive, out of place. I was not trying to fit in. If we were going to turn this ship around, I had to signal at the outset that we were all in for some dramatic changes. I knew my clothes would be a shock, and that was my goal. This was like the cookie company in 1984 and 1985—Caribou needed a revolution.

So with my new team all gathered in the conference room, I launched into my opening remarks: "I've been to more than fifty Caribou stores, and I have yet to have a great experience."

Now, that was true. But if I had to do it over again, I would have phrased it differently. What I meant was that the best of the stores were incredible, but even they were not serving their customers as well as they could. And the difference—going from good to great—was going to be the key to our success.

As you can imagine, this did not go over well. I could almost see what was playing in everyone's head: "Who the hell is this guy?" It was written all over their faces. They saw me as the new CEO who was going to come in and change everything. And the first sentence out of my mouth confirmed all of their worst fears. After that opening remark, nobody was listening. I could tell that some of them had already made up their mind. I was the interim CEO, and they were just going to wait me out until the permanent CEO was found who would be their real leader.

I finished the meeting, but I knew I had failed to communicate a "we can do it together" message. To make matters even worse, I had inadvertently created a new Goliath. Not only did I have to find a way to take Caribou from good to great, but I had to persuade my leadership team to join me. What I thought would be the easy part became a completely new challenge. So I needed to try something else, and fast.

Over the next week, I completed dozens of interviews with the entire management team. I invited them to tell me about themselves, their job, what they thought was good about the company, what they thought could be improved, and what should change immediately. At the end of those few days, one thing that was clear—the people who worked at Caribou loved the company. They loved the brand and the product, but they were frustrated by the company's inability to inspire in other markets the fierce customer loyalty they had in Minneapolis. The company certainly wanted to do well financially, but they also felt an evangelical desire to bring this great product to more people. It didn't take me long to figure out that my leadership team was blinded by their good, and I needed them to see what I had seen during my store visits—the possibility of being great.

This was new ground for me, because I had never stepped into becoming CEO of an existing company. I had not built Caribou, it was not my concept, and I had not hired a single person. They did not know me or understand my vision. Instead of motivating them, I had alienated them and reinforced their sense that I was going to alter the company's culture. After the staff interviews, I realized that we needed a retreat to create a new mission statement and a core set of values together. I felt that if we could bring everyone in a room together, we would build consensus and walk away with the same marching orders. So on the first Saturday that I was at the helm, I brought in a facilitator to work with us at the Marriott where I was staying.

Because of my poor first impression, I am sure that nobody was thrilled to spend a Saturday with me, away from their friends and family. It was disruptive, and I was still trying to be as disruptive as I could be. That is why I wore the suit on the first day, and that's why we held the retreat. We locked ourselves away in a beautiful conference room with floor-to-ceiling windows, and I drew the shades so nobody would be distracted by the scenery. From 8 a.m. to 3 p.m., we pounded away at a new mission and core value statement. The previous mission—"Caribou Coffee: Create the Best Neighborhood Meeting Place"—was nice, but generic. It could have been the mission statement for any area bar or restaurant chain, and it did not tell customers anything about our product or service. After seven hours we had not reached any conclusions, but we had made progress, so I pulled together a subcommittee of five people and charged them to continue working on it. I flew back to Atlanta the following Monday. When I called in to the office on Wednesday to find out the results of Tuesday's subcommittee meeting, the chair I had appointed told me that the team had decided that the old mission statement was "just fine."

I realized that my vision was not penetrating the group. My approach was not working. So without losing my temper, I asked to be connected to Karen McBride, the head of human resources. During my staff interviews, I had recognized that Karen and several others of the senior staff understood what I was trying to do. So I called her, not because she was the head of human resources, but because she was one of the longest-serving team members in the company. She was very well respected, knew what changes needed to be made, and became a very strong ally. She had attended the Saturday retreat, and I filled her in on the results of the sub-committee meeting. Then I asked her to assemble a different group of five people willing to take a second look at the mission. She did, and two days later the group came up with "Caribou Coffee: An Experience That Makes the Day Better." Caribou was not just about coffee—it was about warmth, friendship, and camaraderie. The new mission statement accomplished everything we needed. It communicated something about the experience of customers, employees, and vendors. It spoke to the fact that we were selling not just a commodity but an experience. Now I had at least six people who understood my vision.

In order to get additional key stakeholders on board, I arranged a field trip. I gathered ten members of my leadership team and asked them to pick ten stores in Minneapolis to visit. These were directors and senior directors who were mostly on the fence. They were not opposed to change; they just hadn't yet embraced its necessity. In each store, I wanted them to watch how orders were taken, what happened behind the counter, what customer engagement looked like, and how the product was served. By the time we got to the third store, the differences were really obvious. But we kept going. Then I asked the team to pick one Starbucks store to visit. At Starbucks they saw cleanliness, efficiency, and a warm interaction between customers and employees. They looked at the Starbucks and saw the way each store was carefully organized, but mostly they noticed the professionalism of the staff. After these visits, I asked them a single question, a variation on the one I had asked at the cookie company years before: "If we were going to start a coffee company today, what would you do to compete with Caribou?" That really got them thinking. After a robust discussion, I closed with: "Starbucks is doing the Caribou experience better than we are. If we can do those things and serve a better, hand-crafted product, we will win."

That was when I started to get their attention. I had been there fewer than thirty days and had won over about half of my leadership team. Fifty percent down, fifty to go.

15 This Is the Battlefield

Growing a business is not really that complicated. It's about figuring out what you do really well and doing more of it.

While interim CEO at Caribou, I did a deep dive into the coffee business. I had learned quite a bit about the commodity over the years, but mostly from the perspective of a consumer. I was aware that there were different roasting techniques and different varieties of beans in both the arabica and robusta types. But I wanted a fuller understanding of sourcing, picking, and processing. In my second month on the job, Chad Trewick, the company's Director of Coffee and Tea, asked me to visit a coffee plantation. Caribou was the only coffee shop in the United States to offer the rare La Minita Peaberry from the Hacienda La Minita in Costa Rica.

Coffee seeds, commonly called beans, are the seed of the *Coffea* plant. The pit inside the red or purple fruit is often referred to as a cherry. Peaberries occur naturally when a coffee pit develops into one coffee cherry instead of two, thus soaking up more flavor. This aberration is what makes them so rich and delicious. There is some automation in the industry, but most great coffees are handpicked because the bushes grow on mountainsides. Coffee seeds do not all ripen at the same time, so workers often have to visit the same bush five or six times. You need hand speed and a very good eye to do well in this industry—a bushel of beans should all be about the same color. Workers get scolded if there is too much variation in their baskets, because the seeds cannot ripen off the bush. If seeds are picked too early, they have to be thrown away. Once picked, they undergo an elaborate process to transform them from berry to bean. Peaberries get extra attention, as they have to be hand sorted from the other beans at the processing plants. The coffee is then sold directly to companies all over the world, who rely on importers to handle the shipping.

My visit to the plantation in February 2003 was truly eye-opening. I wanted to understand the whole process if I was going to lead the company. I went into the hills and picked the red berries one by one, learning firsthand how hard the work was. I went into the factory to see how the beans were processed. I really came to appreciate the skill and dedication of the workers. To this day, if I drop a coffee bean on the floor, I pick it up, because I know how much work went into getting it. I returned from my trip to Costa Rica energized. My leadership team was starting to coalesce around the new mission and core value statements that we created in my first month, and I felt like we were poised to take some important next steps on our way from good to great.

I was well aware that gourmet coffee—like gourmet cookies—is an expensive product that nobody needs. Why would someone spend two or three dollars on something they could easily make at home for pennies a cup? In order to run this company well, I had to understand the market and its potential for growth. The Specialty Coffee Association of America, a trade group for the industry, tracked its growth and reported that there were 1,650 specialty coffee shops in 1991 and 31,490 in 2016. In 2000, three years before I joined Caribou, the specialty coffee market was a $4.7 billion business. Two years after I became permanent CEO, it would blossom to $9.6 billion.

Creating a great experience at Great American Cookies was difficult, because customers walked up to the counter, ordered, paid for their merchandise, and were gone. Our employees had about a minute to engage the customers, serve them a good product, and try to encourage them to purchase something like a cookie cake in the near future. Caribou was different—we had at least five minutes from the time they ordered their drink until they were served. And many customers lingered in the stores, reading the newspaper, checking their email, and meeting with friends and colleagues. The first thing I realized was that employees needed to learn customers' names. If you couldn't learn the name, learn the DNA (Drink Normally Asked for). I might not immediately be able to recall the name Sue, but I knew my medium skim latte when she walked in the door. This type of engagement created the "Hey, Norm!" moment from the popular television sitcom *Cheers*. I came up with the acronym; my wife Donna created the definition.

The Caribou mission that was created by a subcommittee of directors and adopted by the company in my first month as interim CEO, "An Experience That Makes the Day Better," became the raw material for a customer-centric equation that I still use in my businesses today. If the mission was about all of the people involved in the company—employees, vendors, and customers—the equation was solely about the customer. It would help us deliver the Caribou experience in every store, every time.

$$P + E + S = Ef$$

This stood for Product + Environment + Service = the Experience factor. I had not taken algebra since high school, but I knew that if you change any one variable in an equation, the result will not be the same. I explained it to my team in this way: If you serve a great product, offer warm and friendly customer service, and have dirty counters or restrooms, you are not offering a superior customer experience. If you have a clean store, a great product, and terrible service, again your equation will yield an inferior result. If this happens with new customers, they will not come back. Existing customers might be more forgiving, but if the problems persist, they will stop coming as well. Brand religion will carry you only so far. All three elements are critical—skimping on any one of them undermines the experience factor. So we had to make sure the equation was working in every store, with every transaction.

The new mission and equation were important, but I still faced a lot of resistance from my leadership team. I held regular meetings at the company headquarters in Minneapolis that included senior directors and directors. At some point during every meeting, someone would say something like "Yes, that's a great idea, but how do we compete against Starbucks? They have thousands of stores, are a publicly traded company, and have endless financial resources." I heard a version of that comment at least a thousand times, and it always stopped the team in their tracks. Just when I thought I was making progress, it would creep into the conversation, often at the end of the meeting, chilling the team's morale. It did not matter what had been discussed before the comment was made, it just wiped out all of our good work. So one day I reached my breaking point.

I got up from my chair and walked up to a whiteboard at the front of the room with a marker in my hand. I am not typically one to use a whiteboard, so this got my team's attention. I faced the board and slowly erased everything we had just put on it. I very deliberately took a long time to wipe away all of our hard work, one swipe at a time. Then I drew two boxes with a line down the center like this:

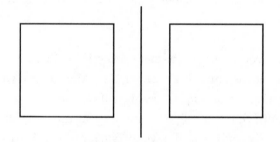

I turned to the group and asked: "Do you know what this is?"

They all stared at me blankly, like deer—better yet, caribou—in the headlights.

"The line in the middle is the road," I said. "The box on the right is Caribou, and the box on the left is Starbucks. This is the battlefield. It's all about which way the customers will turn. If we give them a great experience, they will turn right into our parking lot. If we don't, they'll turn left into our competition's lot. At this moment, the battle is about these two locations. Nobody makes the decision about whether to go to Starbucks because they are a publicly traded company or because they have thousands of stores. We can figure out how to get them to come to us the first time. We can offer buy-one-get-one-free deals and other promotions. But it is all about the experience they had the last time they were at Caribou. This is the battle we face. If we win on this battlefield every day with every customer, we win. It doesn't matter if you're in the coffee business, the cookie business, the doctor business, the banking business, or the lawyer business. You have to find a way to bring your customer back. For us, the secret is the formula P + E + S = Ef. In this war, we are the speedboat and Starbucks is the battleship. We are fresh and nimble; they are huge and corporate. We have a better product; we are creating a better experience. If we do this right, we win."

And winning was all about execution. Now I had a new mission statement, a customer-centric equation, and a battleship metaphor that made sense to the senior management. How were we going to translate that to the Caribou employees in the stores who engaged every day with our customers? How were we going to execute these changes?

One part of execution involved good training—and that was where I began. The new training platform had to be built around the customer experience formula. Deb Jones, director of training at Caribou, was an invaluable ally. She illustrated her approach with this story:

"If you want to get your child to clean her room, you can tell her, 'Before you leave the house, you have to clean your room.' She will go to the room and come back a short while later and declare it clean. When you go to look at it, it is not what you consider clean. Now, you can argue with your child all day long, and you will never get a clean room. What you really need to do is go upstairs and clean the room one time yourself. Then take a picture of the clean room and show it to your child to illustrate what you have in mind. Only then will she fully comprehend what you mean."

So instead of lecturing our employees about the components of great customer service, we decided to show them. We made a three-and-a-half-minute video called "The Caribou Experience." Our marketing department wanted to hire professional actors, but Deb and I insisted that we use real employees and customers. We surmised, correctly, that employees wanted to see real people talking about things that mattered to them. I knew from my visits to more than fifty stores when I was serving as a consultant for Crescent Capital that there were a handful of stores that were doing the Caribou experience well. But I let Deb pick the stores and staff and customers to participate, because she knew them better than anyone else. We used the acronym BAMA to guide the video production:

Be excellent, not average;
Act with urgency;
Make a connection; and
Anticipate needs.

Deb's team was very good, and she put Samantha Viede, who had just completed her master's degree in communications, in charge of the video project. We hired a small production company run by a husband and wife, and Deb worked with them to shoot more than twenty hours of video. They didn't work from a script, but rather let the staff and customers talk about what was important to them. As the filming progressed, it became clear that they were all talking about the great things that were happening in our best stores. When Deb finally showed me the film, I was caught off guard. At only three and a half minutes, I thought it was too short, but she had me watch it a few more times, and I realized that it was just right. It encapsulated everything we were trying to do.

The first fifty-one seconds of the video show an upbeat montage filled with smiling faces, lively banter, and warmth—all examples of how Caribou employees greet customers. The staff members are crisply dressed in black aprons (which we had not yet launched company-wide) and seem to be really enjoying their work. The screen goes dark, and text appears:

At Caribou Coffee we are committed to creating an experience that makes the day better. For every guest. On every visit. What is the Caribou Experience?

The remaining two and a half minutes offers small vignettes illustrating specific ways that employees might help make the day better. There is no omniscient narrator, just staff members and customers talking about what it is like to walk through the doors of a Caribou store.

The first employee says, "When they come to Caribou, they're not just looking for a great cup of coffee. They're looking for an experience." We had not yet rolled out our new mission statement to the stores, and she just nailed it.

The rest of the segments are variations on the same theme. A customer explains, "I love the workers here, they are so friendly, they make you feel so welcome. Every time you come, it's like you're at home."

Another employee echoes the sentiment about why customers come. "They're coming in for a sense of community."

Yet another describes the store's atmosphere. "We've all created this giant living room with a stone fireplace, and we're just here to make everybody enjoy their day."

And a customer gives an example of stellar service: "They have actually brought me my drink out in the parking lot when I got a cell phone call. I am standing out there pacing around talking, and Tony brings me a drink and says, 'Here, you seem busy.'" Note that the customer says, "Tony brings me a drink." This is not some nameless employee, it is his friend Tony.

How many companies today would give their eyeteeth to have a customer remember an employee's name! The vignette involving Tony is not about the employee remembering the customer's name, it's the other way around. It's about the customer making a connection to the employee—and it shows a real bond. I dared Starbucks to take this customer away from us. It was not going to happen if the formula was followed. I remembered what my mentor Irving Settler used to say: "Nobody owns a customer. They don't have a contract with you. You have to constantly earn their loyalty." Anyone watching the training video could see that Caribou was the coffee version of *Cheers*—without the beer and with a whole lot more caffeine.

When I arrived at Caribou, the company's same-store sales were down by double digits. A month after introducing the video and BAMA, we hit positive sales figures for the first time in two and a half years. On the first day of my job, I knew I wanted to stay and lead the company—I wanted to be "Head Bou," as I came to call my position. For each of the hundred days I served as interim, I jumped out of bed energized to turn this company around. I showed up in the dark each morning and left in the evening when it was dark. This was such a big challenge, but I knew we could do it. To be sure, not everyone was happy. Some Caribou employees called Crescent Capital to complain. They did not want change. Change is tough for any company—it's easy to talk about and very hard to do.

During my first hundred days, Crescent hired an executive search firm to find a permanent CEO. Near the end of my contract, I received a call from the headhunters asking me to come to New York for an interview. I told them, "I've been here almost a hundred days, and if that's not a long enough interview, pick someone else. I'm not coming to New York. If I only have a few days left, I need to be in Minneapolis finishing up the work that I was hired to do." And I hung up.

After that call, I made plans to finish out my term and return home. I called Charlie and said, "I've completed all of the deliverables we agreed to and more, and my hundred days are about finished. My plan is to move back to Atlanta."

He said, "No decision has been made about the permanent CEO, so please stay for another thirty days."

And I replied, "I'm not doing it. There has been too much noise about whether I was staying or going, and if I'm not going to be permanent CEO, you need to bring in someone to stabilize the company and implement what we've been able to accomplish in the last hundred days, or it will fall apart. This is a really good company. The team is excited, and they need strong leadership. All of this uncertainty is not good for morale, and it's making it difficult to do the work that needs to be done. Some of the employees who do not want to see the changes implemented are hoping they can wait out my hundred days. The company deserves stability. It's time for Crescent to make a decision. Either we come to terms now, or I'm gone."

Charlie said, "Okay, come back to Atlanta, and we'll talk."

Over the next month we came to terms and, along with a group of friends, I bought into the company. In June, I became a shareholder, chairman, CEO, and, most important, "Head Bou."

Donna and I had been living in the Marriott in Minneapolis, so we started looking for a more permanent residence. We stayed in the hotel for another few months and eventually bought a condominium a block from one of the downtown Caribou stores. I had accomplished a lot in the first hundred days, but now the real work began. Execution was going to be my main task, and the hardest one of all. I had to figure out how to turn the company around and move it toward greatness.

While working on transforming Caribou, I read a number of business books to hone my thinking about what the company needed. None was more helpful than *Execution: The Discipline of Getting Things Done*, by Larry Bossidy and Ram Charan. First published in 2002, it became my bible. I distributed copies to my leadership team, and we constantly referred back to its core message. We held a one-day retreat to discuss the book, because I wanted to make sure everyone understood its core message. I had been telling them much of what the book said, but I knew they needed to hear it from another source. Bossidy and Charan start with a simple question: Why were forty CEOs of top companies such as Aetna, Hewlett-Packard, Compaq, and Xerox recently fired? Why did these smart, capable people fail to produce results? In trying to provide answers, the authors realized that execution bridges the gap between what leaders try to achieve and their company's ability to deliver it.

Bossidy and Charan explain that most companies make a mistake when they assume that execution is a single event, not an ongoing process. It is not something to be delegated to vice presidents and directors while the CEO is working on "bigger" issues. Execution is the "big issue." It has to become part of a company's DNA. It has to touch every aspect of the company or organization, from mission, strategy, and values to hiring, product development, production, sales, and service. Execution has to live inside the company, permeating its cultural fabric, and thus motivating employees constantly to seek ways to improve.

A key component of execution is careful communication. Most companies try to make major changes while failing to adequately explain the reasons. That is a death sentence. That is why my comment about not having a good experience at any of the fifty Caribou stores on my first day fell on deaf ears—I was not communicating well. Companies also fail to understand the role that part-time and hourly employees play in their success. The future of the company is often in the hands of these front-line employees, and if they do not understand why the change is happening, they won't buy into it. It will fail. If the employee is uncertain, the customer suffers. When the customer suffers, the bottom line suffers. Dissatisfaction and confusion are contagious, often wreaking havoc on morale and efficiency.

In *Execution*, Bossidy and Charan begin by focusing on a trio of fundamentals. First, execution is a discipline that depends on the three core processes of people, strategy, and operations. Second, the successful CEO has the main responsibility for running those three processes. Third, execution must be built into the company's reward system and be part of the everyday culture.

CEOs need to have essential behaviors that will help make them successful in the aforementioned processes. They must know every aspect of their business—a lesson that I learned early on from my mentor Irving and from the first two companies I started, Pant-O-Mine and Great American Clothing. Leaders must be realistic and never shy away from admitting mistakes. They must have the ability to set a few clear, measurable goals and priorities and stick to them. They must follow through—avoiding the old trap of overpromising and underdelivering. A good leader gives clear directions, so when subordinates leave a meeting, they all understand their homework. Good leaders should reward employees who are doers in meaningful ways, through either bonuses, new opportunities, or promotions; this helps inspire others to follow their example. Leaders must also understand their role as a coach to help grow the company's capabilities. Finally, good leaders must know themselves and be honest, tolerant, and authentic.

These were all lessons I had learned in my career. I also soon learned that when you become CEO of a company, there is no longer any such thing as an off-the-cuff comment. Whatever you say to someone in an elevator, or in casual conversation, is taken to heart and passed along to others. If you look at the carpet and remark that the color shows dirt, the carpet will likely be a different color the next time you walk into the room.

All companies are reflections of the personalities and beliefs of their leadership. Just like the patriarch or matriarch of a large family, the words

of whoever is on top set a tone that resonates throughout the organization. If the boss is cynical and self-absorbed, negativity tends to hang
over everyone who works for that person daily. If the boss is upbeat and
enthusiastic, the enthusiasm is infectious. The personalities of the workers become a reflection of the attitudes and personality of the boss. Like
all CEOs, I wanted to use my position to build a better company. The old
saying "It is lonely at the top" is true only if the CEO wants it that way. A
good leader is the band director, if you will, of the culture that drives the
company. Whatever the company believes in—its culture, its good and bad
habits—are always driven from the top.

Our company had a heart, and it was something I really wanted to
showcase. One of Caribou's traditions, started in 1999, was a good example. We had a product called Amy's Blend that was sold each spring and
fall as a tribute to a wonderful employee who died of breast cancer. It was
a great program, but it was not well coordinated. I was determined to
expand its reach and thus extend Amy's legacy. So we committed to donating 10 percent of the sales of the coffee and merchandise related to the
blend to cancer research (today it goes to CancerCare). I also persuaded
the Coca-Cola Company to match our donation. So each year, customers
would anticipate the product, connect to the story behind it, and see their
purchase as a small step toward helping those facing cancer. That was part
of the reason why Caribou had such devout followers.

Bossidy and Charan go on to say that most CEOs put virtually all of their
time into budgeting, strategic planning, and financial monitoring and
very little time into talent development. I learned the lesson about cultivating talent while building Great American Cookies. In 1978 the cookie
company was growing. Arthur and I were still not taking a salary, but
we really needed to hire a district operations manager. We calculated the
salary we could afford to pay and ran an advertisement in the newspaper.
We had a number of applicants, but no really strong candidates. Then we
got a call from Tom Lynch. Tom had served in a similar position for a company called Burger Chef, a fast-food company founded in Indianapolis
in 1954. He had a lot of experience running multiunit stores, and he was
impressive. But his salary requirement was double what we could afford.

So Arthur and I talked about it, and I said, "We have to hire this guy. If we are really going to grow, this is who we need." So we agreed to forgo our salaries for a little longer and hire Tom.

We were lucky enough to find Tom even before we needed him. Most companies fail because they hire for the moment, not for the future. They also view employee salaries as expenses, not as capital investments. Human capital is as important as any building or piece of machinery. If you make the right hiring decisions and select job candidates who have the ability to get things done—to execute—then you will make a big return on your investment. Tom was a game changer for the cookie company. Without even realizing it, I had practiced what Bossidy and Charan preached. I did not delegate the responsibility of finding the right person and putting him in the right place. And it made all the difference.

When Tom came to the cookie company, we were still pulling ourselves up by our bootstraps. Tom's expertise would help us minimize our mistakes. With Tom, we would not forget the pot holders. He would prevent us from making a fatal error. The pot holder story from our opening day could have been the end of our business. Jeff Weil, the manager of Perimeter Mall, could have walked up and said, "You guys are done." He would have been within his rights to terminate our lease.

Tom Lynch became a metaphor for how to grow a company. When I started Pant-O-Mine, I did not have enough people around me who knew more than I did about specific aspects of the business. By the time we hired Tom at the cookie company, I had learned to listen to and respect a range of experts who did not shy from sharing hard truths about what was important or necessary. When I came to Caribou, Tom Lynch symbolized my philosophy about hiring. I no longer looked for people who were like me or who made me comfortable. I looked for people who understood the business and could execute.

The rest of Bossidy and Charan's book is focused on the three processes—people, strategy, and operations. It ends with a "Letter to a New Leader" that asks a series of questions I had often faced in my career: How well do you know your organization? Are you among like-minded people in your new job? Do people embrace reality and engage in constructive debates? Are business leaders driving the strategy process, or has it been delegated to nerdy, isolated planning types? You have a budget, but do you have the action plan the budget should represent?

While reading their book, I came across the concept of the Execution Triangle, which echoed many of the observations that Bossidy and Charan detailed. This model was pioneered by a Boston consulting company called the Rhythm of Business. The triangle has three elements: skill set, tool set, and mind-set. Most companies are good at the first one. They do fairly well at finding people who have relevant skill sets for their industry. The problem comes when they put people with good skills in the wrong job—they are talented but cannot execute well. That is a trap. You want to be loyal, but you have to be careful not to place someone in a position to fail. Then you end up concluding that there is something wrong with the product or process rather than the person implementing it.

The tool set is equally important—you need a way to measure success and the right tools at your disposal to do it. In retail, this might involve upgrading point-of-sale software.

The most important element of the Execution Triangle, though, is mind-set. If you don't explain the contemplated change, process, or product in a way that gives your employees or leadership team a clear understanding of its importance and value, they will not support it. You have to lay out why it's good for them, why it's good for the customer and the company, and how it makes their job better or easier. Mind-set is the least expensive and easiest thing to address, but often the most neglected.

16

Service, Service, Service

The customer has told you what we need to do.

With all the pieces in place, it was time to dig into the company and find out what was working at Caribou Coffee and what needed to be improved or changed. The product was the one area that did not need much attention—it was terrific when I arrived. Caribou was already doing four things to create a great cup of coffee. The first was sourcing: Caribou was already using the highest-grade Arabica coffee beans. The company also had artisan roast masters in place who were creating smooth and tasty blends. They craft-roasted in small batches to optimize flavor. And the company used the latest valve technologies to prevent oxygen from draining the flavor from the coffee. I did nothing to change the product; it was a key part of the brand religion and did not need adjustment. My issue was presentation and consistency.

I implemented a set of protocols for brewing in the stores that ensured high standards and a strict freshness policy. Product quality was a key issue that the training platform addressed. At first, there was lot of variation in how employees prepared our products and presented them to the customer. As I did at the cookie company, I had the training team put Caribou employees on the customer's side of the counter and make them look at each latte, iced drink, or cappuccino that was served. What was appealing and what was not? We sold an expensive product, a luxury product even, and it was not being given consistent enough love and attention. Even with the best coffee beans, you can still serve a bad cup of coffee.

When I joined Caribou, cold coffee drinks were gaining in popularity. One afternoon while visiting a store, I was standing behind the counter when a customer ordered a small iced latte. I watched our employee make it and pass it over the counter in its 12-ounce cup. The customer looked at it with a puzzled expression on her face for about a minute. I came around the counter to ask her, "Is this the first time you've ordered this?"

She said, "Yes."

"I noticed that you were looking at it kind of funny," I continued.

"Yes, well, there's certainly not much there. Just a few sips, and it's gone," she replied.

And she was right. We served drinks of 12, 16, and 20 ounces, and the 12-ounce was really too small for iced drinks. So I suggested that we remove it from the menu and change the "small" to 16 ounces.

At first my marketing team said, "If we eliminate it, we'll have to start our price point at sixteen ounces. That will be higher than Starbucks."

To which I replied, "What's your point? Why do we have to be the same as Starbucks? Should they drive our every decision? If we are going to be successful, we should not mirror Starbucks. We have our own identity, and we need to do what's best for our customers." The marketing team also wanted to name the new 24-ounce drink "extra large," but I balked because of the negative connotations of that term.

The marketing team suggested that we do a two-week test in ten Minneapolis area stores. I never thought conventional market testing was very useful, at least not the way it was typically done. A lot of companies test a product without having a clear purpose. You have to test for a specific outcome. If you don't, then you end up with vague conclusions that don't help the company very much. And you've wasted time and money. The good thing about working in the food industry is that testing is pretty straightforward—you take a product to the customers and let them tell you whether they like it or not. The team wanted to test whether the customers still wanted the 12-ounce size, but I insisted that we test only drinks of 16, 20, and 24 ounces and call them "small," "medium," and "large." Even if a few customers wanted to keep the 12-ounce drink, the majority of customers thought it was not a good value, so we risked disappointing them every time we sold one. And most customers won't speak up, they just won't come back.

Jeremy Kugel, an energetic young man in marketing, ran the test on the iced drinks and came back with overwhelming results that the customers loved the change to the larger size. They did not complain about the price or miss the smaller size. Still our marketing team were afraid to roll it out. They weren't giving our customers enough credit for understanding that while our starting price was higher, the drink was also larger. It was like the cookie cake testing we did while I was at Great American Cookies all over again. You have to listen to your customers; sometimes they know better than you do. I finally intervened and said, "Guys, the customer has told you what we need to do. We tested it. If we don't follow through, then we're not giving the customers what they have told us they want. And they won't come back." So we ordered the new 24-ounce cups and kept the 12-ounce ones, though that size was removed from the menu. And not a single customer complained.

Environment, the second variable in the customer-centric equation, was my next area of focus. Because Caribou had no dress code in the stores, the employees did not look professional, and this reflected on the product they were serving. There was nothing wrong with being casual and friendly—that was a hallmark of Caribou's culture. But casual that bordered on sloppy was not acceptable. So we started a dress code. Employees could wear black, denim, or khaki pants or skirts that did not have holes or tears in them. They could wear white, brown, or black shirts. T-shirts, at least at first, were not permitted unless they had a Caribou logo. When you are trying to address an issue or solve a problem, sometimes you have to overreact. This was about changing the mind-set of each employee, and if they had to wake up each morning and think about what they were going to wear, I had succeeded.

The dress code went over fairly well, but the introduction of the black apron with the Caribou logo was much more controversial. This was the one change I made that employees pushed back against. They felt it was too much like Starbucks, just too corporate. But it was an important change that projected efficiency, cleanliness, and professionalism. I did not want to change our culture, but rather preserve and enhance it across the company. If we were going to be better than our biggest competitor, we could not just be about a cup of coffee.

The décor of the stores was popular, making you feel that you had escaped to the mountains, so it didn't require many changes. We updated it, but we kept the lodge-like feeling that so many customers loved. None of our competitors had fireplaces at that time, and I was always amazed by how popular they were. When we opened our stores in the Middle East later during my tenure, we would see customers come in from 100-plus-degree heat to sit by the fireplace. Caribou really was a way to escape from your everyday life, even if for just a few minutes.

The final variable in the equation, service, had the most immediate and broadest impact on the company. Conventional wisdom holds that the key to success in real estate and business is location, location, location. I would argue that in business it is really service, service, service. It is always less expensive to keep an existing customer than to try to find a new one. And service is the key to transforming customers into evangelists for your company. They will not only remain loyal to you, they will bring you more customers.

Good service depends on good hiring practices—finding the right employees for the right jobs. I spent a lot of time hiring dedicated people who embraced the Caribou vision. We looked for people with talent, positive attitudes, and a passion for customer service. Store managers underwent an eight-week training program in which we used the video, the BAMA platform, the customer-centric equation ($P + E + S = Ef$), and the mission and core value statements to paint a realistic picture of what the company was and what we expected from them. We knew that for the changes to become part of the company culture, we needed a deep, well-trained management bench that could continue to grow.

With a few exceptions, I implemented all of these changes with the leadership team I inherited in 2003. I made some adjustments and reworked the organizational chart to add a vice presidential level, but most of the core people stayed in place. I wanted to convey that they each played a part in the company's success, and I wanted their titles to reflect their level of responsibility. To help the directors and senior directors continue to grow, I offered a range of professional development opportunities such as management training, coaching, and mentoring. All of these initiatives were available to hourly employees, store managers, and the leadership team.

My laser focus on product, environment, and service in the first year helped the company soar. After I became CEO, and for the next thirty months, we ran double-digit increases in same-store sales. The leadership team that was so hesitant when I arrived in January of 2003 now was really on board. It was especially gratifying to me that, with few exceptions, we made all of these changes with the existing management team. They were a very talented group—all I had to do was let the genie out of the bottle. Now we had to focus on execution. My perfectionist tendencies came in handy in this phase. At first I was probably micromanaging the changes related to product, environment, and service much more than I would once everything was in place. But there was not one detail in this turnaround that I wanted to leave to chance. I could not "forget the pot holders" until our execution was perfect.

With Great American Cookies, I started the business from scratch. With Caribou, I was asked to expand an existing business. Smart growth would be my mantra. It was my plan to build 50 new stores before December, and over the next four years I wanted us to go from 200 to 500 stores. When I took over, the company was in about a dozen major markets. I was hired to expand beyond that level into states like Colorado, Nebraska, and Iowa and into the Northeast. Opening new stores was a challenge. Each new store cost between $300,000 and $400,000, and it typically employed fifteen people. The biggest hurdle we faced was finding the right locations.

I was hired to grow the company, and I quickly realized that this was not just about new store locations. We needed to create a national brand for the company. There were plenty of untapped opportunities for new business channels—selling packaged coffee to grocery chains, airlines, offices, and big-box retailers, franchising, and licensing. But we could not even consider these avenues until we centralized our operations. This created a facilities challenge, and here I drew upon my experience at Great American Cookies. Just as I had learned to hire for the future at the cookie company, at Caribou I needed to build for the future. We had a main support center in downtown Minneapolis and three auxiliary roasting facilities. Our coffee team kept suggesting renting additional buildings, but that just posed more problems than it solved. We were roasting our beans at several offsite locations and transporting them back to our main location for packaging and delivery to our stores. It was a logistical nightmare.

I gave a small team the mission of developing a plan to centralize our operations under one roof. They found a developer that would be willing to construct a facility to our specifications and then lease it back to us for a number of years to recoup their investment. It was an enormous commitment, a twelve- to fifteen-million-dollar investment. Everything about it was expensive—design, construction, lease, and move. The team had been working on a plan, but we did not make the final decision until after I became permanent CEO. It was an uncertain time, and I remember a meeting with George Mileusnic, our chief financial officer, and Paul Turek, vice president for supply chain, in June 2003. We were sitting at my conference table with all of the documents and blueprints spread out ready for me to sign. We spent about an hour, once again, going over the pros and cons of making such a dramatic decision, as I kept saying, "We have to do this."

George finally said, "This is a really big commitment and could be a huge mistake."

I looked him squarely in the eye and said, "George, if we don't succeed at all of the changes we are going to have to make, this building will be the least of our worries."

I signed the documents, and we broke ground in September 2003. The plant relocated in the summer of 2004, and the rest of the company in the fall. Everything was now centralized.

The new facility was all about calculated risk. I knew retail, I knew the company, I knew our operations, and I knew our competition. The many lessons I had learned over the years gave me the confidence to sign those documents and plan for the future. I had a lot of experience managing and implementing change, and I knew how to execute. But this was about building a facility for business that we didn't even have yet. Opening the first batter facility at the cookie company was not as big a risk. We had the business to justify it. At Caribou, the new building was a huge leap of faith because we hadn't even started expanding the commercial division yet. But I firmly believed that this world-class facility would be the catalyst for change—and it was.

The new building helped us take a giant leap forward. The commercial business allowed the brand to be experienced by people in markets not served by our stores. When I arrived, Caribou had a very small commercial business focused on just one upscale chain of stores, Lunds & Byerlys. I hired Henry Stein from Coca-Cola to lead our commercial sales division. He reached into mainstream grocery stores (Giant Eagle, HyVee, Safeway, Harris Teeter), big-box retailers (Target, Costco, Sam's Club), and sports arenas and fitness centers (Lifetime Fitness, the Target Center, Compuware Sports Arena). We were also successful with office coffee and food service providers like Sodexo, Royal Cup, Compass, and Aramark. In March 2005 we made a deal to serve an exclusive brew of Caribou Coffee on all Frontier Airlines flights. It was a great fit, because it helped introduce Caribou to Denver—a new market—and Frontier's slogan "A whole different animal" dovetailed perfectly with Caribou's brand.

Also in 2005, Caribou signed a master franchise agreement. We took an unconventional approach to franchising, focusing on nontraditional locations such as airports and college campuses. All of our international business was done through franchising in the Middle East and Korea. This was one of the fastest growing parts of the company, and we had plans to build 250 international stores by 2012. The quality of the product and of our training was so effective that even when we opened stores thousands of miles away, the Caribou experience was sustained. Customers would get the same warm welcome and the same latte in Seoul that they did in Minneapolis.

We licensed the Caribou name and developed a robust online market-place. In March 2006 we did a Midwestern launch of Caribou Coffee ice cream. Several months later, in July, we did a nationwide launch for our Caribou Coffee breakfast bar. In the spring of 2007 we did a nationwide launch with Keurig, and later that summer we launched ready-to-serve coffee drinks in cans in partnership with the Coca-Cola Company. All of these efforts contributed to Caribou's brand reach.

We also introduced new food in our stores. When I arrived, we were contracting individually with local bakeries to deliver products to stores, either first thing in the morning or the night before. There was no consistency from one region to the next, and the stores constantly ran out of product. It was common to walk in late in the morning and see empty bakery shelves. Because of the delivery system, the freshest product was a day old when we sold it. So we put together a program called Bou Gourmet, providing muffins, cookies, bagels, and breakfast breads such as banana and lemon poppy seed that were made to be frozen and, once thawed, remained fresh in the case all day long. For the most part, our operations team did not support the change, partly because it was logistically difficult. We had to put freezers in already cramped stores. Edward Boyle, who oversaw the rollout of Bou Gourmet, faced tremendous push-back from the field because so many people liked the old way. I knew that this change had to take place, and we discussed a new $10,000 oven that was just becoming available that would bake frozen products in under a minute. It would produce a great baked treat, not something that came out of a microwave. It was a battle to get there, but it was a good fight for the future. Today Caribou has some of the best food of any coffee chain.

Amid all these transformations, we also took the company public. An initial public offering is a strategic gamble on future growth, and on September 29, 2005, Caribou launched its IPO. The goal was to raise $67.7 million in net proceeds and use that to repay outstanding debt and to fund expansion. Two years after I took over, we had expanded to 337 stores in fourteen states and the District of Columbia. Starbucks had 9,500 locations. We knew that we were never going to match their scale, so my focus was on quality, brand expansion, and the customer experience. The demand for the company's stock the day we went public was five times the amount of stock being offered. The IPO became a validation for the entire management team. In less than three years, Caribou went from a company with negative sales growth to a public company listed on NASDAQ under CBOU.

All of our hard work really started to pay off, and we saw Caribou's brand religion grow and grow. We never ran any promotions encouraging people to send us photographs, but each week we received dozens of them from customers who were holding their Caribou cups at exotic locations around the world. I saw hundreds of vacation photographs showing a Caribou cup against a snow-capped mountain. We would always send the customers something in return, and the photographs kept coming. People held celebrations in our stores. By 2005 we had counted seven weddings at Caribou, and one couple got married at a nearby church and brought their wedding party to Caribou on the way to the reception. We received letters and photographs from hundreds of people who named their dogs Bou. We also received letters explaining that part of the reason they loved to travel was because there was a Caribou in the airport they frequented, and they did not have one near their home.

The brand loyalty even inspired Donna and me to write a children's book. One of the things that I loved most about Caribou was its embrace of diversity—in all its various forms. I was proud of that tradition when I arrived, and I worked during my tenure to enhance it. It was embedded in our hiring and promotion practices. The number of minorities and women in management positions is still notable. We were also one of the first major companies to offer insurance benefits for domestic partners. I firmly believe that the deep respect the company had for its employees is why Caribou's culture is so rich.

We also received a lot of letters about how much parents enjoyed bringing their children to Caribou. They wanted us to develop more products that appealed to this market—from bibs to sippy cups. The embrace of diversity and the family-friendly atmosphere we created became the building blocks of our book, *The Land of the Caring Bou*. We worked with Rob Cleveland and Rick Reitz, and with illustrator Timothy Banks, to tell the story of a group of animals who try to save the forest. They mistakenly believe that they all have to be like the Caribou and start putting on antlers, but the story's message is that strength really comes from the uniqueness of each animal. The characters were based on the Hug-a-Bou plush animals sold in the stores and on the website. We decided that we could tell this story about celebrating your own uniqueness in a way that kids would understand. After we published the book, we would travel to our stores and do readings. It was a fun project, but really just a reflection of our philosophy as a corporate citizen. We felt like this was a way of giving something back. All proceeds from the book were directed to two children's literacy initiatives: Success by Six and the United Way's readiness program. The Spanish-language version of the book was given free of charge to agencies that served the Hispanic community where Caribou had stores or business partners.

The most powerful thing I learned during my time at Caribou was not to rest on your laurels. The four keys to success are information, innovation, implementation, and improvement. The last one is the one that most businesses forget. You have to constantly make your product, service, and environment better so your experience factor never gets stale. Most entrepreneurial companies fail in the first three to five years if they are not sold or absorbed by a larger entity. I had promised to stay at Caribou for five years, so as 2008 approached, I was making plans to step away as CEO and transition to the board. I had a succession plan from the very beginning, and I wanted to make sure we had strong leadership behind me. We interviewed and brought in Mike Tattersfield to replace me, and he was exactly what the company needed—a young, fresh face who could take Caribou to the next level. My role as change agent had run its course, and Mike was a great successor.

I left Caribou with some important legacies, born out of the fact that I practiced what I preached. I made decisions about the company that were focused not on the present but on the future. I refined hiring practices and developed facilities and products to support that philosophy. I also made sure that the management team kept a direct line to the consumer. If you have too many layers, you end up playing an elaborate version of Telephone. This party game involves putting about ten people in a line and giving them a piece of whispered information that they have to pass on to the next person. It's a lot of fun to play, because by the time you get to the end, the original message is completely different. I learned this lesson from reading David Halberstam's book *The Reckoning* about the battle between American and Japanese car makers. Halberstam argues that Japanese companies succeeded because they listened to their employees on the assembly line, and that direct connection kept them nimble and in touch with their core business. The most important thing a CEO or a department head can do is get the best information from the most direct source. Companies fail when they no longer have a connection to what the customer wants. This is why eliminating the 12-ounce iced coffee was so important. Steve Jobs was a genius about many things, but he really knew what customers wanted, often before they did.

I loved Caribou and my time in Minneapolis, even with all the snow and freezing rain. I felt I had created a powerful platform for their future success. I was fifty-nine years old when I started at Caribou and sixty-four when I stepped down as CEO—just when most people were thinking about retiring. But I knew that I was not at that final chapter in my life. Not yet.

17

Love Spoken Here

How do you grow up poor and come to understand philanthropy? My parents were working class, and we had little extra money for luxuries. Like our friends and neighbors, we lived on a tight budget, and there was no real mechanism in place to make community giving more visible. People donated to places of worship, but that was about the extent of philanthropy that I remember as a child. Today, solicitations bombard us constantly—on television, in the mail, via email, on the Internet, and from robocalls. Cities and towns in America hold road races and walkathons and golf tournaments to raise funds for the American Cancer Society, among other causes. The Salvation Army collects donations outside stores during the holidays, and other groups set up tables at community festivals to generate support and awareness. There is just a different culture of giving today.

I never thought about philanthropy in a conventional sense as a child. My father was busy working, and I do not remember any discussions at home about donating money. But I do remember my parents talking about Boys Town, an organization founded by Father Edward J. Flanagan in

Nebraska in 1917. Early in my father's career, he gathered used clothes and rags that were then sold to junk companies for bundling and recycling. My father regularly went through what he collected and gave the better items to Father Flanagan. I have no idea how they came to know each other because we lived in New York and Florida, but I remember a framed picture hanging in our hallway that was signed by Father Flanagan. It showed an older boy carrying a younger boy on his back with the caption "He ain't heavy, Father. He's m'brother." That image is etched in my memory; I must have walked past it three thousand times. But it never occurred to me as a child that it had anything to do with philanthropy. My mother was equally committed to giving back—and most of her donations came out of our kitchen. She volunteered in my classroom and served on the PTA, but mostly she baked. She would donate these incredible cakes and cookies to the school, which likely explains my love of sweets. Whatever I learned about generosity and helping others came from my parents' example, not from any deliberate discussion or conversation.

When Donna and I married, we did not have money to give. We were struggling to make a living in our new home in Atlanta and to raise children, and I do not remember anybody ever asking us for money. Once we established ourselves north of downtown in Cobb County, we began volunteering for causes about which we cared. Donna worked with the Feminist Action Alliance, the Equal Rights Amendment (ERA) Georgia Board, and the League of Women Voters of Georgia. She served as the chairperson on the Legal Status of Women and the Georgia Constitutional Revision committees as well as the Cobb County Juvenile Justice Board and the Georgia Student Finance Commission. Today the Donna Novak Coles Georgia Women's Movement Archives are part of Georgia State University's Special Collections. I helped the March of Dimes, Kennestone Hospital, and the American Heart Association, but I discovered that my real passion was education. Maybe this was because I never went to college, but I wanted to make sure that my community was doing its best to provide for our children so they had an opportunity to thrive. I wanted to do something, to make a difference.

It was not until the Great American Cookie Company began expanding in the 1980s and became more successful that I began to think about philanthropy. I cannot recall where I first heard the concept of the Three W's—Work, Wisdom, and Wealth. Maybe it was at a business luncheon or in a magazine article. Whatever the source, it really resonated. When you are young and just starting out, often the only thing you can afford to donate is your work. As you age and become more stable and successful, your contributions grow to encompass wisdom and wealth. Nonprofits and charitable organizations need community members to donate all three. The most important contributions that I have made as a philanthropist have been donations of work and wisdom; the easiest thing I have ever done is write a check. I do not want to minimize the importance of financial gifts—organizations need money—but they need business and community leaders who understand corporate citizenship even more. I have been on many boards whose members had expertise that the organization never could afford to buy. That is good for the organization, but it is also good for the board member. It is often easier to take a minute to write a check than to really commit to an organization about which you care. If you do not give of yourself, you will never truly understand and embrace their mission or appreciate their impact on people you may never meet. In my work with the Walker School, Kennesaw State University, and the Film and Video and Music Commission for the State of Georgia, I discovered that hard work on behalf a cause you believe in is what matters most.

In 1982 we enrolled our second-grader Taryn in the Walker School, an independent school in Marietta, a suburb of Atlanta. Founded in 1957 as St. James Kindergarten, the school added elementary grades by 1960, and the year after Taryn started, it expanded to grades pre-K through twelve. The school had a caring faculty and staff, small classrooms, parental involvement, and responsible leadership. Walker was like a jewel in Cobb County, with maybe four hundred students. But I really fell in love with it on one of our early visits when I saw a needlepoint sign that said: "Love Spoken Here." It had been handmade by a parent. I looked at Donna and said, "This is the right place for us." But while the school had a lot of potential, the student body was small, the facilities were stretched thin, and there was no room for growth.

Taryn did well, and Donna and I attended parent orientation in the late summer of 1985 just as she was going into the sixth grade. We were prepared to sit through a typical meeting about school operations, student expectations, and parental engagement. Instead I found myself riveted by Don Robertson, the new headmaster the school had hired in July. He spent the whole time talking about the future of the school—what was needed to serve more students. Donna and I both walked out inspired. A few weeks later Curtis Daniel, one of the Walker board members, asked me to breakfast. I listened to his pitch to donate to the annual fund and said that Donna and I would be happy to, but that I really wanted to join the board. I remember Curtis confessing that he was afraid to ask because he did not think I would be interested. Committing to the Walker School board was a turning point for us. Donna and I came to the decision that, while there were many worthy causes in Atlanta, we were going to focus our energy and resources on education. The school needed a lot of things, and I thought I could help. I soon found out that writing the check is the easy part.

I joined the board in September 1985, two months after Don became headmaster, and was asked to serve on the finance committee. Only later would I realize how important this committee could become. Walker was a small, struggling school, and the board was involved in the daily operations. The school also did not have a strategic plan, so in his second year Don arranged a retreat with faculty, administrators, and board members to map out the school's future. We created a five-year strategic plan, and the school hired a comptroller to help oversee finances. As finance chair, I thought we needed to do a cash flow analysis, so that became one of his first big projects. The comptroller quickly determined that because parents pay part of the year's tuition early in June, we had enough money on hand to pay off the mortgage. That was a major revelation, and a fellow board member hosted a barbecue at his home on Lake Allatoona at the end of every school year. In a highly symbolic move, the administration and board burned the mortgage in a fire pit in the summer of 1988. With the mortgage debt retired, we turned our attention to fundraising, as it was painfully obvious that the facilities needed a lot of attention.

The current building, which was the old Sprayberry High School, had three wings. Lower, middle, and upper schools each occupied a wing. We really needed to grow the student population—and the only way to do that was to expand the facilities. We had two main needs. The first was to build a new lower school for preschool and the elementary grades, our largest population of students. Then we would renovate the wing that the lower school occupied, adding laboratories and modernizing the other spaces, and move the middle school into that space. Once this was done, we would use the second and third wings to grow the high school. The second thing we needed was a real athletic center. We had a multipurpose room that doubled as a gymnasium and auditorium, but it was not adequate.

I was now chairman of the board, and I assembled a committee in which Arthur Crow, Curtis Daniel, Tony Gatti, and Don McGowan joined me to help solve this dilemma. We met for several hours and went back and forth about which we should build—the lower school or the athletic center? We debated the pros and cons of each and agreed that building the lower school would be the better financial move. It would help the school grow the fastest. But we also knew that a small, overcrowded gym that doubled as an auditorium would not be appealing to potential students and their families. It was a real dilemma. We had hired a consulting firm to help determine how much money the school could raise, and they estimated less than two million dollars. Cobb County did not have a strong fundraising track record—no hospital, school, or museum had ever raised money on that scale. We just did not have that kind of support in this community. The consultant's prediction meant that we could build either a lower school or a gym, but not both. The report made us feel that we had to choose one option over the other. When the discussion started stretching into the second hour, I finally said, "We need to do both. It will cost us more than five million, and we should take this to the board. We just have to do it." We closed the meeting with a vote to take our proposal to the board the next day.

After the board dealt with the regular agenda, I presented the consultant's report. I did not sugar-coat it; instead I detailed all of the findings and said we really needed to raise more than five million, even though the consultants said we would have trouble raising half that amount. Looking back now, I was pretty naïve. I was sure the board would love this. Because the recommendation came from the committee, it did not require a motion or a second, so I just assumed that we would have some discussion and take a vote. What could be easier? But the conversation kept going and going. A number of members were skeptical about the difficult task ahead of us. After we passed the two-hour mark, Arthur Crow, the oldest member of board and a well-known Atlanta lawyer, finally called out, "Enough talk. Call the damn question." Everybody stopped talking. It was clearly time to vote. And we did. All but two members raised their hands to approve the recommendation. I asked for unanimous consent, and turned and stared at the holdouts. Finally they raised their hands too. We closed the board meeting with bottles of Dom Perignon champagne that I had stowed in a cooler. We popped the corks, and everyone toasted the future of the school. Had they rejected the proposal, I suppose I would have been drinking alone.

Three weeks later, Donna and I hosted a board retreat at our home to develop a detailed fundraising plan. I asked Tim Mescon, dean of the business school at Kennesaw State College, to facilitate. At the end of the presentation and discussion, we passed out sheets of paper and asked each board member to list how much they might be willing to donate. They did not have to put their names on the sheets. We hoped that we could raise about $500,000 from the board to jump-start the capital campaign. After we tallied up the numbers, we had commitments for more than a million dollars. We were blown away. This kind of board support could be the catalyst for a major campaign. In the end, we not only built both a lower school and a new athletic center but made additional changes as well. Walker today is one of the best independent schools in the state. What happened at that meeting changed the future of the school, and it took an incredible team of people who had the courage and the vision to see what Walker could become. I served as the head of the finance committee for five years, and then chairman for another five. In total, I was on the board from 1985 until Don Robertson retired in 2011. I gave the Three W's—but in the end, it was the work I gave that really meant the most to me.

18

The Last Five Miles

Real wisdom comes when you realize that the skills you used to finish the race are exactly the same ones you need to conquer the next five miles.

My volunteer and philanthropic efforts in education expanded when my daughter Jody entered Kennesaw State College in 1986. I knew a little about the school, and I had met its dynamic president, Betty Siegel, at metro Atlanta business events. I had also come to know Tim Mescon, the dean of the business school. Tim had facilitated the retreat with the Walker School board and had spoken at Great American Cookies annual conventions two years in a row. I had spoken on campus a few times, but beyond that I had no formal connection to the school.

I had seen the campus grow and was impressed by what it seemed poised to become. Founded in 1963, Kennesaw Junior College began offering classes in September 1966. It became a four-year college in 1976 and a university in 1996. So when Jody enrolled, it was just twenty years old but was growing in size and stature. Even though she remained at Kennesaw State College for only a year, I maintained an interest in the future of the college. Between the location on I-75, the vision of the president, and the quality of the faculty, it seemed destined for greatness. Two of my friends,

Beverly L. McAfee and Fred Bentley Sr., served on the college's foundation board, and they invited me for breakfast in 1989. It has been my experience that one does not get invited to these kinds of breakfasts without expecting to be asked for something. I suspected they would ask for a contribution. The cookie company was doing well, I had joined the board of Charter Bank in 1987 because I wanted to learn more about the banking business and continue to serve my community, and the success of the 1984 Spirit of America Ride (SOAR) had put me on people's radar. I was not prepared, however, for the invitation to join the Kennesaw State College Foundation board. Without hesitation, I said yes.

It had been an interesting week. Just a few days before, a much larger and more prestigious university in Georgia had invited me to join their board. I had been teaching in their business school several times a year. For a guy who never went to college, this was a really big deal. I found myself with a choice to make. Many successful business and community leaders populated the first board, which had a long history. Joining it would have stroked my ego. I have learned from long experience that, for me, ego-based decisions are always a mistake. In contrast, joining the Kennesaw board would be all about the school. If I took the first offer, my work would not have made much difference. I would have been one voice among many. Kennesaw State was more like a growing business. This school offered a great education at an affordable price, had a good location along I-75, and needed help and guidance. It was on the cusp of becoming great, and I felt that I could really make a difference. Kennesaw needed me more than the other university, and it was in my backyard. I was active with the Cobb Chamber of Commerce, my home was close by, and I knew how much the college meant to the county. I also admired the school's vision and entrepreneurial spirit.

In 1990 when I joined the Kennesaw State College Foundation board, I became good friends with its then chairman, Larry Stevens. Just as at the Walker School, I chaired the finance committee. And just as at the Walker School, I looked around to see what needed to be done. Kennesaw was young and growing, like Walker, and there were plenty of areas in need of attention. One of our first goals was to change the school's investment strategy. For many years the foundation's money had been sitting in low-interest-bearing bonds and certificates of deposit. While boards have a fiduciary responsibility not to take undue risk, the finance committee agreed that we needed to diversify the portfolio by putting some of our money into the stock market.

I chaired the finance committee for seven years and loved serving on the board. During that time I became even more active with the business school. In 1993 Betty Siegel, Larry Stevens, and Jim Fleming came to our home to discuss a major gift. Their timing could not have been better. What they did not know was that Donna and I had already decided to become donors. We had enjoyed watching the school grow and change, and we wanted to help contribute financially to that effort. We thought that a million-dollar gift at a larger, more established university might get us a lunch with the president. A gift of that size to KSC, however, would be transformational and could lead to larger and more significant gifts from other donors later. At the time, our gift was the largest ever made to the college.

The irony of the Kennesaw gift was that I was about to contact Larry to talk about it. But I was the one in for the surprise—they brought renderings of the business school with my name on it. We had discussed a large donation, but we never even thought about a naming opportunity. In 1994 Donna and I agreed to make a gift to KSC, and the Board of Regents named the business college after me in recognition of my "success, leadership, and benevolence." I was really honored, but wanted to do more than just write a check. I was already on the foundation board, and I wanted to go a step further to donate my work and wisdom.

On the day of the dedication of the Michael J. Coles School of Business (later College of Business), I was asked to speak, and I remember being overwhelmed with emotion. This was a big commitment for our family, and I was proud of what we could contribute. It was not just a tribute to me, Donna, and our children—it stretched much further back. My grandparents had come to the United States as immigrants, and here I was standing at one of the largest colleges in the state of Georgia having a business school named for me. I had the same feeling that I did when

I saw the Statue of Liberty during my 1989 Race Across America. Your life is stitched by an invisible thread to those who have come before. Many of my family members were gone, but this business school would symbolize all their hopes and dreams. I was proud but also humbled by the moment.

Soon after we made the gift, Tim asked me to teach a class. I thought to myself, "What would a guy with a high school education teach at a university?" I regularly lectured on college campuses around the nation—Wake Forest, Georgia Tech, Northwestern, Cornell, and UCLA—but a one-hour lecture is not the same as teaching a fifteen-week class. I had wanted to be a teacher—at least that is what I thought in my senior year of high school. Yet I had not thought much about how to translate what I had learned in business into a full graduate school course. Tim and the subsequent Coles College of Business deans, including Ken Harmon and Kat Schwaig, kept encouraging me to teach. We would talk about it casually at cocktail parties and other KSU events, but it would take a while for it to come to fruition. And I still had plenty of other work to do.

After serving on the board for nearly eight years, I became chairman of the Kennesaw State University Foundation in 1998. The foundation had a strategic plan, and it was my job to help implement it. One of my roles was to reenergize and reorganize the board. I assembled a new executive committee comprised of new and seasoned trustees. One of our immediate priorities was to build student housing. In order to transition from a commuter school to a residential campus, Kennesaw State had to have places for students to live. The Board of Regents of the University System of Georgia, the governing body over all of the state's colleges and universities, had already been using public and private partnerships to build housing, so this was a straightforward and uncomplicated task. Our challenge was parking.

I served as chairman of the KSU Foundation for five years, 1997–2002, during which time we focused our energy on infrastructure. Parking was a constant need—but it is hard to raise funds for parking. It is just not as sexy as dormitories, laboratories, or museums. It was a lot easier to talk about giving people a place to live than it was to promote a cement parking deck. We thus proposed using the public-private partnership model, similar to what the state had been using for housing, to fund the construction of parking decks. This was an untested proposition, so I went to meet with the head of facilities for the Board of Regents in the spring of 1999. We received their blessing, and KSU and the University of Georgia became the first two schools in the state to use this model. I stepped down as chairman of the foundation in 2002 but have remained on the board, continuing to lecture in the business school, and enjoying playing an active role on campus.

In January 2012 I finally agreed to teach. The name and theme for the class came to me one day when I was riding my bike. I thought about an article that I had written back in the early 1970s for *Men's Wear Daily* when I was the merchandise manager for Male Slacks and Jeans. A reporter from the magazine asked me to talk about how small companies like Male go up against Goliaths like Levi's and Farah. The article, "From Concept to Counter," was a detailed description of how you take an idea into the marketplace. I thought that this would be a good theme for a course, but I did not want to focus on any specific business or industry. Nor did I want this to be a straight three-hour lecture—I wanted it to have real-world applications for the students. I decided to bring a dozen business leaders to tell their stories and describe to the students their methods and processes, as well as their successes and failures. The course would meet one evening a week for three hours. It would be for MBA students and would focus on these mini case studies to look at the overall theme of business development.

I pitched the idea to Dr. Kathy Schwaig, the Coles College dean, and told her that I would need some help. I had no idea how to organize a class; the concept was foreign to me. I needed a regular faculty member to partner with me. In the spring of 2012, a year before we offered the course, Dr. Timothy Blumentritt, a longtime Coles College administrator and associate professor of management, agreed to help me teach. We created a fifteen-week syllabus that focused on specific segments of conceptualizing, building, and launching a business. The class filled up with forty students on the first day, and we had a long waiting list.

A few months before the class started, in September of 2012, I found a lump in my neck while on vacation in Jackson Hole, Wyoming. I went to see a local doctor, who thought it was an infected salivary gland. He prescribed an antibiotic but suggested that we do an MRI as a precaution. Donna and I drove back to our vacation home in Montana, and the doctor from Wyoming called a few days later to tell me that I had a tumor on my parotid gland. Even though he said they are rarely malignant, I wanted to get back to Atlanta and get another opinion and second MRI from Dr. Michael Koriwchak at St. Joseph's Hospital. The second scan showed that the tumor was not just on the gland but wrapped around my facial nerve, which made the removal a very delicate operation. Again I was reassured that tumors in this region are almost never malignant and that I shouldn't worry about it. So instead of worrying about cancer, I became concerned that I would lose control over the right side of my face. When I spoke to him about my concerns, he said, "I could do this upside down and blindfolded." To which I would reply, "Let's not do that."

While I was being prepped for surgery, Dr. Koriwchak came to see me, and I grabbed him by the arm. "Do you see this smile?"

"Yes," he replied.

"I'd like to see it on the other side," I joked.

My smile was saved, but we later learned that the tumor was in fact malignant. I was once again in the shadow of Goliath, this time fighting cancer. The doctor did not think it had metastasized, but he urged me to consider both radiation and chemotherapy. Our dear friends Lynn and Howard Halpern had a close relationship with the oncology department at Emory University School of Medicine in Atlanta, because Howard had fought a tough but successful battle with throat cancer. They helped me get an appointment with Dr. Fadlo Khuri and Dr. Jonathan Beitler and even went with me to my first appointment. The oncology team recommended radiation, so I went five days a week from November through January. I lost my taste buds and experienced a great deal of weakness and fatigue, but I was still very lucky.

As the first day of class at Kennesaw State neared, January 14, I was putting the finishing touches on my syllabus with Tim while trying to manage the daily radiation treatments. I remember getting up on the morning of the first class worried that I was not going to make it through the three-hour session. When I opened the door to the classroom, I saw forty smiling faces, eager to dive into the material. Somehow I found the same internal strength that I did in 1984 riding across the country. It got me through the first class—and I was so grateful for the students' energy and enthusiasm. I drove home exhausted and finished my final radiation treatment over the next two days. It would take me six months to fully regain my strength and a year to get my taste buds back, but I am pleased to report that I beat back Goliath and today am cancer free.

Despite this major health scare, teaching at Kennesaw State University was a terrific experience. To guest-lecture in the class I invited a baker's dozen of friends who were business leaders from throughout Atlanta: Pat Pittard of the executive search firm Heidrick and Struggles; Barbara Babbit Kaufman of Turtle's Records and Tapes and Chapter 11 Bookstores; Joan Lyman of Whynatte Enterprises; Charlie Ogburn of Arcapita Investment Management; Bob Hope of the PR firm Hope-Beckham; Jeff Levy, a technology entrepreneur; David Bar of Great American Cookies; Joe Rogers of Waffle House; John Williams of Post Properties and Williams Realty Advisors; Lorin Coles of Alliancesphere; Arthur Blank of Home Depot and the Atlanta Falcons; Mark Bell of BrandBank; and Larry Stevens of PriceWaterhouseCoopers. My goal was to have the students recognize that on the other side of success—always looming in the background—is failure. I wanted them to hear from people who had been in the trenches in different industries. These were some of the best in Atlanta's business community—and I wanted them to understand what mistakes to avoid. Each guest presented for forty-five minutes, then engaged in a question-and-answer period with the students. After they left I spent the remaining ninety minutes leading an interactive discussion about the lessons learned, helping the students stitch the various themes and ideas together. Each MBA student's major assignment consisted of writing a business plan or engaging in corporate entrepreneurship by taking a fresh look at how to improve a current practice or process in their own company. The projects were impressive, and the results were striking. Some students started their own companies; others, including one who had his own IT consultancy firm, used the assignment to change how they ran their businesses. The course evaluations were positive, and one student who had already completed the MBA program came back to take the course. Another, Connie Engel, completed her MBA and later became chair of the Kennesaw State University Foundation.

While I was serving on both the Walker School and KSU Foundation boards, Governor Roy Barnes appointed me in May 1999 to oversee the Georgia Film, Video, and Music Advisory Board (now the Georgia Film and Music Board). Roy and I had campaigned together and had been friends for more than thirty-five years. After his inauguration, he called and said, "I'd like to have your help in my administration. Is there anything that you would like to do?" I told him I would think about it, but wondered aloud, "Is there still a film commission?" He replied, "There is, but I don't think it has been very active." There was genuine enthusiasm behind my question. If my voice had not changed when I was a child, I believe I would have ended up in the entertainment business. I did impersonations all the time, largely gleaned from old movies, and even won a radio contest. I had a real passion for movies, so the film board seemed like a perfect fit. I called the governor back and told him that was what I wanted to do. I had sold Great American Cookies and had recently lost my U.S. Senate race against Paul Coverdell, so this appointment came at a perfect time.

I was under no illusions when I signed on that this would be easy. I knew that the film business in Georgia was really in decline. It was born under the administration of Governor Jimmy Carter, and Ed Spivey was the original commissioner. One of the first movies shot on location in Georgia was *Deliverance* (1972), an adaptation of the novel by James Dickey, starring Burt Reynolds. The Carter administration immediately recognized the value of the industry. It was a great way to create high-paying jobs and promote the state. It was nonpolluting, it did not stress the state's infrastructure by creating more traffic or use too much water, and it could bring between two and ten million dollars to a community during production. The film industry was a powerful economic engine that boosted tourism and generated revenue for hotels, tour companies, caterers, car rental agencies, restaurants, and other businesses.

The industry in Georgia did well for a while, but soon other southern states started to take notice and expand their own industries. Hollywood loved the South largely because, in contrast to California and New York, the workforce was not unionized. This saved an enormous sum of money for the studios and production companies. Once ranked number five in the nation, by the time I became chairman of the board in 1999, Georgia had fallen to number nine. In the early 1990s North Carolina, with total revenue of more than $5 billion, was the third largest state for film production, after California and New York. It was home to Screen Gems Studios, the largest film studio east of California. Throughout the decade, North Carolina had become very aggressive about soliciting production companies and offering incentives and building a strong economy around film, television, and commercial production. Because of strong government support, Canada was also becoming a major player, and productions began to migrate from the South to Vancouver and Toronto as well as to Minnesota.

I knew that Georgia needed to make some serious changes to be competitive, but I also knew that I had a lot to learn. My first meeting was with Greg Torre, director of the Georgia Film, Video, and Music Advisory Board, at the OK Café in Atlanta's Buckhead neighborhood. Greg would become my most trusted partner in this enterprise. He showed up to that breakfast meeting with a detailed PowerPoint presentation on his laptop about the history of the board and the industry, and we hit it off immediately. He told me, "We used to have a lot more productions, but now other states are offering tax incentives. Unless we figure out how to compete, this industry will not grow. We might be able to attract films that are specifically set in Georgia or tell a story of notable Georgians like Dr. Martin Luther King Jr., but that's about it." I asked him a question. "I'm not interested in why more people don't come to Georgia," I said, "but why *does* anyone come to Georgia to make a film?" I used to joke that in my early career I thought I knew all the answers, but not all the questions. My work at Great American Cookies had taught me to turn conventional questions upside down. In my first few months, Greg and I did just that.

This was new ground for me, so I needed a thoughtful and coordinated plan of attack. Looking back on my career, I started to think about what made any business successful—and I distilled it down to what I now call the Four I's—information, innovation, implementation, and improvement. I developed this concept at Great American Cookies, and I approached all aspects of my business using this system. These four words became my road map—and they would help transform the film industry in the state.

I had to start by gathering as much information as I could. I called and visited film commissioners in other states to ask: What is working? What challenges are you facing? What kind of public and private partnerships have you developed? What has not worked well, and what did you do to fix it? I learned that if you wanted to be effective, you had to have a strong board that represented many different industries. I also discovered that you had to become an ambassador and get out into the field to talk to different communities about the benefits of having a movie, television show, or music video filmed on location. Finally, it was clear from my conversations that the state had to offer practical, measurable incentives that would save production companies money. After thirty days I told Greg that we had three major challenges—building a board, educating the state, and creating incentives to attract new business.

The board was dormant when I arrived in 1999, so my priority became building one, and this is where innovation came into play. I wanted to assemble the most diverse and talented group that I could, because this was a big job that needed a lot of intellectual capital. Greg used to joke that the reason I was named commissioner was because I had a great Rolodex. And he was right—I did not hesitate to reach out to friends and colleagues, but also to people I did not yet know but thought would be really good contributors. In all we tapped forty people, including Billye Aaron, vice president of the United Negro College Fund in the Southern Region; Bobbie Bailey, who owned Our-Way, an air-conditioning and refrigeration company, as well as a recording and music publishing company; Kay Beck, a professor of film studies and codirector of the Digital Arts and Entertainment Laboratory at Georgia State University; Renee Bishop, a writer and producer for American Artists Entertainment;

Larry Culbertson, vice president of film and video for IXL; Steve Fox, a partner in the law firm Rogers & Hardin; Ronnie Gunnerson, senior vice president for corporate affairs at Turner Broadcasting; Joel Katz, entertainment practice chair in the law firm Greenberg Traurig; Mitchell Kopelman, partner in the accounting firm Habif, Arogeti & Wynne; Whitman Mayo, a seasoned actor who appeared in such television series as *Sanford & Son*, *Barretta*, *Sesame Street*, and *ER*; Pat Mitchell, president of CNN Productions; Marion Ray, Teamsters Local 728 in Atlanta; Joey Reiman, founder of BrightHouse; and Jay Self, director of the Savannah Film Office. I made recommendations and Governor Barnes's office suggested some as well, and when we had assembled our team of forty, he swore them in as a group. It was an impressive team, and they showed up for everything. They were committed to the commission and helped the industry thrive and grow.

Once I had a plan and a board, I needed to focus on implementation. To do that, we had to get out into the field. In the spring of 2000, Greg and I traveled to the AFCI Locations & Global Finance Show, often called Location Expo, a major conference in Los Angeles that is billed as the "marketplace for global locations, filmmakers, and producers." As part of the expo, film commissions from the United States and abroad set up booths to attract producers, studio representatives, location managers, and others in the industry who might be interested in what your community could offer. We also set up meetings with producers and studio executives to talk about why Georgia was so appealing. The trip to California was followed by a series of trips throughout the state to educate communities about the advantages of the film industry. Greg and I went everywhere—Macon, Savannah, Tifton, Columbus, Albany, Dalton, and Valdosta. We crisscrossed the state and met with legislators in each town or city to build support for legislation that we needed to pass to offer tax incentives for the industry. I also wanted them to know that they would catch holy hell from their constituents if they did not embrace the growing film industry that not only created new jobs but also boosted tourism.

I met so many people in my role as chairman, including Robert Redford, who directed *The Legend of Bagger Vance*, which was filmed in Savannah and Jekyll Island as well as in South Carolina. I met him the first time on the set and later at two events organized by CNN's Pat Mitchell in Park City, Utah, around the Sundance Film Festival. Pat was on Sundance's board as well as ours, and she arranged two dinners for us to meet; at the second and smaller event, we talked about his new Harley-Davidson, and I suggested that he hold a second premiere for the film in Savannah, which he later did, at the Savannah College of Art and Design's theater.

We had all the ingredients in place. Now we had to find a way to be competitive again. Georgia had a lot going for it—a well-trained crew base, great locations ranging from sandy beaches to historic towns dripping with Spanish moss to scenic mountains, a large international airport, and the kind of infrastructure the film industry needed. The labor force was now unionized, but that was less of an issue than tax credits for production companies. The problem was that we lacked incentives. Providing them would be a game changer.

If we were going to reach our full potential, we had to focus on improvement, the fourth pillar in my plan. My travel to California and around the state made it clear that we simply were not competitive. Too many other states were outpacing us. This is why House Bill 610, passed during the 2001 legislative session, was so important. This landmark legislation, which I helped push through, granted tax incentives to production companies that shot films in Georgia, and it gave the state a competitive edge in attracting lucrative projects. It offered companies a use tax exemption, which meant that if they bought materials or services in Georgia for a film, video, or music production, these purchases were not subject to tax.

We saw a bump in the business, but we were not going to rest on our laurels. We had to create more jobs and build a stronger industry, and this required additional legislation. I worked on the Georgia Entertainment Industry Investment Act, House Bill 539, though it would not be passed until 2005, two years after I left the commission. This was an industry-specific tax credit extended to companies that spent a certain amount of money. It did not matter where the company was based; the credit was transferrable.

In four years we turned the industry around. The combination of a strong board, outreach, and tax incentives has helped create one of the strongest industries in the nation. In 2017 the *Atlanta Business Chronicle* reported that Georgia hosted more feature film productions in 2016 than any other state or country. Film L.A. commissioned the study and found that film and television shows spent $2.02 billion in Georgia on a range of projects, including *Captain America: Civil War*, *Passengers*, and *Allegiant*. The United Kingdom took the number-two spot, followed by Canada, California, Louisiana, and New York.

The film commission pushed me, changed me, and made me a better businessman. From the time I started working with Irving Settler at the age of thirteen, my whole career had been focused on retail. I did not realize until much later that Irving was really teaching me how to get customers to come back—and that is what we were trying to do with the film commission. We were working to reclaim business we had lost and to attract new companies. Irving always did something a little special for our customers, so they would think of us first when they needed something. I needed producers and studios to do exactly the same thing. They had to think of Georgia first when they were discussing possible locations. My four years on the commission and the legislation that passed in 2001 and 2005 helped them do just that. Even though it was a volunteer position, I worked almost every day for four years to help rebuild the industry throughout the state. I did not know then, but my work with the commission was a dress rehearsal for my time at Caribou Coffee.

If I divided my life into three chapters, I might start with what I call my "learning years," comprising my first forays into retail, various apprenticeships, and my work in the clothing industry that led to the formation of my first two companies. The second chapter, "the earning years," encompasses my time at the helm of Great American Cookies, Caribou Coffee, and Charter Bank. The third chapter is about sharing what I have learned in the past sixty years with my community—maybe best referred to as my "last five miles" that, as in my coast-to-coast races, have prepared me for the next five miles.

When I raced my bicycle for the third time from Savannah to San Diego in 1984, I was five miles from the finish when my body started breaking down. I had covered more than 2,500 miles and could see the finish line. I just could not get there—it was too painful. So I had to break those last miles into component parts. I found myself going block by block, lamppost to lamppost. That is what helped me finish and set the world record. This is exactly the same approach I applied to the Walker School, to Kennesaw State University, and to the Georgia Film Commission. I studied the challenge, broke it down into manageable parts, and tackled them one at a time. The most important part of conquering the last five miles is not the result, though victory is certainly sweet. Real wisdom comes when you realize that the skills you used to finish the race are exactly the same ones you need to conquer the next five miles.

I have only two yearbooks from my time in public school—and together they tell the story of my life. The first is from eighth grade in 1958. The yearbook had a theme, looking into the future, and there is a two-page photograph of me with books in my right hand looking out of the auditorium. It is my one and only centerfold, and I was the least likely student for such a feature. I was a bit of a troublemaker in middle school and was walking back from detention one day when the photographer grabbed me for the photo shoot. It was just dumb luck. But what I remember most about the story is that all my friends bought copies and wanted me to sign the picture. My father had gone bankrupt when I was ten, and we had no extra money. I had been working odd jobs but still could not afford the five-dollar price tag for the yearbook. I had to wait until the next year when the school sold them for fifty cents.

The second yearbook on my shelf at home is from my senior year in high school when I was living with my brother Gerry in Rockport, Massachusetts. The page that shows my senior picture lists my future profession as teacher. I had been inspired to consider the career by my English teacher, Gertrude Miller. I had enrolled in an advanced English class and met with her in the first week of school to confess that I had failed the subject in my first three years of high school in Miami Beach. While I promised to work hard, I was unprepared to write all the book reports she assigned. However, she promised to help me. For my third report I asked her if I could write about Henry Miller's novel *Tropic of Cancer*, first published in the United States in 1961, banned in America for thirty years, and the subject of obscenity trials. I was sure she would balk, and I was curious to see if I could push her, but she said, "I am sure you'll do a very good job of discussing all of the metaphors in the book." I did, received an A, and learned that she was unflappable. More important, I learned that she appreciated my creativity and would cultivate my tendency to think unconventionally.

Rockport had a great high school. Several teachers had doctorates, and they offered extensive testing and career counseling to seniors. One of the testers asked me what I wanted to do as a career. I said I want to go to college and become a teacher; he looked at me for a long time to see if I was joking, laughed, and said, "No. You would not be a good teacher. Go out into the world, make your mark, find yourself, and then teach people about it." I left the meeting thinking, "That guy is crazy. I'm going to be a teacher." Looking back, I see that we were both right. I did go out and make my mark in business through Great American Cookies, Caribou Coffee, Charter Bank, BrandBank, and the Georgia Film Commission. But I also have become a teacher—albeit not in a conventional sense. I do not have a classroom, take roll, or give exams or grades. After I finished my 1984 Spirit of America Ride (SOAR), I started traveling around to businesses, universities, and other institutions where I could share my story, and I have never stopped. Today I talk about my early business career, the accident and my recovery, building teams in my record-setting bike races and in my companies, but also about philanthropy and volunteering. I do this not to extol my achievements, but rather to inspire those around me to take on their own challenges, to complete their last five miles, and to prepare for the next five.

I know you can do it, because I did.

Epilogue

The First Law of Nature Is Growth

Goliath and I have met on many occasions during my lifetime. And I suspect we will meet again.

I have distilled my story down to ten lessons that work for any business or personal endeavor. The experiences that taught me these lessons are woven throughout the book, but here is a snapshot of the wisdom I have gleaned after years of starting and leading companies, raising a family, setting world cycling records, and serving my community.

1. **Take risks early in your career.** When I was twenty-two years old, I struck up a conversation with a businessman on a flight from New York to Detroit. As we made our initial descent to the airport, I asked him what kind of advice he would give someone my age. After thinking for a moment, he said: Take most of your risks in business while you're young, for you can more easily recover if things go badly. The older you get, the more complicated life gets, and risk becomes much harder to stomach. It was great advice, which I still share with entrepreneurs who ask me for help today. You are going to have setbacks at some point in your business or in your life. In the final analysis, though, failure is not about the falling down but about

202

the staying down. The ability to get back up over and over again will set you apart from those who doubt your abilities or tell you that your ideas are unsound. My feeling has always been that these are the same people who don't understand risk, courage, and the power of doing more than is expected of you.

2. **Associate only with people of integrity.** Those without it will undermine your best efforts, diminish your effectiveness, and poison your company. To be that person of integrity, speak honestly, directly, and respectfully to everyone in your life and in your business—family, friends, suppliers, employees, colleagues, shareholders, and customers. I learned the value of this lesson when I worked as a teenager at Dorwins, a clothing store in Miami Beach. The owner, Irving Settler, was the most exacting boss I ever encountered. He taught me a great deal about retail, but the time he fired and rehired our tailor Ralph is something I still think about. Ralph was trying to take advantage of Irving during his busiest season, and even though Irving was angry, he rehired him when given the opportunity. Irving was tough, but he was also fair. His approach to Ralph showed respect for his store, for his vendors, and for his employees. A second example is the day I lied to Bob Luehrs during an interview for H.I.S. Sportswear about how old I was, because I was afraid he would not hire me if he knew the truth. I confessed that same day that I was only twenty, but that brief moment taught me the importance of telling the truth. Years later, Bob told me that he had already decided to hire me, but my confession made him even more enthusiastic. What could have been a disaster turned out to be the bedrock of a great friendship built on trust. Maybe Mark Twain said it best: "If you tell the truth, you don't have to remember anything."

3. **Find a mentor to guide your career. When you make your mark, become one.** I was lucky as a teenager to have found Irving, and he taught me nearly everything I know about retail. I would not have been successful had he not been so hard on me or invested so much time in my education. He taught me the importance of knowing every

aspect of your business, from tailoring to purchasing to merchandising to finance, and especially customer service. Those essential lessons, and my failure to apply them when I founded my first company, Pant-O-Mine, helped make it possible for me to take the risk to start Great American Cookies in 1977. As I have moved throughout my career, I have tried to pay back that debt by giving time and energy to young entrepreneurs, helping them avoid the same mistakes I made. This is why I agreed to teach the "From Concept to Counter" class in the spring semester of 2013 at Kennesaw State University. It is also why, when advising someone writing a new business plan, I focus on setting attainable goals, knowing the competition, building a strong team, and avoiding being incapacitated by fear.

4. **Know what you don't know, and surround yourself with people from whom you can learn.** Some people are intimidated by working with or associating with someone more capable or knowledgeable than they are in a specific area. Others thrive on building relationships with people who have complementary skill sets and conflicting points of view. After making some mistakes building teams early in my career, I learned to hire and empower a diverse group of people at Great American Cookies and Caribou Coffee who possessed exceptional talents and were not shy about challenging me. I marshalled those talents to build the largest cookie company in the nation and later to prepare Caribou to take on the industry giant, Starbucks.

5. **Even in a digital age, customers respond to, respect, and remember the personal touch.** Technology is one of the most effective ways to reach customers, and if used wisely, it can replicate the warmth of face-to-face contact that has defined exemplary customer service over the past century. The companies that have used technology in thoughtful and creative ways to serve their customers will continue to thrive in the digital marketplace. IKEA, the Swedish furniture company, created a mobile app that uses augmented reality to allow consumers to preview a rug, table, or bed in a room before buying

it, saving them time and money. Rackspace, the managed cloud and hosting computer company known for its "fanatically helpful" customer service, had an employee surprise a customer with a pizza while they were on the phone trying to solve a complicated problem. Companies do not have contracts with their customers; they must earn their business with each transaction. I remember shopping for clothes at the Sample Shop on Hertel Avenue in Buffalo at the age of six, a few years before my father went bankrupt. I was always amazed that the owners knew all of our names, our birthdays and my parents' anniversary, and what we liked and did not like. Today, Amazon comes the closest to replicating that feeling. Technology does not have to be cold and impersonal. It can bridge divides and make real connections to customers by using old-school techniques in new ways.

6. **Have a clear mission and vision statement, and make sure your team is fully committed to it.** If your associates cannot explain the importance of your company's mission and why it resonates with customers, you have some work to do. If you are leading a company and discover that there is nobody behind you, you are just out for a stroll. When I was interim CEO of Caribou Coffee, we created a new mission ("Caribou Coffee: An Experience That Makes the Day Better") that took into account our employees, customers, and vendors. It became the raw material for a customer-centric equation that I still use in my businesses today: $P + E + S = Ef$ (Product + Environment + Service = the Experience factor). I learned that you have to deliver a great product and experience, and do not assume it will age gracefully. Be prepared to test it, find its weak spots, and use that knowledge to improve it on a continuous basis. Only then can you build a brand religion.

7. **How you respond to the unexpected is the difference between success and failure.** Regardless of how well you prepare, you will be confronted with uncertainty, failure, and plenty of surprises. When I told my brother, Gerry, that I was going to go into the cookie business, he said, "You've got to remember that success and failure

go hand in hand. You cannot predict what will happen, but you have to take the chance. The worst thing that can happen is that you fail and go back into the clothing business." Well, I certainly could not have guessed that my partner, Arthur, and I would forget pot holders on opening day and burn the first batch of cookies so badly that they caught fire in the oven, bringing fire trucks to the mall. Six weeks later, I could not anticipate that I would be nearly killed in a motorcycle accident. And I never expected that during my 1983 race from Savannah to San Diego that I would be knocked off my bicycle by a dust devil in Arizona and break my collarbone. Instead of giving up or feeling sorry for myself (though I wanted to do both), I learned to anticipate multiple outcomes, remain agile, and keep my sense of humor. To this day, I cannot look at a pot holder without smiling. Facing the unexpected is often a great learning opportunity, even though it may not feel like it at the time. As the noted golfer Bobby Jones once said, "I never learned anything from a match I won."

8. **Trust your employees and give them the opportunity to do their best work for you.** Few businesses invest in human capital in the way that they should, with professional development, opportunities for growth, and a meaningful reward system. Even fewer companies use the most important and cheapest tool in their arsenal—communication. The more you communicate to your associates and colleagues, the clearer the road map, and the more effective your company will be. A few months after founding Great American Cookies, we hired a new manager at Greenbriar Mall in Atlanta. He was very outgoing, and we also discovered that he was a talented artist. So we gave him the creative license to transform our cookie cake business by creating beautiful designs with clever messages, which we soon adopted throughout the company. Hiring well, providing opportunities for growth, and respecting and cultivating talent is the best way to build a strong team. David Hassell, founder and CEO of 15Five, a web-based company focused on employee and manager feedback, argues that 70 percent of employees are "uninspired or actively disengaged" because

they feel "unsupported." Investing in employees helps improve morale, increases retention, drives loyalty, and boosts a company's reputation as a great place to work.

9. **Use the skills that helped you build a great career or business to build a better world.** Your success drew and depended upon community resources, from schools to libraries to banks, so become a good citizen and strive to make your community safer, stronger, and more resilient. With that in mind, find a way to provide opportunities for people that you may never meet. The greatest gift you can give someone else is a chance to succeed, and never worry about who gets the credit. If you have been successful, you have been given plenty of recognition. Give it away.

10. **Never let someone else tell you what you cannot achieve or put limits on your potential.** Do not let people underestimate your abilities because of your youth, and on the opposite end of the spectrum stay sharp, nimble, and relevant. Years ago, I read a great line: "Never rest on your laurels, because the hardest thing on your laurels is resting on them." We often tell our children they are too young to try something new, and our parents that they are too old. I started my business career at the age of eleven and have worked for more than sixty years, and I do not have any plans to sail off into the sunset anytime soon. I stepped down as CEO of Caribou in 2008 at the age of sixty-five. While contemplating what to do next, I kept hearing the same question from friends and acquaintances: "When are you going to retire?" I could not even imagine retiring, and I know that I am not done yet.

Not long after I stepped down as CEO of Caribou Coffee, I was at a cocktail party and my friend Barbara Kaufman came over to introduce me to her future husband. She said: "This is Michael Coles. He's the cofounder of Great American Cookies and the former CEO and chairman of Caribou Coffee. Now he's nothing." We all laughed, but it made me think about how much work defines you. It had been a major part of my identity for so many years that it was hard to think of myself not leading a company. I found myself in an odd position: I was still working, just not full time and not in a high-profile position. I had not retired from my life. I was still doing important work and was especially active mentoring emerging business and nonprofit professionals and chairing the board of BrandBank and Brand Holding Company. And I knew plenty of friends and colleagues who were in the same position. They were working harder than they ever had, just not getting a regular paycheck.

I firmly believe that it is never too late to do something bold. In fact, later may be the best time, because the weight of wisdom and experience are on your side. In 2003, *Jezebel* magazine asked me how I knew if I was successful. I have avoided that word my entire life, because it suggests that your journey is over. It also distracts you from growing and creating opportunities for the people around you. I know I'm more successful than I used to be, because when I go to hotels, I don't take the little bars of soap anymore, so I guess I'm somewhat successful. But I do grab all the little shampoos I can get my hands on.

I wrote this book to help you face your own Goliaths, whatever form they might take. Starting a new company, changing jobs, going back to school, surviving a divorce, or just trying to get back in shape are all stressful events that require courage and commitment. They are all Goliath-like challenges, and the hardest part of facing them is often taking the first step. I've always liked the 1990s Nike slogan "Just Do It" because it demands action in the face of uncertainty. That is why the David and Goliath story appeals to me. The point of the story is not David's victory over Goliath in the Valley of Elah; the point is that David was willing to face him in the first place. We all have the ability to battle giants. The challenge is finding courage to step into the valley.

Acknowledgments

From Michael

I started thinking about writing this book more than twenty-five years ago, but something always stopped me. One day in February 2016, I finally sat down at my computer and wrote a simple question: "What is keeping me from doing this?" My answer was: "I keep waiting to have other experiences to share that might be valuable to a reader." That seemed ridiculous, because if I waited much longer, I would be either dead or unable to remember anything. That very afternoon I picked up the phone and called Dr. Kathy (Kat) Schwaig, dean of the Coles College of Business at Kennesaw State University, and told her that I was finally ready to get serious, but that I needed a coauthor. So Kat is the first person I would like to thank, because she is the one who told me to call Dr. Catherine Lewis.

Catherine has been a professor of history and an administrator at KSU since 2003, and we would see each other periodically at university events. While I didn't know how much she really knew about me, I thought she would be perfect. But it would not be that easy; I had to persuade her that my story was worth telling. She is a distinguished author of more than a dozen books, an active speaker, and a museum curator, and she is really busy. I knew that if she took on this project, we would have to spend a lot of time together. So we compared schedules and found a morning to carve out half an hour. I had a breakfast scheduled at the Buckhead Club with an entrepreneur, and she agreed to come at the end of the meal before her next meeting. Knowing we would not have much time, she asked me to order her a bagel and a glass of tomato juice in advance (amazingly, she does not drink coffee).

Catherine arrived on time, and we chatted for a few minutes before getting down to business. I had a pile of folders, filled with a preliminary book outline and some things I had written over the years. I was ready to discuss the length, content, and schedule of the book, but Catherine had a totally different agenda. She knew how tedious and difficult this process would be, and how much energy it would take to do all the research, interviews, drafting, editing, rewriting, and revising. This kind of project can take years, and coauthors have to really trust and respect each other. So she looked at me and asked me one question: "Are you an asshole?" Now, if you knew Catherine, you would know that this is not her style. She's pretty polished and polite, so I was stunned and fumbled around for an answer. I finally said, "I have a lot of friends who still invite me to dinner, so I think I'm a pretty nice guy." I guess it was the right thing to say, because she smiled and we got down to business. For the next twenty-two minutes we talked about my story, mapped out a plan, drafted a schedule to begin working on the book proposal—and then, like a Tasmanian devil, she was gone. I couldn't believe that this was finally going to happen. To this day, I still have doubts as to whether I passed her "asshole" test.

Since that first meeting, I have come to realize why I had not managed to finish this book myself. It was because I was waiting for Catherine to write it with me. We worked tirelessly for two years, sandwiching meetings and conversations into our busy schedules. Fortunately, we are both early risers, so we fell into a routine of talking on the phone between five-thirty and seven most mornings. She would then draft a chapter for my review, and the rewriting would begin. Catherine has been more than my coauthor; she has become the friend who helped me find my voice and bring this volume to life. So, thank you, Catherine, for turning "no" into "now."

Thanks are also due to my daughter Taryn, for challenging me to a race up the driveway when she was three years old that changed my life, and then joining Donna as one of only two crew members in my 1982 race. She found time to help critique this book even when she had none. To my daughter Jody, whose love, support, and caring nature have meant so much to me. To my brother, Gerry, who stepped in so many times during my formative years and got me back on track. Thanks for hanging in there, Big Bro.

I want to acknowledge my best childhood friend, Dennis "Denny" Couture, who died way too young and whose life was much worse off than mine. We leaned on each other, and together we survived some really rough times. He was also the person who told me I would be successful because I had great hair.

To Gertrude Miller, my very proper twelfth-grade English teacher. I tried so hard to fluster her with my choice of books to write reports on, like Henry Miller's *Tropic of Cancer*. She knew my game and never once criticized my decisions. She taught me that it was okay to challenge authority and to think unconventionally.

To Irving Settler, who was perhaps the greatest mentor any young man could have, and who taught me most of what I know about business and life. To Bob Luehrs, for looking beyond my youth and giving me the opportunity that changed my life. To Tad Kaminsky, for allowing me to help him grow a company that changed the blue jean business forever; his genius is still with us today. To Susan and Arthur Karp, for sharing a great cookie recipe with the whole country. Susan, your Blackfoot Indian great-great-grandmother would be proud. To Jeff Weil, for giving us a chance.

To Michael Shermer, for a lifelong friendship that has endured long after we stopped riding bicycles together insanely long distances with very little sleep. To all my crew members who helped make my bike races possible in 1982, 1983, 1984, and 1989. I want to give a special shout-out to Pete Penseyres, Jim Penseyres, and Bob Fourney, my Race Across America teammates in 1989.

To Gary and Joan Whitaker and the SOAR documentary film crew that went from Savannah to San Diego with me in 1984. Their crack-of-dawn jokes helped me face each morning during that grueling race. To Richard De Bernardis, my dear friend who rode with me from the trailing edge of the Rocky Mountains in California against seventy-mile-per-hour headwinds. To Dave Johnson, who accompanied me on the last five miles in 1984. You all helped me face Goliath.

To Betty Siegel, Dan Papp, Sam Olens, Kat Schwaig, Tim Mescon, Norman Radow, Tommy Holder, Jim Fleming, Jim Dunn, and all of the members of the Kennesaw State University Foundation for their friendship and support for KSU over the years; together we transformed the university. Larry Stevens deserves special recognition for his leadership; he has become one of my closest friends and colleagues. For years, he encouraged me to write this book.

To my late father, David Coles, who met me twelve miles from San Diego to cheer me on. Without telling me, he had followed me all the way from Savannah to ensure that I was okay. It is never too late to say thank you for watching over me.

To all of my friends and doctors who have supported me over the years as I worked to recover from my motorcycle accident and from cancer. I cannot fully express how much your love and support have meant to me.

To all the team members at Great American Cookies and Caribou Coffee and all our franchisees, thank you for your hard work on behalf of two great companies and for making me look good. I also want to thank all those people who bought billions of cookies and oceans of coffee; you helped me to build and lead two great companies. And special thanks to my colleagues at BrandBank and Charter Bank.

To my campaign managers, Kate Head in 1996 and Beth Shipp in 1998, and to all the staff, thousands of volunteers, and supporters who helped us bring so many important issues into the national conversation.

To Greg Torre, Roy Barnes, and the members of the Georgia Film Commission, who helped revive the industry in the state. To my colleagues at the University System of Georgia's Board of Regents and the Board of Trustees at the Walker School, who worked so hard to help improve education in Georgia.

To Phyllis Hendricks for her many years of service as my administrative assistant, and to her husband, Ronnie. They both tolerated numerous late-night calls as we were writing this book. I also want to recognize their daughter, Carissa, who has always offered invaluable tech support.

To Jim Kennedy, for being a good friend and constant supporter during my political campaigns. I am honored to have his foreword in this book.

I am sure I have missed a few names here and there; please forgive any omissions.

To my wife, Donna, for so much. It would be impossible even to begin to describe it all.

And last, but not least, to Elaine Silverman, wherever you are. Thank you for jumping off the pier at Crystal Beach and pulling me out of the water when I was drowning at the age of five. If not for you, there would have been nothing to write about.

From Catherine

Working on *Time to Get Tough* was like seeing a movie of someone's life come into focus. Michael has been a fascinating subject, and his good humor and determination to bring this book to fruition were inspiring. I could not have worked harder or enjoyed a project more. I will never forget how he started most of our morning conversations with "Catherine, Catherine, Catherine." And I am convinced that I will always have his Brooklyn accent playing in my head.

We had several readers who did much to shape and improve the manuscript. My father, Dr. James Richard Lewis, and brother, Dr. Richard Anthony "Tony" Lewis, both edited early drafts and offered valuable suggestions. As I discovered long ago, it is useful to have two professors, one trained in English and one in art history, in your family tree. I am also grateful for my team at Kennesaw State University and beyond: B.G. Dilworth, Dr. Jennifer Dickey, Dr. Ouida Dickey, Tyler Crafton-Karnes, Stefanie Green, Anna Tucker, and Andrea Miskewicz, all of whom helped the book take shape. Finally, Ann Marlowe served as a fine copy editor. Her careful attention to detail helped improve the manuscript in ways that we can never repay.

We would like to offer special thanks to photographers David Caselli and Kate Daly, who helped illustrate this book.

Lisa Bayer, at the University of Georgia Press, was the first person to see the merit and power of this project. We are grateful to her staff, notably

Katherine La Mantia and Jon Davies, to the faculty committee, and to the anonymous readers who offered much enthusiasm for the book. Last, but never least, I want to thank my husband, John Companiotte, a noted author in his own right, and my daughter, Emma, who at the age of eight had to get herself ready for school and entertain herself for endless hours while I revised chapters or talked on the phone with "Mr. Michael." Their support is what made this book possible.

About the Authors

Michael J. Coles is an Atlanta business executive, serial entrepreneur, education advocate, well-known public speaker, and the namesake of the Coles College of Business at Kennesaw State University. After almost two decades in the clothing business, he cofounded Great American Cookies in Atlanta in 1977 and grew it into the largest cookie store franchise in the United States. Coles's story of personal perseverance is as impressive as his business acumen. Following a near-fatal motorcycle accident six weeks after founding the cookie company, he recovered through a self-designed rehabilitation program and went on to set world records in three coast-to-coast bicycle races. Coles's commitment to community service led him to run for the House of Representatives against Newt Gingrich in 1996 and for the U.S. Senate against Paul Coverdell in 1998, the same year he sold Great American Cookies. For the next four years he chaired the Georgia Film Commission and served on the University System of Georgia's Board of Regents, the Kennesaw State University Foundation board, and the Walker School board. In 2003 he took the helm at Caribou Coffee, where he more than doubled the size of the company, opened a commercial sales division and an international market, and took the company public on NASDAQ under the symbol CBOU in 2005. Today he serves as chairman of Brand Holding Company and BrandBank and actively lectures about business, giving more than seventy-five talks a year at universities and corporate events nationwide. He is coauthor of the children's book *The Land of the Caring Bou* with his wife, Donna.

Dr. Catherine M. Lewis is Assistant Vice President of Museums, Archives & Rare Books; director of the Museum of History and Holocaust Education; and professor of history at Kennesaw State University. She received her BA with honors in English and history from Emory University and her MA and PhD in American Studies from the University of Iowa. She is the author, coeditor, or coauthor of fourteen books, including *Bobby Jones and the Quest for the Grand Slam* (2005), *Don't Ask What I Shot: How Eisenhower's Love of Golf Helped Shape 1950s America* (2007), *Jim Crow America* (2009), and *Museums in a Global Context* (2013). She recently completed *Memories of the Mansion: The Story of the Georgia Governor's Mansion* with First Lady Sandra Deal and Dr. Jennifer Dickey (2015). Dr. Lewis has curated more than forty exhibits for organizations around the nation including the Atlanta History Center, Delta Air Lines, the United Way, the Breman Museum, and Augusta National Golf Club. She regularly presents at national and international conferences and serves on numerous boards, including the Women's Leadership Committee at Kennesaw State University, the Yates Scholarship Board for the Georgia State Golf Association, and the Museum Committee for the United States Golf Association. In 2018 she was named chair of the Robert T. Jones Jr. Program, a partnership between Emory University and the University of St. Andrews.